CAMBRIDGE LATIN AMERICAN STUDIES

GENERAL EDITOR
SIMON COLLIER

ADVISORY COMMITTEE
MARVIN BERNSTEIN, MALCOLM DEAS
CLARK W. REYNOLDS, ARTURO VALENZUELA

51

TOBACCO ON THE PERIPHERY

TOBACCO ON THE PERIPHERY

A CASE STUDY IN CUBAN
LABOUR HISTORY, 1860–1958

JEAN STUBBS

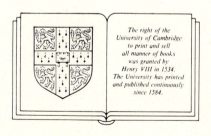

CAMBRIDGE UNIVERSITY PRESS

Cambridge

London   New York   New Rochelle
Melbourne   Sydney

Published by the Press Syndicate of the University of Cambridge
The Pitt Building, Trumpington Street, Cambridge CB2 1RP
32 East 57th Street, New York, NY 10022, USA
296 Beaconsfield Parade, Middle Park, Melbourne 3206, Australia

First published 1985

Printed in Great Britain at the University Press, Cambridge

Library of Congress catalogue card number: 84–19918

British Library cataloguing in publication data
Stubbs, Jean
Tobacco on the periphery: a case study in
Cuban labour history, 1860–1958. – (Cambridge
Latin American studies; 51)
1. Tobacco industry – Cuba – History
2. Industrial relations – Cuba – History
I. Title
331′.04797′097291   HD8039.T62C8

ISBN 0 521 25423 X

Out of the agricultural and industrial development of these amazing plants were to come those economic interests in which foreign traders would twist and weave for centuries to form the web of our country's history and the motives of its leaders and, one and the same time, the shackles and support of its people. Tobacco and sugar are the two most important figures in the history of Cuba . . .

Fernando Ortiz. *Cuban counterpoint: tobacco and sugar*

To Pedro, Ilmi and Sahnet

Contents

Preface

I first went to Cuba in 1968, with the intention of studying the tobacco workers over the period 1914–1958. I was extremely dissatisfied with many Latin American labour studies and with the widely held view that the working class as a whole had become 'integrated' into and 'identified' with the process of industrialization and urbanization. The choice of Cuba and the tobacco workers was a logical one. Before going to Cuba I had spent a preliminary year in London exhausting secondary sources and it was clear that this was one of the most urbanized of all Latin American countries, with a large working class and a well-organized labour movement. The tobacco workers comprised the oldest and, for a long period of time, the largest grouping of industrial urban workers (sugar workers, though numerically greater, formed isolated pockets in rural areas). The cigar makers were among the first to form guilds and strong craft unions, and the militancy of this sector as a whole stood out, not only in the nineteenth century, but also in the twentieth.

I had envisaged a more sophisticated study of social history, looking at the tobacco neighbourhoods of Havana and provincial towns, to relate both in- and out-of-work activities. After a few months in Havana, I found this was clearly out of the question, for little basic groundwork had been done on either the industry or the conditions of the workers over the period.

This was somewhat surprising, given that tobacco was Cuba's second most important industry and that, in certain key periods, the tobacco bourgeoisie appears to have been almost as important as the sugar bourgeoisie. There are some good socio-economic studies of Cuba but most – including the classics of Ramiro Guerra and Alienes y Urosa, plus the more recent works of Julio Le Riverend, Manuel Moreno Fraginals and Oscar Pino Santos – concentrate on sugar and the way Cuba became a mono-producer and mono-exporter of it. They give some pointers as to what was happening in non-sugar

ix

sectors of the economy. Thus, in general terms, it is known that any form of diversified agriculture and manufacturing as a whole was held back; that only the export industries, sugar and tobacco (this in itself being relative), were any exception; and that, from 1925 onwards, stagnation in the sugar sector was affecting the whole economy. Trade and finance were so exclusively structured around sugar that little credit was available for other activities and there was a resulting imbalance toward the trade and service sectors and away fron manufacturing, which was not only small-scale but also extremely backward. As such, however, few sectors outside sugar have been studied in their own right. There are some monographs. Calvache's work on the mining industry is one, a more recent study of the soap industry by Jesús Chía another. In the case of tobacco, there are the works of Fernando Ortiz and Jóse Rivero Muñiz, both of which are useful and informative, though less so as regards the twentieth century – Rivero Muñiz' two-volume *Tabaco* has one chapter of twenty pages or so on the post-1902 period.

As was the case for the industry, it was also soon evident that in Cuban historiography the finer political and social implications of a dependent economy, even in a general sense, had scarcely been touched upon. Issues such as the weakness of the national bourgeoisie, what this meant in terms not only of foreign and home policy but also of the role of the military and the trade unions, are only recently being raised in any depth. As regards labour history, there are a few standard trade union histories and narrative accounts of strikes and other kinds of labour action, as well as what has been written on wider social movements over key periods, and biographies of leading personalities. Tobacco fares somewhat better than other sectors by virtue of the early worker organizations in this sector, but little penetrates below the surface of events or attempts to analyse in any systematic way the growth and nature of the trade union movement and class consciousness in this sector.

Several years of my research in Cuba went into treading considerable new ground to trace the development of the industry, the workers and their organizations. Given the lack of a strong historical tradition and the very course of events in post-independence, pre-revolutionary Cuba, it was not surprising to find that many documents, especially those relating to the twentieth century, had not been kept, had disappeared or had been destroyed (especially over the insurrection period) and that many more were as yet unclassified and often virtually unusable. The Archivo Nacional de La Habana contained a substantial, if unclassified, collection of documents, the Comisión Nacional de Propaganda y Defensa del Tabaco Habano (CNPDTH). This contained little of the actual commission (set up in 1927) and less on the industry in general, but there were many files of the old American Tobacco Company subsidiary in Havana, the Tabacalera Cubana, S.A., acquired by the archive after the Revolution. The files were not complete but did include much company correspondence, reports, some statistics and general accounts, together with newspaper cuttings. These proved to be an extremely useful starting point. The Registro Mercantil de La Habana, also belonging to the archive, and dating back to the 1880s, comprised a relatively well-kept and indexed collection of volumes in which all businesses were required by law to register. This was a mine of information on some companies and supplied essential data on all as to when they were founded, who put up the capital and the amount, and subsequent modifications. It was a relatively easy body of information to handle and, though largely unworked as yet, will obviously constitute a basic source for many studies to come. Much of the old Archivo del Ministerio del Trabajo is intact. A substantial part is catalogued according to the names of individual workers and hence unwieldy, but a good section in the Archivo de Seguro Social is classified by sector and by firm, and contains useful data on the labour force. It was more difficult to obtain information on the labour movement as such. Much of the archive of the Confederación de Trabajadores de Cuba (CTC) was not available, nor were those of older organizations of individual sectors of workers. I had, therefore, to make up for such a crucial deficiency in source material by checking through the newspapers and periodicals and more scanty materials from other sections in the national archive, such as the Fondo Especial, the Fondo de Donativos y Remisiones, the Fondo de Tribunales de Urgencia, the Fondo de Audiencia and the Miscelanea. Sections such as Hacienda and the Secretaría de Agricultura, Comercio y Trabajo corresponding to the twentieth century were uncatalogued; and, when I probed further with a group of colleagues from the Instituto de Historia de la Academia de Ciencias de Cuba, it became clear that they were neither sizeable nor contained documents of primary importance. I also spent some time in the Santa Clara archive but data from the Havana archive constitute the bulk of documentary evidence for this study. I was able to check secondary sources in the Biblioteca Nacional José Martí and the libraries of the former Sociedad Económica de Amigos del País, the Instituto de

Historia, and Cubatabaco, the state tobacco enterprise. I found in these libraries, as well as in the archives, pamphlets that had obviously never been studied before in connection with the subject.

Cuban statistics in general are poor. Few series exist for the nineteenth century and those for the twentieth are often inadequate and hard to locate. From 1927 on, the CNPDTH compiled annual statistics for tobacco, some of which were extended back to the beginning of the century, but these were not always reliable and left some gaps. For the nineteenth century, there were official trade balances for certain years but otherwise I was forced to rely almost entirely on secondary sources and data included in British consular reports, which I was able to check in the British Museum in London. Most statistical data on the workers comes from official censuses, though also from CTC returns, ministry of labour files, the national archive and some secondary sources, as do figures for unionization. Where figures were not available, I was able to build up a fairly comprehensive picture using interviews and other more descriptive material.

Checking wider tobacco sources in England enabled me to verify certain points, especially regarding the structure of the world tobacco industry, which I had only been able to piece together in Havana. I should point out here that although there are some informative straight economic business histories on tobacco in several countries, to my knowledge there has been no serious work done on the changing nature of the world structure of production with the advent of imperialism. Neither, it seemed, had there been any detailed work on tobacco workers in any other country, with the possible exceptions of Holland and Germany (for which language constituted a barrier) and the many biographies of the cigar maker Sam Gompers, of the American Federation of Labour. I had, therefore, no comparative study to aid me. Since then there has been interesting work done on Puerto Rico and on Cuban cigar makers in the United States, which does provide useful points of comparison.

My findings were originally written up in 1975 as a London University Ph.D. thesis under the title of 'The Cuban tobacco industry and its workers, 1860–1958'. More avid readers are referred to it for more detailed information and statistical tables. Since then, I have had occasion to rework several parts, but the study as a whole still focusses largely on socio-economic and political aspects of formal labour history. As such, it is heavily biased toward the better union-ized, better documented, largely male sector of the cigar makers. My findings, however, led me to quite radical re-interpretations of certain key facets of their history, including the complex relationship between growing militancy and the unions and the particular scope and nature of radical ideologies. I have endeavoured to raise some pointers for future work on equally important informal and cultural aspects of that history and other less-documented sectors, especially those involving large numbers of women and children. To round off the study, it would have been important to look more closely at late nineteenth- and early twentieth-century developments in the United States, especially Key West and Tampa, which formed part of a single 'Cuban' cigar-making universe, and also at the post-revolutionary period. I had, however, already rather ambitiously become immersed in a hundred years of Cuban tobacco history, and I had to stop somewhere.

Throughout my research, I have been indebted to many people. In Cuba I had the full co-operation of the various archives and libraries, and in particular the Instituto de Historia and its director Julio Le Riverend. It was he who made it possible for me to go and work there. Evelio Lugo, head of the industrial department of Cubatabaco in Havana, and Marysabel Dueñas, of the Las Villas delegation, enabled me to interview tobacco workers both in Havana and in many of the small tobacco towns. Cuban colleagues Manuel Moreno Fraginals, José Luciano Franco, the Pate Juan Pérez de la Riva, Jorge Ibarra, Jesús Chía and Fe Iglesias all offered hints and suggestions along the way. Professor Jurgen Kuzcinski and Dr Helga Nussbaum, of the Institut für Wirtschaftsgeschichte of the German Democratic Republic, gave me great encouragement at a critical stage in the writing. My thesis supervisor, Professor E. J. Hobsbawm, gave me constant support and help in thinning down much narrative to make the necessary analytical points. And my family and friends were forbearing in seeing the whole task through.

The responsibility for the basic arguments and exposition and for correct translation from the original Spanish (unless otherwise specified) is mine.

October 1984   JEAN STUBBS

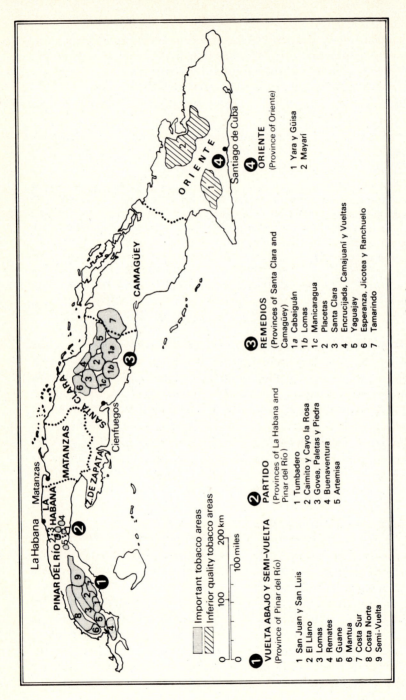

① VUELTA ABAJO Y SEMI-VUELTA
(Province of Pinar del Río)

1 San Juan y San Luis
2 El Llano
3 Lomas
4 Remates
5 Guane
6 Mantua
7 Costa Sur
8 Costa Norte
9 Semi-Vuelta

② PARTIDO
(Provinces of La Habana and Pinar del Río)

1 Tumbadero
2 Caimito y Cayo la Rosa
3 Govea, Paletas y Piedra
4 Buenaventura
5 Artemisa

③ REMEDIOS
(Provinces of Santa Clara and Camagüey)

1a Cabaiguán
1b Lomas
1c Manicaragua
2 Placetas
3 Santa Clara
4 Encrucijada, Camajuaní y Vueltas
5 Yaguajay
6 Esperanza, Jicotea y Ranchuelo
7 Tamarindo

④ ORIENTE
(Province of Oriente)

1 Yara y Güisa
2 Mayarí

Important tobacco areas
Inferior quality tobacco areas

Tobacco-growing zones of Cuba, 1944
Source: *Anuario del tabaco habano* (Havana, 1944), p. 54.

Introduction: A changing world tobacco economy

> I like to regard people both making it and smoking it not only as a sort of friendship, but as a vast domain of democracy wherein we find gathered people of every class and race and creed, having, in pipe or plug or cigar or cigarette, a bond of sympathetic understanding and a contact of common interest and good fellowship. I like to contemplate the business of producing and the pleasure of consuming this exalted plant as really a realm peopled by congenial spirits and ruled only by those kindlier human emotions which the smoke of these fragrant leaves kindles in the hearts of man . . .
>
> Carl Avery Werner. *Tobaccoland* (1922)

It has to be one of history's ironies that in 1933 – the year the Cuban tobacco industry was facing bankruptcy – Doris Duke was called the richest girl in the world. She was the daughter of James B. Duke, who left an estate valued at more than $100 million at the time of his death in 1925. A third of her inheritance was to be turned over to her when she was 21, which was in 1933. She inherited a million-dollar palace built by her father on an estate of 2,500 acres of land near Somerville, New Jersey, on which he was reported to have spent a further $2 million. In 1924, he had set aside a $40-million fund in securities for the benefit of Trinity College, Durham, North Carolina, on the condition it change its name to Duke University. For this, he was hailed as a great philanthropist whose aim was to benefit mankind.[1]

Behind the philanthropist was a businessman rated in 1905 as the 'Croesus of the tobacco trade', a man who in amassing a multi-million tobacco fortune had ruthlessly helped ruin other tobacco companies and countries, Cuba included.

The complexities of this process are part of an even more complex historical relationship between the developed and under-developed areas of the world whose full economic, social and political implications are only just beginning to be understood.

With the technical and industrial revolution taking place in Europe in the late eighteenth and early nineteenth centuries, and subsequently in the United States in the latter part of the nineteenth century, relatively backward economies in the rest of the world were increasingly unable to resist the force of the new centres of wealth, industry and commerce. In the case of colonies, there was no choice; and even those countries which were politically independent were often not strong enough to reject the role cast for them by the manufacturing centres. The whole continent of Latin America, especially after the break with Spain and Portugal, was turned into an almost total economic dependency of Great Britain. Plantation owners were quite prepared to make their money by exporting raw materials and importing foreign manufactured goods. Only when there were any strong manufacturing interests did any conflict arise.

During the last decades of the nineteenth century, a fundamental change took place in the nature of world capitalism. Capital accumulation and the concentration of production in the advanced countries were developed to such a stage that monopoly began to play a decisive role in economic life. This transformation was one of the most important phenomena – if not the most important – of the modern capitalist economy, and was to have far-reaching implications for the already established division between the advanced and the backward areas of the world. Whereas in the old competitive situation manufacturers had vied with each other for a largely unknown market, new concentration allowed for the estimation of sources of raw materials, on the basis of which it was possible to capture both existing and potential sources throughout the world. Increasing amounts of capital were exported to the backward countries, the cheap raw material areas. As the export of capital increased and the foreign sphere of influence of the big monopoly corporations expanded, international agreements between combines to form cartels became inevitable.

These international cartels were to divide the world among themselves, thus producing modern imperialism. They divided in proportion to capital, in proportion to strength, cementing the division of labour created between the manufacturing centres and the suppliers of raw materials on their periphery and closing even further the possibilities of a more diverse economic development and industrialization to the latter. Monopolies were able to guarantee their sources of raw materials and derive the greatest profits when this division involved the loss of political independence, but there also arose new forms of economic and state dependence in countries which were, in formal terms, politically independent.

The vast upheavals in the 'periphery' during the late nineteenth and early twentieth centuries were one more facet of the extraordinary growth of monopoly production, often in what were hitherto little-exploited products. Tobacco was one of these.

The initial impact of the tremendous developments taking place in Europe and the United States during the nineteenth century was the opening up of markets for tobacco. During the first half of the century pipe and cigar smoking became popular in England; more predominantly cigars in Holland, Germany and Spain; snuff and cigars in France and Italy; and plug[2] and cigars in the United States. In all these countries there was a growing industry for such commodities but quite large quantities were also imported. To satisfy these, as well as home markets, manufacturing industries in snuff, plug and cigars (especially the latter) developed in many tobacco-growing countries of the underdeveloped areas of the world – Brazil, Indonesia, the Philippines, Mexico, Cuba, Turkey, and many others. Some of these countries were also producing a new form of smoke, the cigarette. Though gaining in popularity, while still crudely rolled this was considered a somewhat vulgar habit by the more 'refined' classes of the advanced areas.[3]

By the latter half of the nineteenth century, there were already disturbing trends evident in the world tobacco trade for many tobacco countries. Tobacco manufacturing, protected by tariff barriers, was developing at such a rapid pace in Germany, Holland, France, Spain, Italy, England, and finally the United States, that these once major importers of manufactured tobacco goods not only became more self-reliant but also exporters of such products. By the 1890s, Germany was turning out some 6,500 million cigars and 1,100 million cigarettes, and the United States some 4,900 million cigars and 3,750 million cigarettes a year.[4]

It was in the last decades of the nineteenth century when that vulgar habit cigarette smoking was tamed, partly through the discovery of milder (more refined) flue-cured 'Bright' tobacco[5] in Virginia, but more because of the invention of a cigarette machine which not only produced cigarettes more efficiently and at far less cost but also made a better-looking finished product. The extent to which this machine revolutionized the whole tobacco industry cannot be overemphasized.

The earliest recorded cigarette machine – and it may well have been the one developed by Susini in Cuba – was commented on by an English observer at the 1867 Paris Trade Exhibition: 'Its extreme complication was against satisfactory action. It is a first machine and like all first attempts, leaving much to be desired, paving the way only to something better.'[6] Subsequent machines were largely American in origin: the Hook (1872), Emery (1879) and Bonsack (1881). It was an improved Bonsack, rolling off 750–1,000 cigarettes a minute, which, alongside subsequent improved machines for cigarette making, packing, tipping and all other processes of the industry, laid the foundations for the first of the giant tobacco corporations. Production costs were halved and smaller firms swallowed up by larger and far more profitable mechanized enterprises employing cheap, mainly female as opposed to earlier male labour.

The United States led the way in characteristic 'frontier' style. When flue-curing was discovered just before the outbreak of the American Civil War, the Durham Bright belt became a vast centre for that increasingly popular form of smoke, the cigarette. Washington Duke was a small farmer who had stockpiled Bright leaf before being conscripted and later established a family tobacco business. W. Duke and Sons and Co. moved into cigarettes in 1881 and had become prosperous enough two years later to buy exclusive rights to a new and improved Bonsack. Duke gambled on a machine producing finer cigarettes, despite an 1887 rival's comment: 'We don't consider him as a manufacturer of cigarettes: he will be broke before the year is out.'[7] By 1890 his price undercutting had eaten away their sales and profits to such an extent that they were pressured to join a combination called the American Tobacco Company, with Duke as president. ATC took 90% of US cigarette sales and made profits of over $40 million in its first year. Mechanization provided a uniformity of production which allowed the launching of nationwide cigarette brands, backed by national advertising and distribution systems. Any subsequent competitors could be, and were, undercut and bought up.

In the 1890s, Duke extended ATC control over ancillary industries and all other tobacco products. Cigarette profits subsidized even more costly price warfare that also involved buying off political and legislative bodies, controlling judiciaries, circumventing the law and crushing competition and marketing policies. First plug (1894–8) and then snuff (1899–1900) succumbed to the Tobacco Trust, as ATC was also called. The attempt to move into cigars (1901–2) was less successful, largely because production was still a complicated and pricy business, no cigar machines yet having been invented. ATC's American Cigar lost $3.5 million in 1902 and, although operating with moderate profits from 1904 on, cornered only 14% of the total market.

The British parallel to the Dukes were the Wills, who were the first to gain exclusive British rights over the Bonsack, to make extensive use of national brands, advertising and price undercutting in cigarettes, and to amass a considerable fortune, enabling Henry Overton Wills III to become benefactor and first chancellor of the new Bristol University in 1909.

As early as 1894 Wills had been concerned over ATC power on the US leaf market and had discussed and rejected possible amalgamation with ATC. Though it was by far the largest tobacco company in the UK, netting over half the nation's cigarette sales, Wills was far less cut-throat in its methods. It was only when Duke bought up Ogden's, the second largest British company, initiating cut-price and other deals to retailers, that twelve other manufacturers were pressured into an alliance with Wills to form the Imperial Tobacco Company and wage a retaliatory war.

After an all-out war, an agreement was finally reached whereby Ogden's was sold to Imperial, and ATC and ITC agreed to keep out of each other's territory. Each acquired trading rights in the other's brands and patents but, through Ogden's, it was ATC that acquired a substantial minority interest in Imperial and the right to nominate three of its directors. It also had two-thirds control of the new British-American Tobacco Company (BAT) set up for trade in the rest of the world outside the UK and US, Cuba and Puerto Rico, the last two being considered ATC domain.

The pattern was set for the twentieth century. By 1909 ATC alone had controlling interests in 250 companies, 119 of which were actual member corporations (86 in the US, Puerto Rico and Cuba, and 33 operating exclusively in other countries of the world). It has been argued that after dissolution in 1911 under the Sherman Anti-Trust Law[8] the old ATC lost much of its former importance. And yet the major companies to emerge from that dissolution – American Tobacco, Reynolds, and Liggett and Myers – not only maintained their hold over a rapidly expanding home and overseas market but were also, in 1941, again convicted of further Sherman violations. Similarly, although it has been maintained that Wills lost its former glory and much has been made of brand 'competition' between Players and Wills,[9] these were the major companies in that one giant combine, ITC.

There is little doubt that British and American corporations have remained strong in world terms up to the present day. BAT, the early giant creation of ATC and ITC, was rated as the largest in the late

1960s.[10] Great tobacco monopolies were also formed in most European countries. Many, including state tobacco enterprises (such as the Compañía Arrendataria de España in Spain and the Régie Français des Tabacs in France) were also interlocking multinational corporations.[11] Between them, they operated in virtually every country open to private enterprise.

All were concerned primarily with the leaf market and or cigarettes. This in itself is significant. With the advent of the machine, the cigarette became the first tobacco to be mass-produced for the mass market, so becoming the tobacco product *par excellence* of the twentieth century. Cigarettes came to comprise some 90% of total sales of the major companies and by the mid-1920s accounted for well over half of total production in countries like the US and the UK. Aptly enough, one of the most informative works on US tobacco was entitled *The American Cigarette Industry*.[12] Today's cigarette giants are completely mechanized. Compressed tobacco conditioners inject air, water and steam into the tobacco, casks are broken open and tobacco spread out and deposited on conveyor belts to large rotating cylinders in which the tobacco is further moisturized and cut, later to be blended in bulking silos. Rotating paddles carry the blend to the shredding machines, after which it is dried in more rotating drums. The final tobacco mix is then rolled into cigarettes in electronically controlled machines each of which produce some 2,500 cigarettes a minute. These are then machine packed, some being lab tested on complex equipment for firmness, filter efficiency and smoking quality.

With the advent of cigarettes, plug and snuff died a natural death – and pipe tobacco came not far behind. Cigars still held their own as a luxury smoke but, as such, had a far more limited market, even when ATC was able to launch the first really efficient cigar machine in 1929 and produce cheap machine-made cigars in a big way.

Duke never lost faith in a cigar machine and the possibility of standardizing production and opening up new markets. It was a long time coming but when it did it was almost as significant as the earlier cigarette machine and is certainly worth considering in some detail.

The man who worked on perfecting such a machine was ATC's American Machine and Foundry Co. president, Rufus Lenoir Patterson. Logically, a machine presupposes standardized raw material. For the cigarette machine, the tobacco was chopped so finely that for practical purposes it was standardized. But the cigar had to be made of a filler, consisting of big pieces of tobacco in millions of different shapes and sizes, enclosed in a wrapper of one big piece. No two tobacco leaves are exactly alike in form, size, thickness, strength, pliability, texture, or any of the other attributes which play an important part in the manufacture of cigars. Initially a bunching machine was devised for filler, and the wrapper was still rolled by hand. The Fresh Work Cigar Machine of the early twenties was a breakthrough in combining bunching and rolling. Though it was still not entirely satisfactory, its basic principles were incorporated into later machines. Two variants were made: the short and the long filler machines. In simple terms, the machine fed the filler along a moulding channel towards rotating metal plates on which the binder and subsequently the wrapper was placed to be rolled around the moulded blend.

ATC let other companies try out the machine first on a rental basis. Connoisseurs swore they could never be fooled by machine-made cigars but were actually being fooled daily. Finally, in 1929, 'after $8,000,000 and twenty years' grief', as *Fortune* put it, ATC's George Washington Hill launched Patterson's machine and machine-made cigars in a big way. He introduced his famous 'no-spit' campaign for five-cent cigars: 'No spit on these Creme cigars of mine', was the slogan, referring to the old (and already obsolete) method of sealing cigars. 'They are pure. My machine made them so.'[13]

Just a few months earlier, Patterson had commented: 'If I had had the least idea of the trouble the machine would cost, it would never have been made.' But its advantages were soon evident. By 1930, well over half US cigar production was machine-made, and the newly formed ATC subsidiary International Cigar Machine Company was reaping considerable profits from leasing the machine. Along with other machines for stemming and sorting the leaf, the cigar machine facilitated the expansion of large corporations such as the General Cigar Company, the Consolidated Cigar Company and Bayuk Cigars Inc., and the squeezing out of many small hand-producing concerns. Thus, as against 22,159 shops and factories manufacturing cigars in 1910, there were only 5,292 in 1936. A skilled and relatively well-paid labour force was cut by 60% in rolling, 15% in stemming. Male cigar makers were often in the process replaced by cheaper female labour.

Cigar production was given a new lease of life but marketing possibilities were still limited in comparison to cigarettes. According to *Moody's*, over the period 1929–60 (after the introduction of the machine, that is) US cigarette consumption increased fourfold (from 122 to 507 billion). Cigar consumption had, by the late 1950s, only just regained its 1929 level. It was in cigarettes that the great fortunes were being made.

In world terms, the United States – main producer of the mild leaf –

had by the late 1920s come to account for 29% of total world production, handling over 40% of the total leaf trade. Over the next two decades, the US position was consolidated as the largest single world producer of leaf, as it was also by far the largest single world producer of cigarettes. The other major producing countries in the late 1950s were the USSR and Japan, followed by the UK and West Germany, their home industries having suffered considerably during World War II. In the less profitable cigar world, the United States was only marginally in the lead by the 1950s, with West Germany a close second, followed by Italy, the Netherlands and Spain.

In both cigars and cigarettes the output of the many other tobacco-producing countries was becoming comparatively smaller and smaller. For the tremendous growth of monopoly cigarette production and the big cigarette producing nations, restructuring as it did world cultivation, production and distribution patterns, could not but have equally tremendous consequences for the home industry of those countries. By the 1960s there was scarcely a country of the capitalist world unaffected by these large monopoly corporations. The onion-skin structuring whereby 'world economy contains national economies which contain industries which contain firms' was turned inside out by monopoly capital. Tobacco and tobacco economies were no exception.

With the increase in tobacco manufacturing in the advanced countries over the latter part of the nineteenth century, a division of labour was fast being established (the United States excepted) between tobacco-growing and tobacco-manufacturing countries, the latter importing increasingly smaller quantities of manufactured products and increasingly larger quantities of raw tobacco leaf. The tobaccos of smaller producing countries had special qualities. Many were dark tobaccos, such as the high-quality, aromatic Cuban tobacco, used both in cigars and cigarettes but particularly the former; the somewhat inferior tobaccos from Puerto Rico and the Philippines; and the strong Turkish and Greek tobaccos. Sumatra tobacco was elastic and a particularly good cigar wrapper. During the latter half of the nineteenth century, the US industry was based on a blend of these with home-grown tobaccos.

Prior to the consolidation of the tobacco monopolies, the relationship between the manufacturing centres and primary producers was largely mercantile, tariff barriers in the advanced countries playing a major part in protecting home industry. With the growth of the tobacco monopolies, this changed. Companies like ATC, ITC and

BAT either moved directly into tobacco-producing countries – as was the case of ATC in Puerto Rico and Cuba, ITC in Rhodesia,[14] and BAT in Sumatra – or operated through monopoly corporations controlling the international leaf market from Holland.

It is significant that the penetration of monopoly capital in small tobacco-producing countries was largely in leaf. In order to maximize profits and consolidate their monopoly position, tobacco corporations needed not only to guarantee their own, but also control other, supplies of raw leaf. Control over raw materials implied control over the emergence or non-emergence of competing industries.

By the turn of the century, the pattern was set. In country after country, the sheer strength of the monopolies and the protectionism and adverse terms of trade established by them was to increase the imbalance of the home industry toward the export of leaf and away from manufacturing. Any increase in manufacturing was largely in the area of inferior tobacco products for the home market, often considered of such secondary importance as to be left to small local concerns.

By the late twenties, the shift in world production to mild cigarettes began to produce a falling back of world demand for, and drop in the price of, the leaf they produced. With the best tobacco lands either owned or controlled by foreign monopolies, local growers were left taking the risks of a shrinking market, fighting a recurring problem of over-production and keeping prices afloat.

Small tobacco countries – especially those which had come to depend heavily on one, usually the US, market – found their possibilities for development more and more limited. Cuba's Comisión Nacional de Propaganda y Defensa del Tabaco Habano (CNPDTH) published a series of marketing reports in 1931 which brought out certain aspects of this.[15] Sumatra leaf had been used almost exclusively by US industry in the early twentieth century. US corporations bought their supplies through monopolies in Holland. By 1925 nine such corporations registered in Amsterdam controlled 93% of the Sumatra crop. Specially suited for machine-made cigars, Sumatra leaf had a longer lease of life than many others, but manufacturing suffered considerably. Many of the hundreds of small cigar-rolling shops were forced to close down. The only substantial industry was centred around six modern cigarette factories, including the BAT factory, but these used imported leaf, mainly Bright from the United States.

The Philippines had similarly come to supply the US with considerable quantities of somewhat inferior dark tobaccos. By the 1920s exports to the US were declining rapidly and the islands were left with a surplus production. A falling demand for cigars and cigarettes made with home-grown tobaccos put manufacturing in crisis, and factories turned to light tobacco. Even then, increased imports of American cigarettes from the late twenties on constituted fierce competition for local industry.

In 1940, the Caribbean Commission brought out a study on the tobacco trade of the Caribbean region.[16] Of its eight major conclusions, three are particularly relevant: (1) by the mid-thirties, leaf comprised four-fifths of tobacco exports, the only increase in manufactured products coming directly from the temporary stimulation of abnormal war-time conditions; (2) rises in export prices were outdistanced by rises in import prices; and (3) the advanced manufacturing countries, especially the US, maintained a dominant trading position. Over the period 1935–46, imports of American cigarettes doubled and the US share of total tobacco imports came to an average 90%.

Not included in the Commission's brief, Cuba nonetheless presented a common trading pattern. Particularly famed during the nineteenth century for its superior quality cigars – names such as La Corona, H. Upmann and Partagás became household words for the aristocracy in Europe and the United States – manufacturing for export expanded rapidly. With the growth of tobacco manufacturing in Europe and the US however, these once importers of Cuban cigars became importers of Cuban leaf.

It was both the leaf and the superior Havana cigar which provided the motive for the American Tobacco Company to speculate on the crisis years of Cuba's Second War of Independence (1895–8) and the 1890 world depression to move in to control production and export. As a result of the political and economic crisis (and the agreement with earlier British interests), ATC was able to buy up land and businesses. Some manufacturers were just about able to hold out, only to be faced with the falling world markets of the twentieth century. And when ATC finally transferred quality manufacturing to the US in 1932, between them cheaper 'Havana' cigars manufactured in New Jersey and machine-produced five-cent cigars took over much of what was left of Cuba's old market.

The Havana cigar became that famed luxury product which had but a small 'niche', as *Fortune* put it,[17] in the mass consumer market of the twentieth century. Its fame and quality it retained, its price also; but its markets were down. At the same time, the new five-cent cigars were blended with cheaper tobaccos. The result was an oversaturation of

Cuban leaf on the world market and all the concomitant problems of a price drop and over-production at home. Cuba might have retained its image of 'land of the *best* tobacco in the world' but, by the mid twentieth century, it was a much-afflicted tobacco-producing country.

The economic, social and political implications of this for Cuba are the subject of this study. The development of the Cuban tobacco industry was held back in such a way as to maintain an archaic structure of cultivation and production. This in itself wrought considerable changes as regards the nature and composition of tobacco growers and manufacturers, and the workforce in the industry. Over the twentieth century, there was a constantly large outwork sector and increasing numbers of seasonal and casual workers, many of whom were women, in the sorting and stemming sheds. The old, if small, aristocracy of labour rolling the luxury cigars was almost completely broken down and a new aristocracy was to grow up in the only really expanding sector, cigarette production for the home market.

The economic insecurity of both manufacturers and workers became manifest in their struggles and their ideology. Wide divisions were created between the large factories and small shops, and between different trades. The fluctuating and irregular nature of work in much of the industry made for the slow growth of unions in general and for splits within them. It also made for a growing militancy and the emergence of more radical ideologies as an early, if weak, alternative to reformism.

While the structure of the labour movement assured aristocrats and their representatives of greater influence than the broad mass of the workers it was temporarily possible for reformism to be strong in this sector. Even this had its limitations, however, as the burden of dependence was passed down the line.

Class ideologies cut across national ideologies that had particular relevance to the industry. Once largely Spanish-owned, with top jobs taken by Spanish immigrants and bottom ones by slave and indentured labour, and then subject early on to American capital – this history helped make the tobacco industry the scene of early conflict whose ideological ramifications spanned annexationism, abolitionism, nationalism, anarchism, anarcho-syndicalism, socialism and communism. The old Spanish-owned and later American Trust factories were to become initial focal points for worker unrest and organization and veritable battlegrounds for ideology. But, from the late nineteenth century on, there was wider unrest and political radicalism that was often on the margin of any established unions as such. As conditions ripened for the expansion of union organization into new areas and trades, so this radicalism gained a strong foothold in a sector-wide labour movement. Tobacco workers came to be highly active in defending not only their own interests but also those of the Cuban working class as a whole. For this reason, among others, they were particularly targeted in an anti-union war whose effect was ultimately to channel class action into the underground and insurrection.

PART ONE

Development and distortion of Cuban tobacco

1

Don Tabaco, 1817–88

There was a period in the nineteenth century when Cuba was able to develop as a tobacco-manufacturing country in its own right. Earlier moves toward working the tobacco leaf (largely as snuff) had been seriously curtailed by a Spanish crown monopoly. Under the Real Factoría (1717), Real Compañía de Comercio de La Habana (1739), and Nueva Factoría (1761),[1] manufacturing in Cuba was prohibited and all tobacco purchased at a fixed price and exported to Seville for manufacture.

To all intents and purposes, an increasingly strong eighteenth-century oligarchy turned from tobacco to sugar, which was proving to be lucrative in other Caribbean islands. The fact was, however, that in the rush of later eighteenth-century sugar expansion, one area had been unsuitable for sugar cultivation. This was Vuelta Abajo in Pinar del Río province, which proved to combine especially rich soils and climatic conditions suitable for cultivating a fragrant tobacco leaf. This proved to be a particularly fine cigar wrapper and went well with a darker filler tobacco from an area spanning Las Villas and Camagüey provinces, called Vuelta Arriba.

This tobacco and the cigar that was made from it were much coveted on the overseas markets that were being opened up with the technical and industrial transformation of Europe: symbolically, the first big market for Cuban cigars was to be London. Foreign agents began to operate in Havana around the turn of the century, and it has been argued that the Factoría came to be so mismanaged that, by selling off stocks of leaf to individual manufacturers operating illegally, officials prepared for its downfall. It only remained for Arango y Parreño, main spokesman for the new rising oligarchy, to be appointed Factoría adviser and prepare an eloquent report on the abuses of the monopoly which had led to the stagnation of tobacco production, for pressure to be such as to make abolition of the Factoría inevitable.[2]

Somewhat paradoxically, since the cigar and cigar tobacco were the motive force behind the abolition of the Factoría and Cuba's subsequent tobacco development, it was the cigarette that was cause for early innovation and was *the* Cuban smoke. No traveller left Cuba without commenting on its popularity. 'Wherever one goes in Cuba, one encounters the cigarette more frequently than the cigar. In the streets, during intervals of the opera, between the lips of pretty women, between different courses of a meal, and even at the entrances to churches one finds the delicate and fragrant cigarette', wrote one of the more celebrated of such travellers.[3]

By the mid-1860s, sizeable cigarette factories were owned by Bernat Rencurrell, José Mendoza and José Susini y Rioseco. In 1863, Susini's La Honradez factory claimed to have a daily output of 3,000,000 cigarettes, accounting for one-tenth of Havana production (one-twentieth of that of the island as a whole) and supplying the royal houses of Europe. The factory was enormous for its time, employing some 2,500 workers in all, but Susini had also embarked on a technical revolution in Cuba by inventing an elaborate cigarette machine. As a result of this machine, presented at the 1867 Paris Trade Exhibition, the factory's renown spread to Europe. The machine and other innovatory processes such as the special aromatic liquid through which cigarette tobacco and paper passed, the general organization of the factory, including its fine lithograph department, in short its overall 'magnificence', made Susini's factory 'the symbol of industrial progress in the island'. It was described as 'an industrial establishment of the first order, the most important perhaps of the Spanish overseas possessions and one of the greatest in the manufacturing world'.[4]

Susini's machine inevitably helped account for increasing cigarette exports – largely to South America but also Europe and the United States – from just under 9 to 40 million packs over the period 1859–90. In this same period, however, Cuban cigarette production was fast overtaken by developments in the industry worldwide and, at home, soon overshadowed by, and merged with, the manufacture of cigars.

There is no doubt that cigar manufacturing was Cuba's nineteenth-century industry *par excellence*. Catering to a rapidly growing export market from the early years of the century onwards was a rapidly growing industry and some rapidly growing concerns.

The earliest cigar-rolling shop of importance was said to be Hija de Cabañas y Carvajal, founded by Francisco Cabañas in 1810 (although he had been manufacturing cigars since 1797). He was responsible for the first Havana *segar* on the London market where, by the 1820s, quality hand-rolled 'Havanas' had a solid reputation. Equally, by the 1820s, Havana was reputed to have a total of 400 rolling shops and to be well on the way to becoming the 'tobacco city'. Jaime Partagás (1827) and Ambrosio de Larrañaga (1834) consolidated their Havana shops, and London prices for 'Havanas' rose from 2–12 pesos a thousand, according to size and class, in 1828, to 5–20 pesos in 1832, and 12–36 pesos in 1847.

Subject to yearly fluctuations, exports increased from just over 140 million in 1840 to nearly 360 million in the peak year of 1855, with growing demand in Germany, Denmark and France, as well as England, and to a lesser extent the United States and Spain. Some of Cuba's major cigar factories of today date back to the 1840s – H. Upmann's La Madama (1844) and La Corona (1845) are cases in point. H. Upmann marked the first direct German capital investment in Cuban tobacco, to be followed in the sixties by Gustav Bock's Aguila de Oro.

The growth of the industry over this period was, indeed, phenomenal. According to a statistical report of 1861, of a total of 1,217 cigar-rolling shops throughout the island, 516 were in Havana and 158 registered as first class, that is, with fifty workers or more.[5] In some, numbers of workers were already into their hundreds, the Cabañas factory having 300. Similar figures – a total of 1,300 shops for the island and 500 in Havana – are quoted by Hacienda in 1862.[6]

Nonetheless, if by the mid-century this small Caribbean island had gained a reputation for manufacturing the finest-quality and most valued cigars in the world, yet the tide had already turned. Despite fluctuations and abnormally high exports in 1855, from that year on Cuba's overall, long-term export market began to recede, oscillating for most of the latter part of the century between 100 and 200 million cigars a year. The late 1850s European trade recession was but a temporary factor in this. More important was that in the years 1859–70, Cuba's major cigar markets, Germany and France, cut imports by two-thirds and one-half respectively. Only England continued systematically to import, rather than manufacture, cigars.

These trends were largely obscured by the fact that these were years in which there was a fast-growing US market, owing largely to late industrial take-off after the War of Secession, which ended in 1865. In the 1870s, the United States was to become Cuba's largest single importer, and by the 1880s was handling virtually all Havana cigar exports. When US imports began to fall off in the 1890s, Cuba's total export figures stood at approximately half their 1850s level.

More significantly, prior to 1855 leaf exports had risen roughly proportionate to exports of manufactured tobacco, although in quantities far superior to the amount used in that manufacture. In the period 1855–90, there was, as against the drop in cigar exports, a 30% increase in leaf exports to Germany, other European countries and the US. By the 1870s, the US alone accounted for the bulk of exports, pricing Germany out of the market. According to the British consul's Havana trade and shipping report of 1878, the US was by then the only significant importer of leaf,[7] a fact later corroborated in official statistics for 1890.[8] Moreover, the value of exports was consequently inverted: in 1859 the value of cigar exports was twice that of leaf, in 1890 leaf twice that of cigar.

In the early part of the nineteenth century, US manufacturers were producing clear Havanas made with Cuban tobacco and retailing them at four to five times the price of the domestic cigar. During the 1850s, 'half-Spanish' became literally true of the US industry as a whole. The amount of Cuban leaf imported – mostly through New York – was about equal to the amount grown in all of New England and it had become well-established that the Havana leaf was the *sine qua non* of good cigars. The great Havana tobacco warehouses for exporting the leaf date back to the forties and fifties, one of the most important being that set up by tobacco grower and financier Juan Conill in 1840.[9]

It was quite possibly Conill's success and tremendous importance in tobacco, financial and government circles that again helped mask the full implications of exporting great quantities of leaf abroad. There had been, it is true, recurrent problems of imitation cigar brands being manufactured abroad from the 1830s on, and this had led to certain demands for the prohibition of leaf exports. As a response to such early demands, the Sociedad Económica de Amigos del País invited essays on the subject. The winning essay was that of Antonio Bachiller y Morales, who argued strongly against such prohibition.[10] And, in 1851, a major study on tobacco could still compare the stable future conditions offered by the tobacco industry favourably with those offered by other products of Cuba.[11]

Not until the late fifties did a new generation of the more intelligent of the Havana tobacco oligarchy begin to express concern over the future of manufacturing in Cuba. Rivero Muñiz mentions Luis Susini

(José Susini's son) submitting a formal petition to Hacienda in 1857, asking for leaf export prohibition, reduction or duties. 'Very soon, alas, that industry will be finished in this country, so that we will have to resort to purchasing abroad our very own product', he wrote, 'or nationals who depend for a living on that industry will have to go to those same foreign shores in search of work.'[12] It was his fears on this score, no doubt, that led him to a later, unsuccessful venture to establish a cigarette factory in the St Sébastien free-trade area on the French–Spanish border.

In an essay on the agricultural and commercial production of tobacco in the island, written in 1862, Ramón de la Sagra commented on two articles published in the *Diario de la Marina* on 11 and 12 December 1861, referring to the problem of increasing leaf exports and declining cigar exports:

Its author takes stock of these notable or significant differences and attributes the decline in the importance of cigar rolling to the development of similar foreign manufacturing . . . it is to be lamented because of this, that the products of the island's leaf, manufactured beyond her confines, compete with the Cuban products at the point of consumption. It would not be impossible, he adds, for us also to see, if the decline continues and the tariff system so permits, what we need for our own production leaving the ports of this country, to be re-introduced through them in the form of what we need for our consumption, after having been worked abroad.[13]

The extent to which tariffs, especially US tariffs, could hit the Havana industry is well exemplified by that introduced in the United States in 1856, when Cuba's exports dropped by almost one-third. Rivero Muñiz argues that it was as a direct result of this that some of the first manufacturers moved to Key West and New York. Over the next two decades, the high tariff rate was to be a constant problem for manufacturers in Cuba. 'The surcharge of 19 per cent imposed on the entry of finished cigars into the United States', continued the *Diario de la Marina* article quoted by De la Sagra, 'increases day by day the fears of Cuban manufacturers who are already suffering from foreign competition and from the duties with which their artefact is burdened in all parts, when its sale is not absolutely prohibited or stagnant.'

Cuban manufacturers were fast finding themselves in the anomalous position of political dependence on Spain, whose interests lay in protecting its own manufacturing interests, and economic dependence on the US, with an incipient industry embarking along the same protective path.

In 1867, the British consul was still reporting that the value of tobacco had advanced greatly over the past five years and that the demand for cigars of superior brands far exceeded supply. In 1874, however, he was to comment on the falling off of demand for cigars and accumulating stocks in Havana, and by 1878 was prescribing gloomy prospects for the Cuban industry:

Owing to the excessive import duties into the United States, almost prohibitive as regards cigars, 1,500 factories have sprung up in that country to enjoy the advantages of this protection by importing the leaf and selling their countrymen inferior cigars . . .

The secession of the United States from being the greatest consumer of cigars to being a considerable manufacturer, though not as apparent as expected, probably owing to the strikes of cigar makers in that country, is not on that account any less real.[14]

Little wonder that both annexationist and independence movements should find among cigar manufacturers some of their more monied supporters and that there should have been a constant stream of Cuban manufacturers emigrating to the United States for an amalgam of political and economic motives. The historical paradox was that those manufacturers to do so, importing Cuban leaf and able to take advantage of marketing their product without additional import duties, were the ones to prosper. So much did they prosper that by the end of the war Julián Alvarez, owner of the Henry Clay factory and then president of the Gremio de Fabricantes de Tabacos, was lamenting the fierce competition manufacturers in Cuba were facing from those who had emigrated. He calculated their unit costs of production as only 65.7 pesos, as compared with 110 in Havana. Duties levied on leaf were being kept at a minimum as agents for foreign firms set up stemming shops in Havana, so as to reduce the dutiable weight of the tobacco.[15]

Undermined both internally and externally, conditions in the industry were such as to bankrupt many smaller manufacturers who had remained and create an 'almost untenable situation', according to a manufacturers' report of 1886. Eyewitness accounts of the late 1880s and early 1890s may have referred to small cigar-rolling shops on every block in Havana. Even a cursory glance through the Registro Mercantil de La Habana, however, testifies to the ephemeral nature of a great number of these, and many more must never have been registered.

Against this backdrop, renewed US exports provided larger concerns with the opportunity to consolidate their interests. The result was that the latter part of the eighties witnessed a concentration of capital and a fusion of enterprises (as well as fierce industrial conflict, strikes and lockouts) of an unprecedented scope. Some smaller manu-facturers, such as Benito Celorio, Rafael García Marqués, Alfredo Nogueira, Juan Cueto, and José María Galán, who either held out during the war years or started in business afterwards, were able to build up their concerns. The Susini factory – then called La Legitimidad and owned by Prudencio (Marqués de) Rabell – remained one of the most important cigarette factories, although on a scale much reduced as compared with the 1860s. It had largely been superseded by expanding new factories like La Corona, using first an improved Cuban–Spanish machine and then an imported Bonsack.

The giants by then producing both cigars and cigarettes were Cabañas y Carvajal, Henry Clay and Bock, La Corona, Gener, Partagás (then in the hands of the Bances family, one of the largest banking houses of the time, with considerable tobacco businesses)[16] and Murías. By the late 1880s, the first three of these were turning out 12 million cigars a year for export and employing 1,000–2,000 workers, Their greatness was such that their factories were palaces of great architectural splendour, setting the tone of building for the period. La Corona, in Aldama Palace, was described in an 1890 pamphlet as especially outstanding for its 'rich, panelled ceilings, excellent paint-ings, notable watercolours and frescos', and it was noted, 'with all the manufacturing there, the marble floors are shining clean and only the fragrance of cedar wood prevails'.[17]

For these export giants, at the zenith of their manufacturing history, Havanas were lucrative business.

2

Enter monopoly capital, 1888–1902

Monopoly capital first penetrated the Cuban tobacco industry in the last decade of the nineteenth century. The very structure of world tobacco production and the internal economic and political conditions of Cuba, by weakening Cuba's manufacturing potential, favoured that penetration on a large scale and set the pattern for the future development of the industry as a whole.

In 1888, British interests began to invest considerable sums of capital in buying up tobacco concerns. That year, both Henry Clay and Bock and Partagás were secured and London companies set up under the same name. Bock, Alvarez and Bances became shareholders and directors, Bock and Bances the Havana managing directors, of the respective new companies.[1]

The penetration of British capital was fostered by official British policy in Cuba. In 1890, the British consul found hope for British enterprise in tobacco. 'It would be regarded favourably by the Spanish and the Cubans', he commented, 'because they understood that the interests of Great Britain are of a purely commercial character, and their development can, therefore, tend only to the preservation of social order and security of property.' Although the interests in Partagás – which had been largely directed toward its leaf growing property[2] – were liquidated in 1896, two years later the London company, Havana Cigar and Tobacco Factories Ltd, was set up, subsuming Henry Clay and Bock and Co., and again with Bock as Havana managing director. This company came to control some of the largest factories in Havana, including Aguila de Oro, La Corona and La Legitimidad, and some 35 cigar and 18 cigarette brands.

Until this point, relations between the United States and Cuba as regards tobacco had been almost exclusively mercantile. This changed dramatically, starting in 1899, when the Havana Commercial Company (promoted by H.B. Collins and Company of New York) bought up one cigarette and twelve cigar factories in Havana, bringing them under one organization with the important leaf business of F. García Bros and Company.

It was this company which facilitated the later absorption of Havana's tobacco industry into the American Tobacco Company. In 1901, ATC moved into Havana, combining some twenty factories under the newly created American Cigar Company and, by 1902, had absorbed Havana Commercial. That year, a new subsidiary, the Havana Tobacco Company (later to become Cuban Tobacco) was set up to consolidate all ATC Cuban holdings. Havana Tobacco subsequently bought the capital stock of two important factories, the Marqués de Pinar del Río and Hija de Cabañas y Carvajal, their owner Leopoldo Carvajal (Marqués de Pinar del Río) becoming shareholder and director. Henry Clay and Bock and the Havana Cigar and Tobacco factories remained officially registered British companies but financial control passed into ATC hands.[3] What was to become ATC's important Havana subsidiary, the Cuban Land and Leaf Tobacco Company (formally established in 1903), came to control sorting sheds, a large stemmery and important tobacco lands (previously belonging to Henry Clay, Cabañas y Carvajal, Havana Commercial, and other individual companies). It thereby came to control supplies of the much-sought-after leaf in the Vuelta Abajo region of Pinar del Río province.

British capital had first moved into what was a prosperous and expanding Havana export industry. The period in which later British and American capital secured a monopoly over Cuban tobacco, however, is significant. The relative prosperity of manufacturing in the late 1880s was cut short as US protectionism reached its height in the McKinley Tariff-Law of 1890, increasing duties from $2.50 to $4.50 per lb on cigars imported into the United States and maintaining a 25% *ad valorem*. It has been calculated that on 1,000 cigars, weighing 14 lbs and valued at 80 pesos, 83 pesos were paid in customs duties and internal taxes. The result of this was that yet more manufacturers emigrated and, importing the Cuban leaf, began to consolidate their position in the manufacturing world of the United States. The decades of the 1880s and 1890s witnessed the growth not only of the great tobacco-manufacturing centres along the east coast but also of a whole area new to tobacco, namely Tampa.

It was in this period that the Tampa Board of Trade and municipal government, interested in the industrial development of the region, initiated a policy of fostering the tobacco industry. Attracted by the Board's policy, Cuban manufacturers already in the States and others coming directly from Havana settled in Tampa. Among them were the émigrés Hidalgo Gato and Vicente Martínez Ibor, around whose factory Ibor City was founded. Tampa subsequently developed as a leading cigar-manufacturing area in its own right, producing a large proportion of quality cigars made from imported Cuban leaf. The region escaped the 1890s depression somewhat, precisely because of its rapidly growing and prosperous tobacco industry.[4]

In Cuba, there is no doubt that the 1890s represented a second turning point and initiated a prolonged collapse of the cigar export industry. US protectionism in the form of the 1890 McKinley Bill combined with particular resistance on the part of the Spanish colonial authorities to any attempted renegotiations of either internal taxes or the terms of the US tariff. An indication of just how badly the industry was hit during this period can be seen in the series of reports drawn up by leading tobacco manufacturers of the day. '. . . before the rigours of the new US tariff, which places the tobacco of the Island in the most precarious circumstances, and having moreover almost completely closed to it the market of the Peninsula, help should be given to this important source of wealth', they pleaded in 1891. Their recommendations – the immediate suppression of export duties and a new trade treaty with the United States – met with a rather unhelpful announcement from Madrid to the effect that 'the criteria of the Government would be based on the necessity of harmonizing the interests of Cuba with those of the regions of the Peninsula largely favoured by the trade legislation in force in such a way that the former are producing as little as possible'.[5]

The Compañía Arrendataria de España was at the time buying only half the stipulated amount of leaf tobacco, and the entry of manufactured tobacco into the Peninsula was strictly limited. Taxes on tobacco manufacturing in Cuba were being raised so much that in 1893 the manufacturers delivered an ultimatum to the Madrid government which read: '. . . if the repeal of new and increased old taxes is not achieved within a short period of time the cigar manufacturers will find it impossible to continue carrying out their industry'.[6]

The full tobacco dilemma was again spelt out in a subsequent manufacturers' report of that same year:

. . . the most alarming fact, and that which best shows the decline of the industry, is that to the extent that cigar exports decrease so do those of the tobacco leaf increase . . . That increase in the export of the raw material brought with it, as is natural, a considerable decrease in the supply and, as a logical consequence, the increase in price of the product, which was damaging to the industrialists in Cuba and beneficial to those in other nations; for, while the price of the raw material is the same for all, there is a disadvantage as regards other conditions, for import duties levied on tobacco are greater for cigars than for leaf, and export duties here are of the same character – that is, they are greater than for the manufactured product with which we freely concede a premium to foreign industry. Due to this is the strange fact that a cigar made abroad exclusively with Cuban raw material is cheaper than the cigar manufactured in Havana and exported. It is primarily to this that the development of the tobacco industry with Cuban leaf in Germany and the United States must be attributed . . . and the successive closing down of cigar- and cigarette-rolling shops . . . here.[7]

Their eloquent words fell on stony ground, while the US government took steps to take advantage of the situation. As the Cuban manufacturers' union put it:

Government officials in the United States, endowed with a practical spirit which leads them to push with extreme perseverance and incessant activity for all that which lends itself to the grandeur of their country, observe, step by step, the rapid decline of the Cuban industry, and, eager to sap its last strength and carry it to total extinction, make the following offers to Cuban industrialists . . .[8]

The offers included a three-storey building, 60 feet long, and a $100,000 credit at 7% annual interest. The manufacturer was committed to producing 10 million cigars over a period of three years, at the end of which he became legal owner of the said properties. 'These, made to an industry on its last legs', the Cuban manufacturers cried, 'could not be more tempting for the immediate acceptance of those who are on the verge of seeing their interests, which they had been able to build up over long years through constant effort, being annihilated.'

Again tobacco was a major factor in the Second Independence War of 1895–8, from which it was also to suffer such dire consequences. Overall figures for the tobacco crop were down 20% by the end of the war, as much as 90% in some tobacco districts of Pinar del Río. According to a report drawn up on the Pinar del Río situation by Bock in 1899, the scarcity of rural labour produced by recruitment into the liberation army and an overall population drop of 60% in some tobacco areas, plus government seizure of oxen, land being laid waste and cuts in credits, all meant that many tobacco farms were ruined and tobacco growing limited to extremely small zones.[9]

Without a crop, without the raw material, many tobacco factories faced insuperable economic difficulties. Politically, manufacturers were again drawn into the war with Spain and again the object of political persecution. Others, foreseeing an increasingly bleak future, preferred to follow the example of those before them and either transfer manufacturing to the United States, often supporting the war from there, or simply sell out.

Thus it was that American Tobacco speculated on the crisis years of what was soon to become a Spanish–American–Cuban war, to effect the earliest onslaught of monopoly capital on any one sector of the Cuban economy. It was a war which marked US imperialism's first major offensive whose pay-off was a sphere of influence for US investment over the whole of Central America. In Cuba, this and the ensuing military occupation from 1899 to 1902 consolidated already existing interests and also new financial ventures. General reports on investment possibilities were the prelude to major US companies, including American Tobacco, moving in.[10]

Contrary to other sectors, tobacco fell to the US onslaught without any prolonged rivalry with earlier British interests.[11] Backed by its ITC agreement, ATC bought up land and businesses that included the major cigar and cigarette factories of La Corona, Cabañas y Carvajal, Henry Clay, Murías and La Legitimidad. By 1902 it controlled 90% of all cigar exports and had effectively eliminated or co-opted some of the most active and influential members of the tobacco oligarchy into its two subsidiaries, Cuban Land and Leaf and Havana Tobacco, whose Cuban president was Gustav Bock. Through the former it successfully guaranteed supplies of prime tobacco leaf and through the latter embarked on a concentration of production and modernization of manufacturing plant in Havana.

The motive force behind Duke's policy in buying up the Havana industry has long been the object of speculation, and the general assumption has been that he overstepped the mark. Virtually every account of the industry in this period points to two things. Whereas in 1902 the Trust exported 90% of cigar exports, the figure was down to 52% by 1904. From 1906 to 1922, Havana Tobacco ended each year (with the exception of 1920) with a deficit. The company failed, it is argued, because production costs were high, tariff barriers prohibitive and workers well-organized, traditionally well-remunerated, and determined to see things stay that way, staging some of the biggest known strikes in 1902, 1907 and 1908.

In the light of subsequent developments, ATC's long-term Havana policy can be seen to have been fourfold: (1) buy up major factories, (2) streamline manufacture, (3) transfer production for export (especially to the US), while (4) guaranteeing leaf.

A major concentration of production took place. In 1904, Bock referred to a total of 23 factories.[12] Within a year, there were only seven – Cabañas, Henry Clay, Manuel García Alonso and La Intimidad, Aguila de Oro, J. Murias, and La Carolina. Occupying their former buildings were only Henry Clay, Manuel García Alonso, and La Intimidad. Cabañas cigars, along with Villar y Villar, Pedro Murías, Flor de Inclán, Flor de Cuba and Flor de Murías, were moved to the company's new building in Zulueta, aptly nicknamed *El Panteón*, as all the factories were being 'buried' there. The former Aguila de Oro factory was transformed into the general stemmery and drying department.[13] Over the years, this process continued, and by the 1920s only the Henry Clay (La Corona) factory, housed in Aldama Palace, and the Zulueta factory remained.

And yet, the least successful part of Havana policy was modernization, for the obvious fact that the cigar machine had still not been invented but also for reasons that will emerge in chapters to come. With the advent of the US machine in the 1920s, and widespread opposition to it in Cuba, ATC was again able to take advantage of the crisis years of the late twenties and early thirties to withdraw its cigar export production. In the process, it left for domestic manufacture and a tiny fraction of export production only 200 of what was at the turn of the century a workforce of 5,000.

The point remained that ATC strategy was able to fit in with a world situation it and other tobacco monopolies had helped create. It was a situation with which Cuban manufacturers who had managed to hold out were hardly equipped to cope. Fiercely proud of their past and their quality brands, the 'independents', as they were called, plunged into a head-on rivalry with the Trust and were to spend the next fifty years on the defensive, fighting for piecemeal measures to keep the old industry going.

3

Legacy to past prosperity, 1902–24

When the American military occupation ended in 1902 and the first independent republic of Cuba was set up, the tobacco industry was indeed in a critical state. The magnificent buildings in which the tobacco factories of Havana had been established stood as a legacy to nineteenth-century prosperity. The fortunes that had been made within their walls had been undermined. Devastation from the wars, foreign competition and investment, and the closing of overseas markets had taken their toll. The promises of future prosperity on the part of the occupying US government had hardly been fulfilled. The tobacco industry was no exception and tobacco manufacturers in Cuba found themselves threatened on all sides.

In 1900, Rafael García Marqués, owner of the Real Fábrica de Tabacos Independientes, La Belinda, and then president of the Unión de Fabricantes de Tabacos y Cigarros (which excluded the Trust), wrote a particularly eloquent *Account of the grave situation of the tobacco industries, the causes of their decadence, and measures which are considered necessary to save them from the ruin that menaces them* for the president of the United States, W. H. McKinley. 'Excellent Sir', his report began:

When, on the 1st of January, 1899, Major General John R. Brooke took possession of the government of this Island and announced that the government which he inaugurated proposed among other things to establish confidence, aiding the people to return to their peaceful occupations, promoting the cultivation of the abandoned fields and encouraging commerce, The Cigar and Cigarette Manufacturers' Union, over which I have the honor to preside, awaited in confidence the realisation of these purposes, because it thought it saw a sincere desire to restore the wealth of the country, and hoped to obtain at last the official protection which was so much needed for the prosperity of the cigar manufacturing industry. But a year has passed since these purposes were proclaimed and the country has not seen the promises fulfilled.[1]

At the time, the official commissioner, the Honourable Robert P. Porter, had under study the customs tariff in force. For this reason, the manufacturers' union felt it was an opportune moment to expose the precarious situation of the tobacco industry 'to the end of obtaining the measures of protection that are needed to be saved from the ruin with which its existence is threatened'. Over the past ten years, argued García, the manufacturing industry had declined considerably, owing in large part to the 1895–8 war, foreign competition, especially from the United States, and the lack of official protection. 'Unfortunately happened to us', wrote García, 'just the same as to one who builds castles in the air:

. . . that a heavy wind from the *North* swept away such agreeable hopes; and that heavy *North* wind had been your Excellency's Bill which has caused so much ruin in the Cuban fabrile tobacco industry, that, in 1893, the number of factories who closed up their works totally, were so many that they produced to the Government the fall of *twenty per cent* by this estimation, in the list of tax-payers . . .

Commencing in 1890, it began to drag along a languid and unlucky life, whose end will be, if we do not move soon, the disappearance of such a valuable factor of our public wealth.

The loss of the US market was aggravated further as, with the US occupation, the Spanish government classified Cuban cigars as foreign and more than doubled import duties, and as Cuba lost her markets in Mexico, Argentina, Brazil, Puerto Rico and other countries when the Americans moved in. The English market was about the only important market left – and there import duties were rapidly increasing. 'Such seems to be', concluded García, in flowing terms,

that our tobacco industry is condemned, by providential unimpeachable design, never to be free of the prostration in which it is submerged. All calamities fall on it! All misfortunes besiege it!

Formerly it was that the tobacco industries made rich many persons, and under its shade a great many fortunes were accumulated, and the country enjoyed the benefits of that era of prosperity and flourishing of some industries near to be ruined today. In that time, the working man did not make any complaint, neither declare himself in strike to demand better wages. The work was well-compensated as the life necessities were attended at little expense. There was richness in the country and everything was abundant. Nobody haggled a five-cent piece; money was expended with prodigality, and what one acquired in the cigar and cigarette factories on coming into circulation by the consumption helped the retail trade and the small industries given them life. What times those in which so many valuable fortunes were raised up, as those which represented those great cigar and cigarette manufactories whose products have run over triumphantly through all the world's markets, conveying from the one to the other end of the globe the everlasting fame of our rich solanaces. Today, all is grief, discouragement, ruin . . .

To counteract this situation, the manufacturers' union demanded a reduction of duties on imported tobacco into the United States and annexed territories, total suppression of the export duty fixed on manufactured tobacco in Cuba, and the negotiation of reciprocal trade agreements with other countries, particularly the United States.

García's account of the industry and measures for its survival backed up a report prepared earlier that year by Abad, special commissioner for the Asociación de Cosechadores y Comerciantes del Tabaco en Rama, Unión de Fabricantes and other tobacco interests. His statement was submitted to the Committee of Ways and Means of the US House of Representatives at the end of January, arguing the case for a reduction in the import duty of both manufactured and unmanufactured tobacco coming from Cuba into the United States. The reduction, it was thought, would benefit the two countries, but particular attention was drawn to the very considerable benefits for the latter:

It is a fact endorsed by the exporters of this country [the US] that a cigar made exclusively of American tobacco is an inferior article. Add a little Cuban tobacco to it and you make an acceptable and marketable article. The difference between the two products is so great that the money made by the Cuban producer is of no account compared to the money made by the American producer, because of the mixing of the poor and flavourless leaf with the other, which is not only of superior quality but is unique in the world. The price of producing our tobacco is high and we do not compete in the quantity of our crop nor in the price but in the quality. As General Wood states in the last report of the Department of Agriculture of Cuba, the cost of cultivation of our high grade tobacco is more than 200 dollars per acre, and there is no competition with the United States in the price of production.[2]

An increased trade in manufactured products could not possibly compete with American production and would, on the contrary, benefit US commercial interests.

In regard to the cigar and cigarette production, our production is from 200,000,000 to 250,000,000 of cigars per year; the consumption of the United States is over 6,500,000,000. At present, our import is not more than 40,000,000 of cigars, or two third of one per centum of consumption. A drop of water in the ocean. With a reduction of duty, the consumption of this article would increase without any detriment whatever to domestic production and much to the benefit of the American trade. For every cent that the Cuban manufacturer makes on cigars sold to the United States, the American trader makes *three cents.*

Abad, as García before him, reflected feeling running high among Cuban manufacturers: that the only solution was to push for increased trade with the very nation which was rapidly and irrevocably closing its markets to them. Thus it was that the manufacturers' union, alongside the growers' association and other bodies, were instrumental in putting trade relations between Cuba and the United States on a basis of preferential duties. These were first laid down in the Reciprocal Trade Treaty signed by the first republican government of Estrada Palma in 1903. And yet, the already enormous difference in manufacturing potential between the two countries and the very terms of the treaty meant that Cuba was inevitably the unequal partner. In effect, Cuba opened her doors wide to American imports in return for exports of her primary products, tobacco and sugar. The treaty simply exacerbated a trend which had been developing during the late nineteenth century, and so for the next fifty years Cuba's foreign trade relations were to be US-dominated with a vengeance.

Despite the fact that among the main reasons for the treaty were the supposed benefits for Cuban tobacco, the real nature of these 'benefits' soon became apparent. The United States continued to import large quantities of leaf but not cigars. For a brief period, it did seem as though the treaty had improved the situation in the cigar sector: cigar exports to the US rose from 50 to 80 million in 1902–5. By 1908, however, they were down to 39 million, less than the 1900 figure. Overall cigar exports were equally down, while total leaf exports rose from 28 million lbs in 1904 to 49 million in 1909.

It was against this backdrop that a particularly bitter rivalry developed between the independents and the Trust, in which Gustav Bock became a highly controversial figure. In 1904 he wrote a small pamphlet entitled *La verdad sobre la industria del tabaco habano*, claiming in his forty-six years in Cuba 'to have devoted all my time to discovering the most insignificant detail, the best method for producing better quality Havana cigars' such that 'the cigars manufactured under my personal direction in the twenty-three factories of the Havana Tobacco Company cannot be equalled in aroma, quality and manufacture by any other cigar in the world'. The following year, the independents published a reply of the same title 'to put things in order and show the world that the purity of manufacture of the Havana cigar, in the form and established production methods which secured fame for the product, is preserved only in the factories which do not belong to the Trust and which are already known by the name of "independents"'. Bock was 'an active and competent salesman, who has the advantage of knowing European and American markets well', but 'here, in this capital . . . nobody considers Mr Bock to be an able manager of cigar factories' and 'regarding agriculture and industry he is more than mediocre'.

Bock resigned in 1909, the year before his death. By then, the Trust had already begun to transfer production to the States. The independent manufacturers withdrew into a protective shell, 'falling back on their former reputation', and there developed a certain scandalous 'laissez-faire' in manufacture, as was early remarked in Europe.[3]

Internal problems such as these, along with overall export problems, were behind the setting up in 1909 of a national commission to study the state of tobacco as a whole. Comprising the presidents of the Sociedad Económica de Amigos del País, the Cámara de Comercio, the Unión de Fabricantes de Tabacos, and the Liga Agraria, the commission designed a questionnaire to establish the causes for, and possible means of counteracting, the decline in the industry. It was distributed to growers, dealers and manufacturers, and on the basis of the returns the commission drew up its 1910 report.

Attention was drawn to the fact that the great increase in leaf exports had not developed without adverse effects on the crop itself:

The present situation of the cultivation of the tobacco plant in the territory of the Republic progresses, as it has increased considerably, having expanded in the different localities or regions dedicated to it; but it is undoubtable that this extensive cultivation impairs the credit of Cuban tobacco, in a certain sense, because paying more attention to the quantity and not the quality of the product does not always satisfy the demands of the various consumer markets.

The quality of the tobacco had dropped so much, according to the report, 'that it not only had to be sold at a ruinously low price, but by its very use inclined to the discredit of Cuba's tobacco, which up to the present day has been considered without rival'.[4]

Measures – such as the introduction of irrigation schemes, the use of fertilizers, and greater publicity of new agricultural techniques – were suggested to ensure the quality of the tobacco. Attention was drawn to the need to reduce production costs, which had been increased considerably by 'the latest strikes of the cigar makers, especially the one known as the "American currency strike", which raised the cost of labour, thus increasing the sale price', and the fact that special steps should be taken toward setting up arbitration courts between labour and capital.

The main emphasis, however, was on combatting imitation Havana cigars abroad and reducing import duties in foreign countries, in response to 'the general clamour of those who fear the loss of what up until the present has been considered to be our second source of wealth'.

As in the latter part of the nineteenth century, there was an element of prosperity in the industry during this period. A few relatively large 'independent' companies were able to make headway on both the export and the home market. Many of these, even those that changed hands over the early years of the republic, had continued Spanish capital backing.[5] Thus, Ramón Cifuentes y Llano, who bought the Partagás factory in 1900, Ramón Argüelles y Busto, who took over Romeo y Julieta in 1903, and Eustaquio Alonso, who became managing director of Por Larrañga (all three of them Spanish in origin), rebuilt their tobacco concerns over the first two decades of the twentieth century. Romeo y Julieta increased output from 2 to 18 million cigars a year over the period 1903–16. Partagás' output remained constant at around 18–20 million cigars, although this was little in comparison with output during the late nineteenth century. Smaller concerns such as Cano Bros (founded in the 1880s), Rocha's La Competidora Gaditana (1893) and García Marqués' La Belinda managed to corner a considerable part of the market, as did some new companies which were later to be of importance, including Fernández y Cía (1905) and Rodríguez Menéndez y Cía's El Cuño (1907).[6]

Significantly, some of the older companies – Partagás and Gener are examples – moved into cigarette production on a much larger scale and there were, by the 1920s, several growing concerns catering for an expanding home market. On the strength of production during these years, Calixto López, El Cuño, Partagás, La Escepción, La Competidora Gaditana, and La Moda (of another firm founded by Spaniards Villaamil, Santalla y Cía) became big names in Cuban cigarettes.

Most new capital, especially over the decade 1910–20, tended to be directed toward the leaf sector; and among the important leaf handling companies set up during these years were Menéndez y Cía (1910), which later bought up H. Upmann and Díaz (1913), Junco (1916), and Toraño (1919).

None of these companies – whether in cigars, cigarettes or leaf – were to feel the full long-term effects of Cuba's position vis-à-vis the world industry until the 1920s. And yet again it was probably this, together with the continuing political importance of the large manufacturers and leaf dealers and exporters during this period, that has continued to obscure particularly disturbing wider trends. The value of exports of manufactured tobacco was, on the whole, greater than that of leaf exports over the first fifteen years of the century (exceptions were 1903, 1904, 1909, and 1913). However, cigar exports, although more than doubled over the years 1900–4, fell drastically between 1904 and 1924 from 215 to 84 million. Only during the abnormal demand situation created in the aftermath of World War I did they pick up at all. With the 1920–1 crisis, the artificial market collapsed and exports dropped to little over 59 million. The partial recovery of the early twenties was to be no less short-lived. During the same period, overall export levels for leaf maintained a fluctuating but fairly steady average of around 35 million lb. In terms of value, leaf exports were by the 1920s two to three times greater than those of cigars.

Figures such as these contrasted significantly with those of the nineteenth century. By the 1920s, total cigar exports were but one-third of what they had been over the late 1880s. Leaf exports were twice as great. Moreover, taking the period 1904–24 alone, the percentage of leaf being exported – though declining as a result of increasing *home* production of cigars and cigarettes – remained high, more often than not around the 50% mark and over, while the percentage of cigars exported was more than halved, from 54% in 1904 to 21% in 1924. Manufacturing for export was in a very weak position even before the onset of the world depression of the late twenties and early thirties.

4

Mechanization and recession, 1925–33

It has been said: 'It cannot be thought a great contribution to Cuba's development that, after a quarter of a century of participation of American capital, the tobacco industry is just where it was when that participation began.'[1] In many ways it was actually worse off.

The cigar export industry in particular entered its third and most decisive crisis in the period 1925–33. Government legislation, trade treaties and publicity drives all amounted to an ineffective attempt to bolster a long-past world position for Havana cigars. The 1920s cigarette boom in Europe and the United States and the advent of the cheap machine-made cigar combined with the onset of the 1929 world depression to bring much of the industry to a standstill.

In December 1925, Cortina, the liberal leader, proposed the setting up, alongside the national sugar commission, of the Comisión Nacional de Propaganda y Defensa del Tabaco Habano (CNPDTH), which could undertake marketing studies and promote the Havana cigar in countries throughout the world, by means of trade exhibitions, information brochures, trade treaties, and the like. Cortina viewed the future of the industry with considerable optimism. 'Cuban tobacco has been favoured by the social changes which have taken place in mankind', was how he introduced his proposal for the commission:

The rich or powerful classes grow constantly, the workers obtain high salaries, and industry increases the middle class which can allow itself material satisfaction. When travelling abroad one observes that the world has given Cuban tobacco an absolute monopoly. There is not a single sumptuous party in the universe without the Havana cigar being offered as a choice product. We have the most original monopoly which exists in the world for an article of increasing consumption and great importance.[2]

This feeling was widely reflected in the press. 'Tobacco is . . . the second wealth of Cuba, but perhaps it should be the first. If, instead of Cuba being an immense canefield, it were an immense tobacco field, it

might be better economically for us Cubans.'[3] Sugar was manufactured throughout the world, but Cuban tobacco was unique. All that
was needed, it was felt, was an overseas campaign against the tobacco
mixes of other countries passing for 'Havana'.

Because of this Cortina maintained there was no need to worry
about competition from cheap cigars:

The fact that it is an article of refined living implies that the Havana cigar does
not constitute a threat for local industry in many countries, since, as it is an
expensive cigar, it cannot and should not worry the foreign tobacco manufacturers who produce cheap cigars for popular consumption. Our country
should not aspire to be a producer of large quantities of cheap cigars abroad,
since in that struggle it may easily be defeated.[4]

In this context, the attempted introduction of the cigar machine in
Cuba in 1925 was highly controversial. That it should have been
attempted by Por Larrañaga is significant. From Por Larrañaga board
minutes over these years,[5] certain facts come to light: (1) Por
Larrañaga, the oldest of the independent factories, was one of the few
to have grown considerably over recent years – from an authorized
capital of $200,000 in 1913, the date on which the company was newly
formed, to $1 million in 1919; (2) this increase in capital backing came
from the Antilles Cigar Corporation which was subsequently Por
Larrañaga's major shareholder; (3) in 1925 Por Larrañaga had signed a
special marketing contract with a London importing company, Morris and Morris, giving them exclusive handling of Por Larrañaga
cigars;[6] and (4) also in 1925 an intermediary company, the Cía
Tabacalera Nacional, had been set up,[7] with a special contract with the
American Machine and Foundry Company. Of all the independent
manufacturers in Cuba, Por Larrañaga was the one with financial
backing and marketing contracts for such a venture.

It must have pleased American Tobacco to have others take the
early risks in Cuba, just as they had in the States, in attempting to
introduce the cigar machine. But the backers of Por Larrañaga had
underestimated the opposition such a measure would arouse among
the rest of the manufacturers, workers and public opinion in general.[8]
Not to have opposed Por Larrañaga would, for many other manufacturers, have been suicidal, as was made patently clear in a 1926 report
drawn up by Francisco Pego Pita, major partner in Cifuentes and
president of the manufacturers' union at the time.[9]

A lengthy report, it dealt with both export and home production
and what the machine signified for worker, manufacturer, general
public, and national economy. The drop in exports was attributed
largely to imitation Havanas abroad, lack of adequate advertising, and

the high price and decreasing consumption inevitable in a luxury product. Nonetheless, Cuba's greatest overseas demand, it was argued, came precisely for the superior, high-priced Havana. Since the quality and subtle difference in taste of this superior cigar depended on the fine craftsmanship of the Havana cigar roller, it was evident that mechanization could not help increase exports. What was needed was constant vigilance of foreign imitations, intelligent advertising and renewed attempts to reduce high duties on Havana cigars by importing countries. The vast majority of manufacturers stood to lose since production would be concentrated in the hands of the few who could afford to mechanize. It would mean large-scale unemployment, and the home consumer stood to gain little as even machine-made cigars could hardly outprice the cheap cigars hand-rolled for the domestic market.

Their words were well-chosen: 'risking what we have today', they were being 'patriotic in declaring that the machines have not reached a sufficient degree of perfection to replace manual labour, and for having publicly expressed the fear that that kind of manufacturing might jeopardise the well-earned reputation our cigars enjoy the world over'. The report vividly concluded:

. . . what seems to be beyond doubt is the immense damage that change in our method of manufacturing would inflict on the national economy. For the production of 70% of the cigars which are at present made by hand, more than 300 machines would be needed. Costing close to $2,500,000, this would be a major sum leaving the country. In addition, some $48,000 a year would have to be spent in payment of royalties of $1.60 per thousand cigars . . . for the use of patent, and to this has to be added the enormous sum to pay for spare parts to replace those which are worn out. On the other hand, experts would have to be brought in to set up the machines and teach us how to handle them, since they are unknown to us. All these inconveniences would have one possible compensation, that of obtaining a large increase in our exports, something we think we have shown to be highly problematical to achieve. It would be a different matter if the machines were made in Cuba with Cuban materials and Cuban workers and were exploited by Cuban companies; but the reality is such that it means Cubans would be left with a new annual drain without any kind of compensation, leaving many people here, moreover, without jobs, to give them to workers from another country.

The report left the question open to further study, but considerable pressure was brought to bear on Por Larrañaga from all quarters to discontinue machine production. It was finally a presidential decree which compelled Por Larrañaga to use an additional cigar band on their machine-made cigars.[10]

Hope for improving the situation of the industry was centred on the

CNPDTH, finally set up in July 1927.[11] Exports continued to fall, however, and there were continued debates over the question of mechanization. By 1929, a new feeling was growing, to the effect that 'our tobacco problem has no other solution but that of trying to increase production by all means possible to be able to sell cheaply. Nowadays, to oppose the use of machines . . . is to be against progress.'[12]

New impetus was given to a mixed commission comprising government representatives of both executive and legislature, the manufacturers' union and the cigar makers' federation, to embark on a new study. Dr Eugene Molinet, secretary for agriculture, commerce, and labour and president of the commission, openly expressed his sympathy for the machines, considering them to be 'a symbol of progress'. Manufacturers, less financially solvent than before, still firmly believed mechanization could not solve their problems. They presented their case in a lengthy document to the commission, in which they concluded:

the idea would be excellent . . . but in practice all that would be achieved is a lowering of price, never the placing of our cigars at those reduced prices on the foreign market . . . If, many years ago, certain precautions had been taken in Cuba, aimed at least at blocking industries growing up abroad using our tobacco leaf as raw material . . . that one measure would have served to promote our national industry proportionally, or at very least to have maintained the production of the time . . . We can guarantee that the day the machine arrives will be the day the 'De Profundis' can be sung to our industry.[13]

The report had the desired effect. It convinced the CNPDTH of the importance of maintaining the special band on machine-made cigars and of the limited possibilities of mechanization given the gravity of the current crisis. Even Molinet confessed to having changed his opinion completely.

With or without the machine, the 1929 depression caused the almost total collapse of world markets. Cigar exports dropped by some 60% over 1930–2; the US market was down to a rock bottom of 11.5 million cigars, and even England, that non-manufacturing country, was only taking 21.6 million. Por Larrañaga was finally forced to discontinue machine production of the factory's most famous brands, including Por Larrañaga, and by 1936 no machines were in use.[14]

Instability and defensiveness were to pervade the industry. Closures became the order of the day. Export factories in Havana introduced a new type of 'standard' cigar, hoping to increase sales on the home market. By the end of the year, many manufacturers were cutting back production and laying off workers. 'The industry we represent, as you and the public know well', manufacturers declared, 'is passing through such a prolonged and intense crisis that the industry may well disappear completely within a short period of time.' The manufacturers were 'firmly determined to make the greatest sacrifices to preserve what was still left of a once flourishing industry', but they added, 'our resources are not sufficient to face the depth of the crisis'.[15]

Largely at the instigation of the Trust, manufacturers began to threaten closures if substantial wage reductions were not introduced. In doing so, they brought upon themselves a strike paralleled only by those of 1887–8, 1902, and 1907–8. The strike was broken as the large Havana manufacturers moved their factories out to surrounding towns – with the exception, that is, of Por Larrañaga,[16] which no doubt hoped to consolidate its position on the strength of this. The Trust transferred home production to Santiago de Las Vegas and what was left of export production to Trenton, New Jersey.

'The situation of our second industry – and allow me to say "our" because I feel as Cuban as any, now that I have lived among you for over 40 years', stated Trust director Stuart Houston, 'is, at the present time truly agonizing; and I believe that as long as the current economic depression continues all the sacrifices of which industrialists and workers are capable are necessary to maintain the life of our industry, if we really do not want to lose it forever'.[17] At the end of that month, Houston officially informed Molinet of the company decision. A group of employees of Henry Clay and Bock, he blithely explained, had conceived the idea of organizing a Cuban firm for the elaboration of their trade marks, limiting production to the home market. Henry Clay accepted the proposition of ceasing production for export in Cuba and handed over home production to the new company, Tabacalera Cubana, S.A. The company did so, its owners maintained, given the difficulties facing manufacturing in Cuba, namely: (1) the high customs tariffs, which had grossly increased the cost of the Cuban product in every one of the international markets; (2) the depreciation of currencies in countries which had gone off the Gold Standard, thus increasing the cost of Cuban cigars in terms of the value of their respective local currencies; (3) the depression which so adversely affected the consumption of Cuban cigars and which, together with (1) and (2), meant that their price was prohibitive; (4) the fact that high production costs made it impossible for manufacturers to reduce the current prices for export.[18]

As a result of this, Houston maintained, the company was presented with the alternatives of retiring from the export business altogether or transferring manufacture of export brands to the United States, where production could be carried out under conditions which guaranteed substantial reductions on sale price. By adopting the latter, the company would be able to sell its cigars on the US market at much lower prices. At the same time, the appreciable reduction offered to the consumer would produce a considerable increase in demand for one of the most important agricultural products of Cuba, the leaf tobacco.

The move to the States was to be effected in a style which only a monopoly corporation could provide. Leaf operations were in Cuba, but the processing of cigars was to be carried out in a custom-built model factory in Trenton, New Jersey, simulating 'the ideal conditions of uniform and constant temperature which nature provides periodically in Havana', commented Houston in a company report. He concluded:

We can, therefore, assure the Republic of Cuba that, under the new conditions referred to, the cigars which this company will sell, grown and prepared in Cuba and manufactured in the United States, will maintain in every way the credit of the Cuban cigar, which tradition has made famous.

We sincerely hope that this measure will greatly contribute to the prosperity of Cuba and we nurture the hope that the industrial conditions of this Republic will, sooner or later, allow us to again establish in the Island an important part of our industrial activities.[19]

Despite the professed sentiments for the future of the industry, however, the underlying reasons were quite clear and quite anti-Cuban. For those who might feel sympathy with the Trust, this was the way *Fortune* magazine recounted the La Corona story:

In 1933, in the old colonnade palace of Don Miguel de Aldama in Havana, were made 18,000,000 of the world's most sought-after cigars with nearly ninety years of magic in their name, a small number indeed compared to the yearly production of the preceding decade (39,000,000 in 1925). But, of these only about 5,000,000 were sold. Between twelve and thirteen million remained in the warehouses of the Cuban capital. In that fact, and in the idea which it gave the Cuban Tobacco Company's (and American Tobacco's) George W. Hill, lies the germ of one of the most radical changes in the history of fine cigar manufacturing: the transfer of the rolling of La Corona and its related brands from Havana, Cuba, to Trenton, New Jersey.

In January 1932, this was the situation: La Corona cigars were being made in Havana by a subsidiary of the American Tobacco Company. La Coronas were at this time enjoying their greatest prestige as the smoke par excellence, but they were also enjoying their highest recorded price (sixty cents apiece for La Corona size) . . . and as a corollary, their lowest recorded sales. The cause of the high degree of prestige of La Corona brand was sixty-year-old Don Emilio Rivas, of whom more presently. The cause of the high price of La Corona cigars was largely the activity of the Federación Nacional de Torcedores of Cuba, which had forced up the wages of cigar makers . . . And the cigar maker, in addition to his wages, generally rolled for himself to smoke, out of the same tobacco that went into their product, a provision which, during production in Havana, cost the Cuban manufacturing subsidiary of Mr. Hill's great tobacco chain some $25.00 per month. La Corona cigars were being produced entirely in Cuba. In this production were involved some 142 operations; in the rolling of the leaf and the exporting of cigars to their chief market, the United States, was centred the great bulk of production costs which had made it necessary to keep retail prices high and had kept consumption down. In 1929, the net income of operating companies controlled by Cuban Tobacco, after interest and taxes, was $558,335 in 1930, $314,016 in 1931 (1932 figures will show a heavy loss) and its common stock on the New York exchange reached an all-time low of $1. Of the retail cost of Havana-made La Coronas the cost of rolling per thousand accounted for $54, the cost of import into the US and the internal revenue on their sale in the US, $127.90, and the cost of the leaf about $87.

Mr. Hill saw an opportunity to do something. Exasperated by the cost and irregularities of Cuban labour, he figured that by transferring his rolling activities to the US, he could save on (*a*) labour, by getting greater regularity of production and by eliminating the enormous number of cigars smoked by workers, on (*b*) import duty, by paying only 10% on its finished cigar, and on (*c*) the internal revenue tax (which is based upon retail price), since the reductions in labour and import duty would enable him to sell the cigars at a lower retail price . . .

In three months, 200 apprentice girls had made a million cigars, some good, some bad, some indifferent. These practice cigars were packed into boxes and sold anonymously at fifty cents per hundred. Mr. Gold, from his sunny desk in Trenton, then announced that he was ready to produce La Corona for the trade. On September 13, 1932, the first shipment of American rolled La Coronas left the Trenton plant. George Washington Hill and his lieutenants were ready for their campaign which resounded in the advertising sections of the press. Its theme: La Coronas can now be bought at three for $1 and are actually better quality workmanship than Havana-rolled cigars.

Fortune also commented:

When George Washington Hill goes in for something, he goes the whole hog. No half-ways, he assures. He realised in moving his La Corona rolling to Trenton, he would, in order to maintain the tradition of his No. 1 brand, have to have something unique in the way of a plant. He got it. The new La Corona factory – or 'rolling plant', as it should be called – is unlike any other cigar factory in the world. Within the $500,000 tile-roofed stucco, U-shaped tropical looking building, it was necessary to reproduce the atmospheric conditions found within the walls of the old Aldama palace in Havana where, from 1882 to 1932 La Corona, the cigar of kings, was rolled. This was done by engineers and architects, Francisco and Jacobus. Here, with the windows closed, in the moist fragrance of imitation Caribbean air, 2,000 carefully taught Trenton girls roll La Corona cigars, 1,000 with the left hand and 1,000 with the right, the wrapper leaf being split in two, one half having to be rolled in the opposite direction from the other.[20]

By moving into the Trenton plant, ATC cut the price of what was long considered the finest cigar available for American smokers by nearly 50%. To the charge of the Cubans that US consumers would not differentiate between ordinary cigars and La Coronas, Hill gave three reasons as to why they would: (1) Out of the 142 operations involved in the production of La Corona cigars, only one, rolling, was to be performed in the US. The rest would be carried out as they always had in Cuba. (2) The tobacco for La Corona still came from the famous Vuelta Abajo district (largely owned by La Corona producers). No other tobacco made such fine cigars and no other company could get enough of it to put out cigars in an appreciable quantity. (3) Don Emilio Rivas, cigarman of almost 50 years' experience with the company, who worked with the blending of La Corona, making it in the early 1900s the world's leading cigar, went with the company to the States and supervised production in Trenton, just as he had for twenty years in Havana.

La Corona in the States couldn't lose: quality leaf, lower costs of production and an open market, backed by one of the largest world tobacco corporations. La Corona in Cuba was to produce for the 'safer' home market on a 'sounder footing' under a newly formed Tabacalera Cubana, S.A.[21]

5

New Deal for tobacco, 1934–58

What happened in 1932 has been commonly referred to as the sudden 'withdrawal' of the Trust from Cuba, the most severe blow to the industry. Yet Trust policy had simply come home to roost, as it retained in Cuba only its more profitable sectors. As a block, TCSA and Cuban Land remained one of the largest groupings within the industry. There is some evidence that in 1943 the company was seriously considering selling out but, with the post-war introduction of the cigar machine, it was again showing signs of expansion.

While ATC could use the depression to bring Havana production into line with world monopoly tobacco production, Havana manufacturers tried desperately to find ways of implementing their 'natural monopoly' theory.[1] In February 1936, the Havana trade journal *Cuba Importadora e Industrial* initiated a spate of tobacco articles thus:

Many years ago Mr. Thomas Marshall, at that time Vice President of the United States, made his famous statement that the greatest need of the industry was a 'good five-cent cigar' . . . The problem is to find a method for popularizing among the masses the idea of smoking real 'Havana cigars'.[2]

In the May issue, CNPDTH spokesman Francisco Masiques Landeta dramatically contrasted past and present of the Havana cigar and of Cuban tobacco in general. The situation in all tobacco sectors was such, he argued, that 'the greatest of attention has to be paid to this, our second industry'.[3] He called for a form of New Deal for tobacco, and from then on there was increasing 'national concern' over the whole 'tobacco question'.

The concern should not be underestimated. While by the 1920s leaf exports had almost doubled their post-turn-of-the-century level, cigar exports had dropped to roughly one-third, and their 1920s value was little over one third that of leaf. From then on, this proportion was roughly maintained but the levels of both greatly reduced. More specifically, for every 100 cigars exported during the years 1906–10, only 15 were exported in the years 1936–40. In the case of the UK market, the ratio was 100:5. The Spanish market was affected by the Spanish Civil War, and during World War II the UK stopped importing Cuban cigars altogether. As a result, over the years 1937–46, only 10% of the crop was used in cigar manufacturing as against 54% which was exported directly. In the immediate post-war period, 66% of the total crop was being exported and leaf accounted for almost 80% of total tobacco exports. This trend was reversed somewhat over the years 1947–58, as cigar exports doubled and leaf exports increased by only one-third. The US was by then taking 60–70% of leaf, while ironically Spain had come full circle as Cuba's main market for cigars, taking almost half the total trade. In overall terms, the only periods in which the 1920s level was regained in either cigar or leaf exports were the late World War II years of artificially created demand and the post-war boom of the 1950s.

The first disturbing signs for leaf had come from the US market, as more of the cheaper, inferior Puerto Rican leaf was imported for the cheaper machine-made cigars. Puerto Rican leaf imports rose from 15 to 35 million pounds between 1916 and 1926. In January 1927, the *El Mundo* correspondent in New York, López Segrera, reported:

Cuban tobacco seems destined to lose its former predominance in the US market, if active and shrewd initiatives are not soon taken in order to prevent the bulk of this volume of the tobacco trade being definitively channelled in favour of Puerto Rico, is the opinion of Cuban tobacco importers in this city.[4]

A price drop for Cuban tobacco was accompanied by falling exports, which by 1931 were down to 18 million pounds, a figure comparable to that of the 1870s. The improved Cuba–US Reciprocal Trade Treaty, with its reduced tariffs on Cuban tobacco, soon had its effects anulled under the Costigan–Jones Law and the US Tobacco Control Program. The latter in particular established a quota on Cuban leaf that was lower than existing import levels. Tobacco tariff reductions were abandoned eighteen months later under the Agricultural Adjustment Act, and 1902 duties brought back into force.

As a result, Cuba's overall leaf exports fell from 1931 on, with a spectacular 27% drop over 1935–6. Larger leaf handling companies were not adversely affected as they profited from lower prices on growers' surplus crop. The new US-backed Ruppin (1928), Duys (1935), and Rothschild–Samuels–Duignan (1938), plus manufacturing subsidiaries such as the US General Cigar, all came to control extensive tobacco lands and stemmeries in these years.[5]

They could make light of the situation. 'Although the statistics

show how the manufacture of high-quality cigars is constantly declining in the United States', wrote Lee Samuels, president of the
Chamber of Commerce for leaf tobacco in New York and Vice-
president of the Rothschild–Samuels–Duignan tobacco importing
firm, 'the manufacturers have been able to incorporate a certain
amount of Cuban leaf in the lowest priced *vitolas*. This creates, in my
opinion, a very encouraging situation, if we consider that we will
undoubtedly thus be able to educate a large number of smokers,
bringing them to know Havana tobacco and appreciate its superiority'. He continued:

It's true that such a situation will eventually produce bankruptcies for the
growers and holders of Cuban tobacco. It's obvious that for the Havana leaf
to compete at all with domestic or Puerto Rico tobacco, it has to be sold at a
low price level. However, we have to consider this merely as a transitory
situation. Looked at closely, our aim is to construct for the future; and, if that
can be achieved, we must be ready to make sacrifices.[6]

It was clear that Cuban growers were the ones to make the sacrifice.
Unable to protect themselves against a falling market and falling
prices, many faced bankruptcy and loss of land. It was on their behalf
that, towards the end of 1936, Marcelino Garriga (member of the
House of Representatives for Pinar del Río province) proposed a law
for delineating tobacco zones, classifying each according to the
quality of the land, establishing minimum prices and, most important
of all, crop restriction. Another proposal was to create an Instituto
Nacional del Tabaco and implement a Ley de Defensa del Tabaco.
Both were strongly rejected by the Asociación de Cosechadores y
Comerciantes del Tabaco en Rama (in which the large companies
predominated) and by the House.[7]

The issue was temporarily dropped. But by 1939 the problem of
over-production was so acute that Garriga, then speaker for the
House, again began to press for new legislation. He stressed 'the need
that exists to dramatically restrict the tobacco crop' and argued, 'The
problem is so serious for the peace and stability of my province and for
the national economy, whose second industry is in danger, that I
consider that from this moment on, all other problems are
secondary . . .'[8]

The editorial reply to Garriga came down firmly against restriction,
arguing that the draft law 'aspires to solve legally, by means of state
intervention, a situation which is a natural state of affairs, but for
which official bodies are also to a large extent responsible'. The

solution, it was suggested, lay in the area where state action was weak
– in the promotion of trade treaties and, in particular, a modification
of the 1934 Trade Treaty with the US.

December's *Cuba Importadora* reproduced a letter from the leaf
dealers' and growers' association to the president of the republic,
addressing itself to the critical tobacco situation and reiterating the
need for a strong government marketing policy. 'We are not unaware
that the picture we present for your consideration is sombre; but you
may rest assured we have not exaggerated in the least', the letter
concluded. 'If we do not have recourse to measures . . . the tobacco
wealth of Cuba will culminate in absolute and definitive
bankruptcy . . .'[9]

The 1934 Cuba–US Treaty was targeted for particular pressure, and
the new Supplementary Agreement of December 1939 stipulated a
larger quota. It came 'to correct an injustice', commented *Cuba
Importadora* that month, and occasioned renewed hopes in the tobacco
sector. Hopes dampened, however, as exports continued to plummet,
and House discussions were again heated on control, regulation and
restriction of production – though also this time on the manufacture
of cigarettes.

The relative prosperity of cigarette manufacturing for a growing
home market had been such as to attract new capital at a relatively late
date. The Havana-based Partagás (1927), Gener (1937) and H.
Upmann (1947) were examples of this. Perhaps most spectacular of all
was Trinidad y Hermanos, the only really large tobacco factory
outside Havana. Founded in 1922 in Ranchuelo, Las Villas province,
it gained such a rapid hold on the local and then national market that in
1930 output was greater than that of any other cigarette factory. That
year, Trinidad y Hermanos, along with the Trust, accounted for 50%
of total cigarette production.

Prosperity was, however, relative. Increasing taxes, relatively high
production costs, and falling per capita consumption were some
problems cited by manufacturers.

There seems to have been little explicit awareness in Cuban tobacco
circles as to why there should be such a small overseas demand for
Cuban cigarettes, the export situation being attributed to secondary
factors such as poor selling techniques. Manuel Rodríguez López,
agent for Havana tobacco in Europe and the US, rather naïvely
commented, 'It's incomprehensible that a country like Cuba, which
produces the most famous leaf in the world, does not have foreign
markets for her cigarettes'.[10] A 1935 *Tabaco* trade journal editorial ran:

Better cigarettes have probably never been produced in Cuba, both in terms of presentation and quality. The true cause of the bad state of that industry is rooted precisely in other causes, the principal one, which stands out, being the absolute lack of publicity in favour of our cigarettes abroad, the brazen imitations which are being made of them in virtually all the countries of the globe . . .

In so far as manufacturers of Cuban cigarettes suicidally neglected advertising their product, their foreign colleagues dedicated enormous sums to the development of one of the most striking, intelligent and continued publicity campaigns which has been recorded in the commercial world.[11]

There was particular concern over increasing imports of American cigarettes. Even in Cuba, 'land of the best and healthiest tobacco in the world', there were already smokers who preferred foreign cigarettes. 'Why?' asked Roberto Quesada, in the manufacturers' journal *Habano*. 'Are they superior to ours? Is it their quality which has won them millions of consumers? No. It's simply a matter of that abstract thing we call fashion.'

A campaign was started in Cuba against aspects of the blending process of 'fine' mild cigarettes which endangered health, comparing the much better 'pure' Havana products. Another *Habano* article, penned by editor Ricardo Casado, backed Quesada:

. . . those other cigarettes which seem so mild, whose greasy fibres perhaps inspire greater confidence, are positively noxious, and it is not that we are saying this to defend what is ours, it's a matter of the testimony of foreigners . . . Such that, aside from the particular aroma and flavour, in this question there is another aspect of vital importance, because it directly concerns health, the greatest treasure which should be sought on earth.

Indisputably, the most healthful thing a man can smoke is a Havana, but if he doesn't smoke cigars and prefers cigarettes, it is equally indisputable that the most appropriate cigarette from the hygienic point of view, is the Cuban cigarette, free from molasses, glycerine, scents . . .[12]

Other attacks were levelled at the smoker of foreign cigarettes. 'We write these lines in the knowledge we shall give those who like to stand out an unpleasant time', began one article in *Avance*, 30 January 1940.

A largely defensive outcry, it must be concluded, given that imported US cigarettes constituted 0.1% of total cigarette consumption in 1939 – though in all fairness imports had increased in five years from 300,000 to 300 million and mild cigarettes were invading the world. The manufacturers had reason to react strongly to leaf credit facilities funded by an increased cigarette tax. 'We should not stop arbitrarily in one link of the chain to disarticulate and jeopardize a whole industry', they protested:

The crisis which the agricultural sector of tobacco registers is only one of the aspects of the problem. The manufacturing sector is ruined, in perfect and absolute bankruptcy, and it is to be deplored that fact is not considered in the projects. All the more so, that the so-called stabilization of leaf production, at the cost of the industrial sector, would not benefit the leaf but rather bring with it a new bankruptcy of industry.[13]

Proposals on the tobacco industry were endlessly debated in the House. How little was achieved can be summed up in Batista's presidential address to a tobacco workers' rally in April 1941:

When we came to power we were profoundly concerned with the problem of giving stability and permanence to the nation's industries; we considered that the tobacco industry was a basic industry of the country. But, however great our wish to achieve this may be, I cannot promise you today the immediate fulfilment of all our desires. The situation in the tobacco industry responds more to the influences of foreign markets than to our designs.[14]

A changed war-time marketing situation pre-empted the debate. 'What would they say now, the proponents of a drastic restriction in planting . . .' asked *Habano* in July 1943. 'The fact is that there is both overseas and domestic demand.' Leaf exports were up to 34 million lb in 1943, and cigar exports from 18 to 66 to 181 million in 1942, 3, and 4. 'The year 1943 will be hallowed in the annals of our tobacco as its rebirth', wrote José Perdomo in the February 1944 *Habano*. He was quick to qualify it the year after with 'the circumstances which have determined growth . . . are purely transitory'. Ominously, in 1946 cigar exports were down to 60 million, leaf to less than 26 million lbs.

Sudden market changes brought equally sudden changes in policy. Export expansion revived the whole problem of large-scale export of leaf, especially to the US, which was taking over 80% of the total. With increased war demand, US cigar manufacturers were pressing for a new supplementary treaty to suspend the tobacco quota altogether. With an eye to home manufacturing, the Cuban government initially opposed suspension but newly expanded markets had by 1945 caused a change of heart.

Strong conflicts ensued between manufacturers and growers. 'We are advocates . . . of a just, equitable and remunerative price for the Cuban tobacco grower', manufacturers clamoured:

. . . but, in times of shortage and threat and the increasingly serious threat of an absolute lack of raw materials, as is happening right now, we can in no way be advocates of giving or pretending to give facilities in order that these raw materials be extracted from the country in greater quantities, and the nation's industry be condemned to confront a crisis whose extent is difficult to appreciate *a priori* but which we do not doubt will be of enormous dimensions.[15]

The growers counter-argued:

When it was a question of Congress legislating in favour of the growers, the cigar manufacturers, amongst others, opposed the concession of these measures, arguing that the tobacco problem was one of *markets*; today they want to close the circumstantial markets we have, basing themselves on the argument that we should be an INDUSTRIAL COUNTRY AND NOT AN EXPORTER OF RAW MATERIALS; but they think they can maintain the industry in such an antiquated and outmoded form that expansion in industry is practically impossible . . . It has been said that mechanization will produce unemployment . . . but neither do we want wretched growers.[16]

In this the growers were expressing opinions which were gathering increasing support, and war-time conditions had given the tobacco industry a new lease of life certain manufacturers were determined not to lose.

Mechanization of the cigar industry was an issue that had smouldered throughout the thirties as overseas markets were created for other countries' machine-made cigars. There were manufacturers already convinced of the need to mechanize when war-time production gave them the capital to make the necessary investment outlay. A Havana export manufacturers' report of February 1944 argued that the *only* means of recovering overseas markets and averting a coming crisis was by being able to manufacture cheaper machine-made cigars. In October 1945 a special commission was set up to study manufacturers' proposals that Cuba should produce two types of cigars – the high-quality, hand-made Havanas and a cheaper machine-made cigar for the mass market. The proposals were based on a study of mechanization in the United States and a manufacturers' visit to mechanized US factories. 'The Cuban tobacco industry urgently needs to change its present costly methods of production . . . to prepare its defence weapons against the gradual and intensive mechanization of the North American industry', concluded the delegation.[17]

It was also clear that by mechanizing production large manufacturers hoped to capture the home market as small businesses were squeezed out. Such was the opposition, however, which the larger manufacturers themselves had once helped foment, that the final decision on mechanization was delayed until 1950. Only 20% of home production was included in the final decree of that year, and even this later withdrawn.

Splits in the cigar manufacturers' union over this issue were such as to occasion government intervention, and mechanized production and exports forcibly remained a small proportion of total production. In 1953, out of a total production figure of 375 million (exports of 50 million), total mechanized production stood at 20 million cigars.

While the cigar mechanization debate raged on, the cigarette industry again became the object of subsidization schemes for both cigar mechanization and leaf. After much to-ing and fro-ing among manufacturers, growers, and dealers alike, the final form the Fondo de Estabilización took was very much a compromise. Financed by a certain increase in cigarette prices, it was to guarantee minimum domestic leaf prices while promoting higher overseas prices, and to restrict crop cultivation.

Enforcement to this was left to the CNPDTH and the fund, the latter of which soon became notorious for its irregularities in policy and in the buying and selling of leaf, assigning the best quotas to growers selling to the fund and then defaulting on payments. By 1951, a national embezzlement scandal broke, to the tune of $7.5 million. Faced with the new task of re-organization after the scandal, the fund's new president, José Irisarri, confirmed cheques paid to fictitious persons. Articles in the press exposed fund dealings. One charged 'certain privileged manufacturers' with 'abstaining from buying in the field because it was more convenient to do so illegally from the fund', claiming: 'When notice was served of the inevitable closing of the fund . . . it was agreed to wait until the economic stranglehold on growers compelled them to sell below the minimum price'.[18]

Crop restrictions were dropped, as new fund regulations covered price and quality controls. And yet, 'It's difficult to conceive how a minimum price policy could be put into practice, commented *Cuba Económica* in December 1951, 'for a crop which in the previous year evidenced extraordinary oversaturation of the market, without allying it with crop restriction'.

Steps were taken to 'clean up' the fund but the great new hope for the late fifties centred around the Estación Experimental del Tabaco. Set up in 1937 in San Juan y Martínez, in the heart of Vuelta Abajo land, the station had come to carry out considerable research on the growing and industrial processing of mild tobaccos. As a result, considerable capital was being ploughed into the cultivation of light

Burley leaf, both by parastate financing bodies and individual companies producing new mild cigarettes. Partidos and Vuelta Abajo became important Burley producers, such that between 1956 and 1958 Cuba upped production fivefold, jumping from seventeenth to eighth place in world Burley production.

It had to be the final paradox that this should happen to Cuba, by nature the world's great producer of a strong, aromatic, dark tobacco.

6

The peripheral mode of production

In the global context of tobacco, Cuba's mode of tobacco production lagged well behind. 'The raw material comes from a peasant thurrow (small-scale mercantile production) and is fashioned in both artisan workshops (also small-scale mercantile production) and large factories with wage labour (capitalist production)', was how it was described not long ago.[1] What might have resembled an earlier phase of capitalist development, however, was essentially the product of a systematic process of deformation.

Visibly poor peasant agriculture obscured foreign and home capital which, while creating some large plantations, used and even propagated a most extreme form of sharecropping. The fact that luxury manufacturing for export was held back resulted in an archaic industrial structure with only a few relatively large, on the whole family, concerns and a proliferation of small sweatshop and outwork production of inferior cigars for an unstable and fluctuating local market.

Fernando Ortiz, in his classic *Cuban counterpoint: sugar and tobacco,* placed great emphasis on the delicacy and unique nature of tobacco growing and production. Because of this, he argued, it was particularly unlucrative, unsuited to large-scale investment, unattractive to foreign capital and therefore more Cuban. Pinning his whole work on the contrast between sugar and tobacco, he concluded in one of his more famous passages that tobacco signified 'liberty' and 'national sovereignty' as against the 'enslavement' and 'colonial status' of sugar. Paradoxically, he was much nearer the mark when he noted:

By the end of the nineteenth century capitalism was beginning to invade the tobacco industry to an ever greater degree, introducing changes in all branches of its cultivation, manufacture and trade. Even in the ownership of the land, foreign capitalism had been getting control of the vegas. In the last fifteen years, the number of land-owning tobacco growers has dropped from 11,200 to some 3,000. The landowner is disappearing from the vegas and the *guajiro* [peasant] is joining the ranks of the proletariat, becoming undernourished, poverty-stricken, preyed upon by intestinal and social parasites. The economic system of tobacco is gradually approaching that typical of the sugar industry, and both are being strangled by the heartless foreign and native tentacles.[2]

In fact, in tobacco, one of Cuba's leading export products, the capitalist phase of development began early, incorporating elements of feudalism and slavery. Curiously enough, given the spiralling development of tobacco and the general shortage of labour throughout nineteenth-century Cuba,[3] the latter in particular has almost invariably been played down.[4] And yet in both agriculture and industry, it would seem to have been considerable. In 1827, a figure of 7,297 slaves was quoted for tobacco farms. By 1862 – technically well after the slave trade was abolished (1807) – the number had more than doubled. The total number of slaves recorded that year in cultivation was 17,675, plus a further 28,527 free coloureds, out of a total of 75,058. By far the greatest single concentration of slaves was in Pinar del Río province: a total of 12,174 alongside 9,024 free coloureds, out of a total of 36,766.[5] This would corroborate other accounts of large tobacco manufacturers (Partagás was one) operating large tobacco plantations in Pinar del Río based on slave labour.

Small growers, many of whom are said to have been attracted to Cuba from the Canary Islands by the tobacco boom, were soon at the mercy of buying and credit mechanisms controlled by middlemen. Friedlaender wrote of the 1820s–1840s:

The picture was the following: a certain number of Havana merchants (some of whom probably had warehouses) bought tobacco directly from the tobacco grower or from the local shopkeeper, from whom the tobacco grower obtained his supplies, the price (in the latter case) being set more or less arbitrarily, related more to the debts which the tobacco grower had run up in the shop than to the worth of the plant.[6]

Both Rivero Muñiz and Arredondo describe how increasing tobacco cultivation to satisfy both home and foreign markets was accompanied by latifundism. Neither goes into detail, but agricultural statistics available would corroborate a large increase in not only the number but the size of holdings. In Partidos, between 1800 and 1862, the number of tobacco *vegas* or farms increased sixfold and capital invested two-hundredfold, as average capital per farm increased from 11 to 400 pesos.

In the period 1862–77, which was when manufacturing concerns such as H. Upmann, Bock, Murias, Gener, and others consolidated tobacco lands for their thriving tobacco factories, a 40% drop in the number of tobacco farms was registered. This corresponded to new sophisticated systems of land-leasing – *censo, partido, arrendamiento*[7] – which made poor tenant farmers and sharecroppers out of growers. Initially, most were still able to have oxen, livestock, and a small subsistence plot, but an increasingly large part had to be given over to the cash crop as landholders took their substantial cut.

The tremendous increase in the demand for Cuban leaf on the US market from the 1870s on, coupled with the abolition of slavery in the 1880s, help account for why sharecropping would seem to have developed with a vengeance in the eighties. The press of the time was full of articles on the plight of growers, whose subsistence farming dwindled as the pressure for cash crop production increased. An article in *La Voz de Cuba* ran:

All the small tobacco growers, no matter how poor, tried to have as many fruit trees planted in their vegas as the best situated and more hard-working; they grew for their own subsistence, starch, dried beans, corn, millet and many root vegetables, together with all manner of fruits; they raised large numbers of fowl, as well as cattle, and other animals which, whether tethered or enclosed, never wanted in times of drought . . .

There are now hundreds of vegas whose rents are nearly equal to what they bring in. In such a year as the one just passed their crops were sold to speculators at utterly ruinous prices.[8]

The sort of conditions this produced made it easy for companies like Henry Clay and Bock to absorb extensive lands in Pinar del Río in the late 1880s. And large-scale foreign capital investment in agriculture during the Second War of Independence (1895–8), absorbing lands that included those of the old Henry Clay, Cabañas and Partagas, carried this process even further – possibly to the extent that only lands with foreign capital backing were kept under plough.

Indeed, as both domestic and foreign capital moved in, the stage was set for a land scramble that reached its peak in the war years and their aftermath. In 1898, the Honourable Robert Porter might still have written, 'A tobacco plantation or vega as it known, with its kitchen garden, its platanos for feeding the hands, its flowering and fruit trees, its stone walls, its entrance gates and pretty houses, is the most charming agricultural sight.'[9] But direct buying, plus price and credit fixing, was creating a very different situation, which Arredondo so vividly described:

It was a struggle and there was competition: in other words, the tobacco grower was given ample opportunity for easy credit. But when the 'American

Tobacco Company' won out, reaching a monopolistic agreement with the group of 'independents', there was no longer any need to continue buying land or paying any attention to the credit demands of the growers. These were either forced to sell tobacco at the price set by the Trust or, unable to find buyers, face hunger and starvation. When faced with this cruel alternative, the dealers also fell victim to their own selfishness, excepting those who had sold or mortgaged their warehouses and had become mere administrators or agents for the large factories. In the initial stages of the struggle, the dealer laid down the conditions to the manufacturers. And these accepted, for the law was not discussion but control. However, once the monopolistic agreement went into effect, the manufacturers got the upper hand. The dealer had to sell or go under. And even though he might have had great economic power and a great capacity to accumulate tobacco, in the long run he would fall, bound hand and foot before the formidable might of the manufacturer. As is obvious, the burden which the dealer bore he immediately passed on to the grower. In this case, the latter became the most exploited element in the whole production process . . . If trader and industrialist possessed the means of defence to evade the crisis, the grower found himself alone, isolated, defenceless against the brutal determinism of economic reality.[10]

The land scramble produced a fusion of trader and industrialist capital over the early decades of the twentieth century. Instances include Cifuentes, the Santalla Brothers (in leaf since 1889 and who contributed much of the capital in promoting Villaamil, Santalla y Cía in 1905), leaf dealers Rodríguez y López and Menéndez y López behind El Cuño in 1907, and Digon y Dosal (once with Cifuentes) promoting La Competidora Gaditana in 1917.

This, together with the particular growth in leaf concerns over the second and third decades of the twentieth century, served to consolidate some large-scale plantation agriculture with wage labour but also the sharecropping trend. Thus, between 1899 and 1929, the total tobacco land area remained roughly unchanged while output was more than doubled and the number of farms almost halved (from 9,500 to 4,000 in Pinar del Río province and from 15,000 to 9,000 in Santa Clara). Land ownership was quoted in the region of 25% over the whole period.[11] This made for tobacco-producing firms that could have the substantial annual payroll of 400,00 pesos for the year 1935,[12] but also for sharecropping taken, in Arredondo's words, 'to the limits of extraordinary cruelty and the sharp rhythm of monocultivation'.

As the 1930s depression set in, general concern over the leaf sector also focussed public attention on the lack of trade ethics, unscrupulous buying agents and illegal practices. '. . . the grower was at the mercy of speculators and the landowner, to whom he paid rents that were exaggeratedly high', wrote Manuel Fabian Quesada in 1935:

In those conditions, the system for growing tobacco became lackadaisical. An ill-intentioned struggle began between the grower and the speculator, honesty being cast aside by both.

The honourable grower was victim to the greed of buying agents, paid by their employers more to rob than to buy; and decent buyers became the victims of the cunning and unscrupulous grower . . . The economic re-sources of the dealers allowed them to organize *en bloc* in order to compensate, rather dishonestly, for their losses, throwing this on to the grower . . .

The methods used for buying the leaf from the vegas can be defined as gangster-like.

The buyer was usually well paid so that he would become attached to his job. Once an expert was employed; now a strong-arm man was chosen. He paid for the tobacco; but on receiving it all kinds of dishonest tricks were open to him: tampering with the weight of the leaf during transport, damaging it to make it an inferior product, and even at the wave of a Colt there was the typical, 'I'll take this'.

I do not exaggerate. Decent persons were eliminated from the business. Trade practices sowed the seeds of revenge in the countryside. And it has been known for the buyer to go off with a few well-delivered blows from an uncompromising grower.[13]

Subletting of land became common and almost certainly accounts for the wide discrepancy in statistics in the 1940s. In 1942 Raggi y Ageo put the total number of tobacco farms at 4,417. Alienes y Urosa claimed 3,852 in 1943 and 5,732 in 1945 (the increase being attributed to abnormally high wartime demand). CNPDTH quoted 22,750 in 1945 and the agricultural census of that year, 34,437. Land ownership was set at around 20%.[14]

More descriptive accounts of this period throw these figures into relief. Cuban Land, with the largest expanse of administration land, was quoted as having, in addition to 3,300 wage labourers, *partidarios* who could keep for themselves only one-half of their shade tobacco crop, three quarters of sun tobacco. A 405-hectare farm, El Corojo, near San Luis, Pinar del Río, had 500 wage labourers plus *partidarios* who paid 30% of their crop. *Tercedarios* and *cuartidarios* in the Remedios area paid rent to absentee landowners and sub-rented to *partidarios* who paid 50% of their crop. In such cases, the *cuartidario* furnished a place to sleep and board, and the *partidario* was essentially a farm labourer paid in kind.[15]

It was this subletting and sharecropping system that made the tobacco grower all the more vulnerable to market gluts of the kind in this popular peasant refrain of the 1940s:

Once it's been harvested
And stacked up high
Comes the eternal cry
That tobacco's nigh
Down and in Havana stockpiled.

No-one wants to buy
And wait we must
In our fate trust
For all comes to dust
After a hard year's try.[16]

Under these conditions, many were the tobacco growers who for part of the year at least had to sell their labour power – or that of their family – in local sorting, stemming and rolling shops and the like. Some were forced off the land altogether; others, while never completely landless, came *de facto* to swell the ranks of the rural proletariat.

Intensified sharecropping had its industrial corollary in outwork and small sweatshop production. Much of the early nineteenth-century cigar and cigarette production had been hand-rolled in the prisons and the barracks, or in the home. In cigarette production, in particular, there is reference to no more than 45 workers in rolling shops in 1848; and, of the 65 'factories' registered throughout the island in 1862, only six employed 50 or more workers. Much rolling was still done by women on an outwork basis and, to all accounts, by slave and indentured labour.

Slave labour in cigar rolling was probably much more prevalent than established opinion would have it. Piecing together scant figures for the 1860s, for example, it is possible that one-third of the island's, one half of Havana's, cigar makers were at the time slaves, and a further 13% and 18%, respectively, free coloureds.[17]

Cigarette factory owners like Rencurrell and Susini made a point of claiming not to use slave labour but had no compunction in using indentured labour, complaining they could not get the women into the factories. In addition to 300 indentured Chinese, Susini has been recorded as distributing material to some 500 soldiers in the Havana barracks 'who, in their moments of leisure, took to rolling cigarettes' and to 'femmes delaissées' with small children to keep, and several poor families of the surrounding area. Also on record is that he requested the governor for 50 orphans to 'feed, clothe, educate and teach them a craft'.[18]

The technical revolution in cigarette manufacturing, first centred on the Susini factory, slowly began to change this, but even in the

1890s, outwork in the cigarette industry was common enough to produce the rather unusual poetic introduction to a 1898 La Corona Album:

> In this land in all truth
> So poor is it oft sold
> Both lung and life it doth
> destroy . . . be I so bold!
> Manufacturers I know much
> who in white paper pair
> shredded tobacco with hair,
> nails, cockroaches and the such!
> They send tobacco to prison
> where the convicts fashion
> cigarettes oh so slimy
> with their hands all grimy.
> To the hospital of St Lazarus,
> yet much fouler still,
> whence comes a large fill
> of contagion and illness
> and a stench so loathsome
> as the smoke arises from them.
> La Corona is different;
> its building is spacious,
> its machines prodigious,
> its halls well airy,
> where in two hours barely
> are made twenty thousand a cigarette;
> Graceful clean women
> And decent workingmen
> Who care for each sheaf
> of Vuelta Abajo leaf.[19]

In none of the 36 factories recorded in 1890 had hand-labour been completely eliminated. A case in point was La Legitimidad, which employed a total of 700 workers, only twelve of them on the six machines in use.

The relatively scant plant modernization undertaken in the ciga-rette sector after the American Tobacco onslaught at the turn of the century meant that other tobacco interests in Cuba – La Competidora Gaditana, El Cuño, and Villaamil, Santalla y Cía are good examples – were able to build up without great competition. They did not, however, dispose of large quantities of capital to invest in extensive plant equipment. This in turn meant that other, smaller factories sprang up both in Havana and the provinces, especially during the 1920s. Almost all catered for a strictly local market and were never significant in size; many eventually faded out of existence. The great exception was Trinidad y Hnos of Ranchuelo, which, from the time of its founding in 1922, gained such a rapid hold on the local market that in 1930 the factory's output was superior to that of any other Cuban factory.

Nonetheless, a great majority of the small factories were able to survive for a surprisingly long period of time. There were 29 factories in production in 1930. Two, Henry Clay and Bock (Trust) and Trinidad y Hnos, accounted for 50% of total production, but the other 50% was still fairly well shared between the 27 small and medium-sized factories.[20] The 1945 tobacco workers' census still listed 24, although by 1958 there were only 12. On the strength of the post-war home market, three factories in particular – Domingo Menéndez (El Cuño), Ramón Rodríguez (Partagás), and Trinidad y Hnos – expanded sufficiently to make considerable capital investment in basic plant equipment, including the first and only air-conditioning and electronic purifying plants in the El Cuño and Trinidad factories. Together, the three accounted for some 60% of total production. Output of the old Henry Clay factory was down on a par with Dosal y Cía's old favourite La Competidora Gaditana, with an expanding H. Upmann and Villamil, Santalla y Cía (offering a new, mild cigarette 'Royal') close behind. Eight of the twelve factories accounted for some 95% of total recorded production.

Outwork and small sweatshop production had a much longer lifespan in cigar manufacturing, where the technical revolution was much delayed. Late nineteenth-century concentration of production in the export sector brought with it certain changes in the manufacturing process, including a division of labour and the 'detail worker'. Sorting, stemming and blending the leaf became important preliminary stages in quality manufacturing, which also became equated with new specialized skills, such as that of master cigar maker and sorter. Placing the bands on the cigars and decorating the cigar boxes also became jobs in themselves. At the same time, a new category of virtually unskilled work was created in the rolling process, which was the bunching of filler tobacco.[21]

Such changes apart, manufacturing for export continued to be carried out in much the same way but under much depressed conditions and on a much depressed scale in the 'independent' factories of the twentieth century. Thus, as against those 158 factories with over

50 workers in 1862, some 98 in Havana alone by 1890, there were in 1945 only 60. As against those 1890 factories of 1,000–2,000 workers, there were in 1945 only nine with over 200 workers, the largest of which was the H. Upmann factory with 800.

At the same time, if, subject to both seasonal and cyclical fluctuations, overall twentieth-century cigar output remained fairly constant, this was because there was an increase in the home market for a growing population. This was by no means a market for expensive cigars, such as those made for export, and it continued to be largely catered to by small, second-rate, local concerns and private home rollers scattered throughout the island, as it had been in the nineteenth century. Hence the striking comparison between figures for the industry over the span of a century. In 1862 a total of 498 cigar 'factories' were recorded in Havana, 1,302 for the island as a whole. These averaged 8–10 workers in general, in Oriente province 3, and in Pinar del Río 1–2. In 1945, there was a total of 1,050 'factories', 701 of which were small shops of less than 25 workers, a further 289 with no wage labour at all, and 1,382 were private rollers. In Las Villas, the average shop employed not more than six workers, in Oriente province, 1–2.

It was this local and outwork sector that was producing what the 1910 report on the cigar industry referred to as the problem of 'inferior quality cigars marketed in boxes of accredited brands'. Over the next twenty years, an estimated 80% of total domestic output came from this sector. From the thirties on, there were constant references to sweatshop production. 'Few are the rolling shops, with the exception of Havana, Bejucal, San Antonio de los Baños, and Artemisa, where the number of workers passes 50', commented a *Tabaco* editorial of August 1939. 'The majority are small shops or *chinchales* in which a dozen or half dozen rollers rot under terrible conditions.'[22] Twenty years later, the Tobacco Commission estimated that of 1,902 'factories' recorded over half were on the margin of all tobacco legislation.

On the one hand there were the large 'independents', few of whom were ever able to expand greatly in the face of twentieth-century foreign competition and who, on the strength of this, developed their own reluctance to change. On the other hand, there was a proliferation of small sweatshop production, often ephemeral in nature. It stood to reason that overwhelming numbers of both, for very good if historically outmoded reasons, should resist any attempt to introduce the cigar machine, successfully opposing it in the 1920s and even in the

1950s, after a six-year-long battle, still managing to ensure government limitation on its use for the export market alone.

The result was that even during the fifties the overall structure of the industry was little affected. Only eight factories installed machinery, and by 1958 only six continued machine production. In only two of the six – H. Upmann and Gener – did output top pre-1920 production figures. Output from the Partagás factory was significantly lower. Combined, all six accounted for less than 20% of official estimates of total cigar output for that year, possibly more like 10% of the real total.

By the late 1950s, while cigarette manufacturing could be classed as one of the more advanced sectors of the Cuban economy, cigar manufacturing was one of the most backward. According to BANFAIC figures for 1954, two tobacco factories were among the 14 plants employing more than 500 workers: H. Upmann cigars (800) and Trinidad cigarettes (535).[23] Reviewing 1950s manufacturing as a whole, O'Connor placed the cigarette industry in a top group of nine manufacturing industries in which the average plant employed between 201 and 500 workers, and cigar manufacturing in a bottom group of 12 industries in which the average plant employed 50 or less.[24]

Perhaps most telling of all, in the context of colossal world tobacco corporations, was that in the mid-twentieth century the most advanced form of capitalist manufacture in the Cuban tobacco sector as a whole (excepting foreign subsidiaries) was predominantly that of the small family firm. Cano, Cifuentes, Romeo y Julieta (the Argüelles family), Gener, Villaamil y Santalla, and many more were family concerns that had been passed down from generation to generation, their glory waning over time. H. Upmann, one of the oldest and more prosperous of the family firms of last century, that had changed hands twice in the twenties, was finally bought up in 1937 by the leaf-dealing Menéndez family. They subsequently established themselves in both cigar and cigarette manufacture, but the latter in particular. Leaving aside Tabacalera Cubana and Cuban Land and Leaf, their relatively modest family concern – Menéndez y Cía (cigars), Menéndez y García y Cía (leaf) and Cigarros H. Upmann – together constituted by far the largest single bloc within the industry.

Not one of the firms could compare with the grandeur of those nineteenth-century tobacco concerns. This in itself was symptomatic. Tobacco was trapped in a process of de-industrialization and distortion.

PART TWO

Relations of tobacco production

Tobacco:
My ills have no remedy
Either with you or without you.
With you, you kill me;
Without you, I die.

Popular 1930s refrain

7

The tobacco peasantry and proletariat

It goes without saying that a very considerable proportion of Cuba's population was involved in tobacco growing and manufacture. Rivero Muñiz claims that about half the total population of the island was dependent on this one crop around the 1850s; reports of the 1890s claim one-third; and by the mid twentieth century there were still whole geographical areas and towns in Pinar del Río, Las Villas, and Havana provinces for which this still held. Because this was so, de-industrialization and development of tobacco was to have such profound and far-reaching consequences.

Overall decrease in numbers, radically changing composition, increasing fluidity among sectors, general beating down of conditions: all further complicated the make-up of what was already one of the most heterogeneous and complex sectors of the Cuban peasantry and proletariat by virtue of the many different stages and modes of production in the processing of tobacco from the leaf to the finished product.

Sharecropping and outwork, which came to be so prevalent in the tobacco sector, is characteristically done by the family unit as a whole and thus involves much hidden labour on the part of women and children. In nineteenth-century Cuba, this was compounded by slave, indentured, and tied labour, plus a much-abused system of apprenticeship and living-in, features of which were carried over into the twentieth century. These more nebulous aspects of work in tobacco have yet to be explored in depth. However, in both agriculture and industry, certain trends can be postulated.

First, those involved in tobacco-growing comprised numerically the largest sector by far, even if numbers dwindled into the twentieth century. A total of 120,000 – some 58,000 (out of a total population of 69,000) in Pinar del Río alone – were reported as engaged in cultivating the tobacco leaf in official 1862 statistics. Clearly this figure implied that virtually every man and woman, and many a child too, was involved in tobacco in that part of the country. By the same count, there were relatively few in jurisdictions of what was later to become Las Villas province, less it would seem in the Eastern Department. As the demand for inferior quality tobacco filler from that area grew, so also did the numbers in the tobacco growing sector there.

Any growth in numbers was, however, relative. Despite increasing output, the very nature of capitalist development in agriculture, producing as it did on the one hand some large plantations with more scientific farming but also sharecropping in its most exploitative form, meant that the numbers declined considerably in comparison with mid-nineteenth-century figures. This was becoming evident in the latter part of the nineteenth century but, for the most part, was a process which took place over the early decades of the twentieth century. The 1899 figure of 80,000 was almost certainly more a reflection of the state of agriculture at the end of the war, especially in Pinar del Río province. By the 1940s, however, the figure was not much higher: in the region of 80,000–90,000 – some 33,000 in Pinar del Río and 49,000 in Las Villas.

Large plantation agriculture and more intensified sharecropping also meant that the small peasant grower class disintegrated to a large extent, giving way to a new semi-peasantry, semi-proletariat which spilled over into other tobacco sectors, especially the swelling leaf-sorting[1] and stemming[2] sectors for the export market.

Thus it was that in the twentieth century a vast, largely seasonal and rural workforce grew to such proportions that by 1944 there were, in addition to the 88,000 reported in tobacco growing, some 51,000 sorters and 20,000 stemmers.

Of the 51,000 sorters, 19,000 and 28,000 (38% and 56%) were to be found in Pinar del Río and Las Villas provinces. At the height of the harvest, hundreds could be found in a single sorting shed in some of the provincial tobacco towns – 400 in the General Cigar Company shed in Cabaiguán in July 1945. Of the 20,000 stemmers, over 8,000 worked in stemming sheds in Las Villas, over 5,000 in Pinar del Río. While the greater part of stemming thus came to be carried out for the leaf export market, with stemming sheds in small provincial tobacco towns, many stemmeries were also located in the larger towns and especially Havana. Moreover, all the large cigar and cigarette factories had their own stemming departments, often in the main factory building. Thus, the 1944 figure for stemmers in Havana alone was 5,000 (one-quarter of the total) and there were almost 4,000 (one-fifth) in factories. This meant that, as a sector, stemmers straddled the rural and industrial proletariat.[3]

As to the industrial proletariat proper, tobacco was the *one* industry in the nineteenth century to have produced a class of industrial wage labourers on anything like a large scale. It also did so on a scale completely unparalleled in the twentieth century. That the tobacco workers remained one of the largest sectors of the Cuban working class right up until the 1940s and 1950s was an indictment of the development of Cuban industry in general, not a measure of progress in the tobacco industry itself.

Certain sectors of tobacco workers were hit harder than others. The very fact that Cuba's manufacturing potential for quality cigars was cut short inevitably meant a considerable decrease in the numbers of cigar makers, the industry's most predominant industrial grouping. This was especially marked in Havana, where the large export factories were concentrated. At the same time, the backwardness of the industry as a whole meant that the overall number of workers did remain relatively high, with a large sector scattered throughout the island and a continued high proportion of home and small shop workers to factory workers as such. Thus, whereas figures for the 1860s point to some 15,000 cigar rollers in Havana, 20,000 in the island as a whole, the 1899 figure for Havana had dropped to 10,000, although still 20,000 in all. In 1919, only 3,500 (60% less) were given for Havana and this drop largely accounted for the drop in the industry as a whole to 14,000 given that figures in certain other tobacco provinces doubled over that same period. According to 1944/5 statistics,[4] the overall figure was just over 12,000, and the Havana figure, just over 5,000.

These figures compare with an approximate overall twentieth-century figure of 2,000–3,000 cigar sorters and ringers, box decorators, general employees, warehousemen and the like, and a further 2,000–3,000 in the manufacture of cigarettes. It should be said here that, while grossly inadequate, mid-nineteenth-century estimated production figures would point to an estimated 7,000–10,000 cigarette rollers. The 2,500 in Havana's factories throughout the early twentieth century were probably only meaningful as hand and outwork labour was completely beaten down across the island.

Computing overall occupational figures on a percentage basis, it can be seen that by the mid twentieth century over 50% of those involved in tobacco were in growing, some 30% in sorting and 10% in stemming, while only around 6% were in cigar rolling and a tiny 1% in the manufacture of cigarettes.

The fact that the 6% and 1% tobacco proletariat retained a particular importance in both Cuban tobacco and the Cuban economy and society as a whole merits attention on many counts, not least the particular shaping of its historical makeup. In this context, it is worth reflecting on the peculiar interlacing of race, gender, and skill in the industry.

Cigar rolling is skilled work,[5] but there is little to indicate it was originally considered as such in nineteenth-century Cuba. With the lifting of prohibition in 1817 and a rapidly increasing demand for cigar makers in times of acute shortage of labour, many of those cigar makers were not only found in the barracks and the prisons and people's homes. Considerable numbers of slaves, Chinese, and free coloureds were brought into the growing number of rolling shops alongside white waged labour often under quite appalling conditions. In this, the early cigar industry differs little from the cigarette industry.

Rivero Muñiz mentions Chinese in the tobacco industry from the beginning of the nineteenth century, and numbers almost certainly increased after 1847, when the first indentured Chinese were brought over. Although the Chinese in tobacco were considered to be among the most dextrous of workers and better off than the majority of their fellow countrymen, they were also reputed to be among the hardest worked and the lowest paid. In occupational statistics, they would seem to have been classified as whites, and no overall figures have been handed down. But perhaps the most eloquent portrait of the Chinese workers is the one from Hazard in the 1860s, referring to those rolling cigarettes for Susini:

It is curious to see those Asiatics, with their blue uniforms like the ones prisoners wear, some of them with their hair completely shaven, others with plaits sticking up and out, and the least meticulous of them with their long black hair left flowing. All, however, appear to be scrupulously clean in body and apparel, in compliance with the rules of the establishment. Their sleeping quarters are a model of cleanliness and order. Each worker has a small bed with spotless sheets and pillows; all that is contained within those quarters is kept as clean as possible. The most curious objects of daily Chinese life and customs can be seen in them; all kinds of musical instruments, game-tables . . . All the workers have to wear a special cap, with the name of the factory affixed. The whole establishment is subject to a notable degree of precision and military order. For the Chinese indentured labour, there is a punishment system based on fines . . .[6]

Although they were little better than slaves, the factory handbook points out that they were allowed to cook and bathe.

Descriptions of the early cigar industry are less euphoric. Rivero

Muñiz writes of early 'wage labourers' living in, side by side with slaves and contracted Chinese in overcrowded, unsanitary conditions in badly ventilated galleries over the rolling shops receiving only part of their pay in money form, having leave of absence only once a week. And graphic illustrations of the period testify to this, if occupational figures do not. Whereas 1836 returns gave a breakdown of 1,622 free labourers and 612 slaves out of a total of 2,234 cigar makers, from that point on slave labour disappears. Thus, of an estimated 14,000 cigar makers quoted for 1846, there were over 9,000 whites and just under 4,000 free coloureds, but no slaves. Nonetheless, *Diario de la Marina* of 8 December 1857 advertised: 'A negro of repute and good appearance, creole, 30 years of age, good cigar roller of Londres, earns 1 peso a day, has known no owner but the one for whom he was born and the present, for the price of $1,000 for the seller, healthy, with no taints and no debts . . .'[7] Moreover, widely varying figures for the 1860s for a like number of cigar-rolling shops point to the possible existence of over 7,000 slaves and/or outworkers of a total of 15,000 cigar makers in Havana, and a similar figure out of a total of 20,000 for the island as a whole.

There was also in the 1860s a significant percentage of free coloureds among cigar makers: 13% in Havana and some 18% throughout the island. In all, this would seem to point to the astonishing figure of over 60% of Havana's workforce, 55% of the island's, as non-white, when whites far outnumbered blacks in the population at large.

By 1899, that percentage had dropped to 30% and 37%, respectively. Clearly it was to be expected that, against the backdrop of 1880s abolition and 1890s depression and war turmoil, blacks would be hit most, especially in Havana, where the workforce was fast on the decline. But it is equally clear that there had been an entrenchment of white workers rolling quality export cigars, swelled in numbers by an influx of Spanish immigrants to the better Havana factory jobs. Thus, in the 1899 census – the first to distinguish between native and foreign-born – one in five of Havana's cigar factory operatives was classified as foreign white, the majority Spanish-born. And, of the further two out of every five who were white native-born, it is reasonable to assume that one at least was first-generation only.

Martínez-Alier makes the point that the large numbers of free coloureds in the crafts in nineteenth-century Cuba served to make the whites in them correspondingly inferior in status,[8] and certainly this element was tied in with the racial make-up of cigar rollers. Conversely, white entrenchment served to consolidate superiority and strict demarcation lines as to skill levels. Stringent requirements needed to be met to become a master cigar maker, sorter or box decorator, as entry into the cream of the cigar trades became restricted along race and craft lines, as much by the white workers as the manufacturers themselves.[9] Correspondingly, this was when the 'skill' of cigar rolling most came into its own.

Throughout the declining twentieth-century cigar industry, the quality rolling skill was maintained in theory but not always in practice. In this context, the racial component was to a certain extent broken down. Significantly, the ratio of 1 : 5 foreign against native-born cigar makers in 1899 had dropped to 1 : 10 in 1907, 1 : 15 in 1919 and 1 : 50 in 1943. Despite the new wave of Spanish immigrants into Cuba after independence, few were attracted into the tobacco industry, and this, together with the fact that many Spaniards already resident opted for Cuban citizenship, helps account for the initial drop. Other factors were the returning Cuban-born cigar makers from Tampa, Florida, and Key West (although by no means all were able to find work), and the proliferation of local rolling shops catering to the home market. Thus there was an increase from 30% to 38% in the proportion of blacks in Havana between 1899 and 1907. In the relatively prosperous years between 1907 and 1919, this dropped back to 30%, only to increase over the depressed 1919–43 period to constitute 40% of Havana's workers by the latter date.

Throughout the industry, percentages of blacks were higher in the provinces. This held for the 'blacker' cigar makers as well as for the more exclusive factory trades where there were significantly higher percentages of whites: cigar sorters,[10] for example, registered 19% blacks in Cuba, 11.5% in Havana.

Clearly a racially differentiated industry, cigar manufacturing was also gender-differentiated. There is little reference in either nineteenth- or twentieth-century Cuba to women cigar rollers, although a preponderant outwork industry would suggest the existence of at least some. Not a few women interviewed in the late 1960s certainly spoke of being taught particularly by their fathers to roll cigars in the home and of being sporadically employed in cigar rolling in smaller local concerns. Interestingly, there seems to have been no attempt to employ women in the newly mechanized factories of the 1950s, as was very much the case in other countries with the advent of the machine, especially in the United States. The particularly volatile nature of the whole mechanization issue, against a backdrop of un- and underemployment, was clearly what ruled this out at the time.

More interestingly still, in this respect, is the cigarette industry. While to all accounts many women were involved in home cigarette rolling in the nineteenth century, mid-century complaints were registered to the effect that women would not be brought into the factories. Susini was a case in point. The earliest reference to 'a shop exclusively for women cigarette rollers under the supervision of a lady of known repute'[11] was that established by Pablo González, owner of La Africana. However, the continuing reluctance of women to be brought into the factories and the continuing predominance of outwork up to the turn of the century may help explain how men came to dominate the factory jobs and continue to do so even after mechanization. Twentieth-century Havana cigarette machinists were an overwhelmingly white, male workforce who, like cigar makers before them, hastened to ensure control over their 'skill'. They were doing so when, in the cigarette-manufacturing countries of the US and UK, the male workforce had already been considerably beaten down and substituted by cheap female labour. A similar process of white male entrenchment was to be observed in later years in the only other major cigarette factory outside Havana, namely Trinidad y Hnos of Ranchuelo.

Of course, women were over time drawn into the tobacco factories. They were employed as cigarette packers, as well as to place the bands and cellophane and metal tubes on the cigars. More significantly, they accounted for the vast majority of that considerable sector of stemmers. The first signs of female factory labour on anything like a substantial scale came after the Ten Years' War of 1868–78, and in stemming. The Henry Clay factory is reputed to have been the first to employ women stemmers, in 1879. The shortage of labour produced by the war and the exodus of cigar makers to Tampa and Key West may also have occasioned male factory stemmers to move up to the more prestigious work, causing a particularly acute shortage in a newly expanding sector. Over the years, stemming came to be seen as a woman's job in Cuba, such that by the mid twentieth century 90% of stemmers were women. Straddling the industrial and rural proletariat, as it did, and employing large numbers of black women (30% in Havana, 40% in Las Villas in 1943), stemming was far from being recognized as the skilled job it clearly was.

To take our point further, a general breaking down of skill in the industry by the mid twentieth century had as its corollary the very high percentage of the overall labour force that was black (35% in 1943, which compared with an average of 31% for manufacturing as a whole) and female (44% in 1953 as against 14% for other manufacturing industries).

And so, the particular demarcation or otherwise of skill differentials was intricately tied up with the particular historical configuration of Cuban tobacco along race and gender lines. This, in turn, was to leave its mark on wider developments within the workforce and labour movement, some of which are dealt with in chapters to come.

8

Labour aristocrats?

Myth and legend surrounding Cuban tobacco must surely be at their height where cigar makers are concerned. A strong elite of workers hand-fashioning, from a particularly strong, aromatic leaf, a quality product that carved a lasting niche in the luxury world market is what they have been made out to be. The myth of manufacturing stands dispelled; what of the workers?

Clearly, the much-touted theory of an aristocracy of labour in cigar rolling has to be looked at more carefully. Accepting the validity of the term 'aristocracy of labour' as it applies to a distinctive upper stratum of the working class, better paid, better treated, and generally more respected than the mass of the proletariat, it is a term that has been quite misused as far as Cuban cigar makers go. Slave and semi-slave labour (ranging from explicit indentured labour systems to living-in and apprenticed 'wage' labour) produced a variety of restrictions of movement on cigar makers. One of the more famous was the 1851 *libreta*, a compulsory card on which was noted the name of the employer and any money owed to him. As long as there was money owing, the worker could not leave the factory nor any other manufacturer employ him, unless he liquidated the debt. The effectiveness of the *libreta* as a control indicates clearly that wages were, if not always, at least pretty often, inadequate.[1] Certainly average 1852 rates quoted in the order of 1–3 pesos a day were not substantially higher than the 1–1.50 pesos for day labourers.

From the late 1850s and 1860s, there were definitely growing wage differentials. The 1861 figure gave 4 pesos a day for a master cigar maker, as against the 1–3-peso average cigar maker's pay. De la Sagra's 1862 figure set this differential somewhat lower, as 2 : 1. By 1890, however, top cigar makers were quoted as earning 10 pesos a day as against the average cigar makers' 2 pesos, a differential of 5 : 1. This would help explain the widely varying descriptive accounts of those years. Rivero Muñiz comments on this period:

I don't want . . . to say that among the cigar workers there weren't those who liked to wear *flus* [a suit normally comprising trousers, jacket and waistcoat] and five-peso shoes . . . but they were in the minority; they were those who made the *regalía* cigars. Because what is certain is that the vast majority of the tobacco workers led terrible lives in no way superior to those of the rest of the Cuban proletariat.[2]

Muñiz also maintains that the abolition of slavery changed little as regards general conditions in the industry 'since the slaves who worked in it were paid the same wages as the free workers, with the sole difference that while the latter received their wages themselves, the slaves' wages were paid to their masters'.[3]

At the same time, the attraction of top cigar makers' money meant that there were always those ready to serve an apprenticeship in the industry. During their training period, these apprentices were often notoriously taken advantage of: many of the rolling shops frequently had more apprentices than workers, and many apprentices were cruelly exploited, having their apprenticeships extended and receiving sums which were usually 20% or less of what their work was really worth, as Rivero Muñiz puts it.

At the other end of the spectrum comes the description of the artisan

> In Cuba, if his hands are quick,
> The cigar maker is one of those
> Artisans who, history shows.
> Can, if he wishes, make quite a lick
> Of money. Suave and slick
> And spruced up to the nines. . .
>
> . . . Such a toff is cheery, gay,
> And in fine clothes is apt to strut
> So much that there are cases, what
> Of cigar makers who are confounded
> With the doctors and merchants with whom they're surrounded
> Because of the fine figures they cut.[4]

Such men were obviously worlds apart from the majority of cigar makers and common labourers. Indeed, a sizeable number were later creamed off into professorial or managerial ranks, a tradition that continued well into the twentieth century. Suffice it to mention Rafael García Marqués, a cigar sorter who went on to establish his own cigar rolling shop, La Belinda; Eustaquio Alonso, a cigar maker who worked up to become manager of La Corona, partner in Partagás, and eventually president of Por Larrañaga; José Aguirre, who began as a cigar maker editing a workers' bulletin in the mid-1880s to become a leaf broker and edit the industrial magazine *El Tabaco*.[5]

The very prominence of such men was what helped propagate the wider myth. 'These intelligent men', it was said of them at the turn of the century, 'have reached such a state of perfection that they have a good job assured them for the rest of their lives.'[6] But, it was also said, 'Illusion is here today and gone tomorrow.'[7]

Abad's 1900 report referred to the Cuban worker in the industry who 'remarks with surprise, and without being able to explain it, that while the Stars and Stripes float on the Morro Castle, there is less bread and butter in his home and he is worse off than under Spanish domination . . . Under the Spanish regime there were 125,000,000 cigars exported to the United States. Now there are only 40,000,000. Therefore, now the labourer earns but one-third as much as he did before the Revolution. Or, in other words, to three men kept working before, there is today one who works and two unoccupied.'[8]

For the repatriate cigar maker returning to independent Cuba, there was little work to be had in the large factories. And for those entrenched in them, these were to be years of cut-backs in production and costs. In the initial years, this was manifest in less direct ways, such as expecting first-rate workmanship from second-rate leaf, payment in Spanish currency, which was worth less than the American money in which most goods were priced. A short 1905 pamphlet reported gloomy answers from cigar makers as to their future prospects:

. . . that the leaf was small and hard to work, that much was demanded of them at a low rate and when work was limited, sometimes having no more than 60 or 100 inferior quality cigars and 25 to 50 *regalía* cigars to make, that there were to be few shreds when filler was bad; that they were liable to be thrown out of the factory for trivia, and when they looked for a job they had to have the backing either of cigar makers in the family or others who could find them something, or be friends with those who had influence with factory managers.[9]

Later, when there were increasing numbers of unemployed, more direct methods were to be used, such as demanding very substantial wage cuts and transferring factories to cheap labour areas, especially in depression years.

Over the first few decades, wages in the Havana factories still remained probably among the highest of all industrial wages. There were, however, some very considerable cuts. In 1915, the Trust, reputed to pay the highest wages, reduced rates by 50% because of 'war difficulties'. By the end of the war, there are records of average

wages for cigar makers of 2–6 pesos a day. Increases in the order of
10% were registered in Havana factories during the 1920s but the
outstanding salaries for which the industry was earlier renowned were
rare because there was limited work available and often few days of the
week were worked. In 1932, manufacturers succeeded in making even
top cigar makers accept reductions which put them back to 1917 rates.
Wages outside Havana were estimated to be some 1–1.50 pesos a day.
In the post-depression years wages were no higher. In 1936, it was
reckoned that a top cigar maker would find it difficult to earn more
than 2.50 pesos a day, and average factory wages were quoted as
around 1.10 pesos.

The cigar maker of the 1930s, then, was to have little in common
with the image of his nineteenth-century predecessor. This was
reflected in the literature of the time. 'No vestiges are left of that
romantic figure who used to grace the street corners', wrote García
Galló in 1936. 'There remains only a washed-out caricature that has
degenerated so much that it can no longer be considered a cigar maker.
What remains is the rake hanging out on street corners, given to
vulgar language and effeminate gestures, who, out of sarcasm, smokes
American cigarettes, if not marijuana.'[10]

García Galló might have been a bit hard on the poor cigar maker
but such caricatures of the 1930s compared to those of the 1890s and
early 1900s sum up the situation only too eloquently. By the late 1930s,
the semi- and non-factory worker was predominant. Cigar makers laid
off from the factories turned to making a living as best they could,
even if this meant rolling the cheap *tabaquitos a kilo* (one-cent cigars)
and hawking them on the streets. In so doing, the cigar maker entered
that vast underpaid reserve army which the manufacturers could tap
whenever they wanted to put pressure on the remaining relatively
well-off factory workers. In 1930, this cigar maker might have been
earning no more than 40–50 centavos a day against the average factory
worker's 1.10 pesos. The odds were that this worker would also find
it difficult to get back into the factories again on a permanent basis.

During the 1940s, along with much legislation and a pension and
insurance scheme for the industry, industrial wage rates were introduced for cigar makers and increases to the tune of 50% or so. This in
itself meant that wages were only being brought into line with those
prevailing in the 1920s and 30s, and there is little evidence to indicate,
with the exception of the large factories, that the official rates were ever
paid. The August 1939 editorial of *Tabaco* ran: 'Certain *chinchaleros*
[sweatshop owners] have only three or four workers in their shop,

handing out the leaf to be worked to a greater number of cigar makers who roll the cigars in their own homes as self-employed "private" workers, whereby they evade having to comply with the law, defrauding the exchequer and exalting their system of production.'[11]

Home workers had no way of reclaiming a minimum wage, and small shop workers were not much better off. 'The so-called *media breva* is the one most worked in the small factories and *chinchales* [sweatshops]. The official rate for the *media breva* is $13 per thousand . . . Do all the small factories and *chinchales* pay $13 . . .?' asked *Cuba Economica y Financiera* in 1951.

Well the workers know to their own grief, that the majority only pay six or seven per thousand. There aren't many workers who can produce 300 *media brevas* in a day. What then is their daily wage? The few who can manage 300, in a day of eight or more hours, earn $2.10 if they are paid at $7.00 per thousand, $1.80 if they're paid at $6.00 per thousand. But if they produce less than 300, their daily pay is no greater than $1.50 and in no case is there any question of paid holidays or other rights. And those workers labour on average no more than two or three days a week . . .[12]

This, added to the unstable, seasonal nature of the work, meant that if the number of workers in the factories was maintained at all it was often at the expense of a shorter working week. Time sheets for La Corona factory in the early 1950s, for example, show individual variations of between one and 26 days worked, according to the time of year. Take-home wages, then, could fluctuate enormously.

This made for a situation of great flux in the labour force in this sector. Interviews conducted in the late 1960s confirmed that only a tiny few of the cigar makers had held down factory jobs all their working lives. The great majority had at times worked in factories, at times in small shops and at times at home on their own. Outside Havana, many worked on the land during harvest time.

Beaten down as they were, how did cigar makers fare in comparison with other sectors in the industry? The tiny few employed as cigar sorters, box decorators, and the like continued to be better off. A major sector that was clearly worse off were the stemmers. There is little evidence in the late nineteenth century of stemmers being particularly low-paid. 'It's true that they don't make as much as the cigar makers', wrote Estrada y Morales in 1892, 'but this doesn't mean that they don't get a good day's wage.'[13] In 1905, however, former stemmer Manuel Rodríguez Ramos was writing that stemmers were accorded 'the same treatment as the lowest of workers in the factory and yet they had to do their work well to get a day's wage that

barely sufficed to meet the most pressing of their needs'. He claimed
that because of the size of the hands they had to work, stemmers were
able to earn little more than the equivalent of 50–60 cents a day, when
the average unskilled day labourer's wage was $1 a day. At the height
of the depression stemmers, along with other workers in the industry,
were forced to accept reductions which put them more or less back to
1917–18 rates, and the mid-1930s produced the following rather
poignant poem:

> **The stemmer:**
> Her beauty untrammelled, come what may,
> In her home-made dress to work did fly
> At six in the morning, nimble, fey,
> The stemming shop worker in times gone by.
> The rose of her beauty – delicate, shy –
> The frenzied work robs of its blush away
> Just as the gold wings of the butterfly
> Lose their dust in the light of day.
> In front of the barrel, for ten hours she
> Toiled in the dirt and humidity
> That on her meagre strength did pall.
> She did this back-breaking work – for shame! –
> For a pittance . . . Yet there are those who claim
> That Cuban women don't work at all![14]

Women stemmers outside the factories naturally fared no better.
Indeed, in many of the tobacco towns where stemmeries were set up,
wages were considerably lower. In the 1940s, official scales were
introduced. These were higher in Havana than in the provinces and
varied according to the type of tobacco worked. The 1943 census
(which was carried out in July when the tobacco season was still not
over) quoted 60% of all stemmers as earning less than 30 pesos a
month, and a further 38% from 30–59 pesos. Much depended on the
number of days worked. In the Las Villas stemmeries of the General
Cigar Company, the average monthly wage quoted during the late
forties and fifties fluctuated from 3–8 pesos in February to 20–30
pesos in March and April, when the tobacco harvest was in full swing.
A similar situation existed even in the large factories, where the
number of days worked and, correspondingly, the wages received,
could vary tremendously, from as little as three to 26 days and from a
few to 17 pesos for the month.
    Leaf sorters were particularly vulnerable given the extreme
seasonality of their work, in what were almost entirely tobacco towns

with a backdrop of local unemployment. Official sorting rates were low, and payment by weight and type of leaf could be easily tampered with. 'The sorting shop has opened in town. Soon there'll be festivities', wrote García Galló.[15] But the men could earn little more than 50 cents a day and women from 20 to 25 cents (as against official minimum agricultural rates of $1.20 a day).

It was in the cigarette industry, if anywhere, that a new twentieth-century-style aristocracy was to grow up. The first direct reference to wages in the cigarette industry was for the Havana factories in 1890, which were no more than 90 cents a day. It was only as twentieth-century cigarette manufacturing developed that wage scales began to increase, as also differentials between skilled machinists and other workers. In the early years, a machinist could probably get from 1.50 pesos for a day's work of 14–16 hours. By 1920, top Havana machinists were earning around 7.50 pesos a day and their aides 4–4.50 pesos for an eight-hour day.

Over the difficult years of the twenties, Havana manufacturers were able to impose some considerable wage-cuts, one of 20% in 1926. And by 1930, wages in Havana were around 5 pesos for machinists, 3 pesos for their aides. Women packers earned an average of 3 pesos and floor labour 2–2.50 pesos. In many of the factories in the provinces, wages were much lower: in the Trinidad factory in Ranchuelo and others, machinists were paid as little as 2–2.50 pesos a day. Over the depression years, Havana manufacturers tried to cut wages to the levels in the provinces. The strength of the workers, however, was such that standard wage scales finally adopted for the whole island were only slightly lower than those established by Havana workers during the 1920s. Increasing labour costs were put forward as one factor in eliminating some of the smaller provincial factories over the next couple of decades.

In the remaining factories, and especially in Havana and the Trinidad factory in Ranchuelo, money wages more than doubled over the next couple of decades. In 1945 *Tabaco* estimated machinists' wages to be over 10 pesos, floor labour around 5. By the late forties, monthly take-home wages in La Corona were 200–400 pesos (7.50–14 pesos a day), and top wages reached 600 pesos. In 1952, it was claimed that the minimum wage in the Trinidad factory was no less than $10.85 a day and that machinists' wages were up to 16, 20, 25 pesos and more. 'It is worthy of note', the *Libro de Cuba* commented that year, 'that many founder workers – the veterans of the factory – receive, for a six-hour day's work, a wage that is greater than that for six whole weeks in 1922.' At the same time, the factory paid sick leave and was the only one to have introduced a 40-hour week with 48 hours' pay. It was easy to see the prosperity the factory brought:

When the traveller reaches Ranchuelo and becomes aware of the well-being in a hundred and one ways; when he sees the great number of workers who possess cars and their own house; when the comfortable air of the place, the feeling of general content hits him in the face; when he feels . . . the decent life they lead, it will not take him long to realize that all this is due to the Trinidad y Hermanos factory.[16]

And even today, to enter Ranchuelo, with its clean, tree- and flower-lined streets, and to enter the homes of cigarette workers with their little porchways, gardens, and garages, equipped with television and other appliances, is – having come from the other tobacco towns of Las Villas – like entering another world. The cigarette factory, a large imposing building on the main street, is, and obviously was for decades, very much the centre of the whole town.

There is little doubt that in the 1950s, the sort of wages and conditions prevalent in the cigarette industry as a whole meant that workers in this sector ranked high in the industry's labour force, putting them on a par almost with Cuba's white collar workers.

Daily factory wage differentials (in pesos) for the aristocracy of labour debate can be summed up as follows:

	1860	1890	1900	1920	1930	1945	1955
Sorters and master cigarmen	2	10	—	5–7	2.50–3	2.50–4	2.50–6
Cigar makers	1	2	—	2–6	1.50	1.50	1.50
Cigarette machinists	—	0.90	1.50	2.50–7.50	5	10	14–20
Others	—	—	—	1.50–4.50	3	5	10

These figures do not take into account the number of days worked, nor are they indicative in any way of real as against money wages. In the absence of any cost of living index, it can only be pointed out that during the twentieth century there was a strong inflationary pressure on prices and corresponding deflationary pressure on money, such that money wages were undermined. From 1937 to 1949 the purchasing power of the peso in terms of foodstuffs dropped by almost 60%.

And so, even top cigar makers who had once shared in the

prosperity of *the* industry of Cuba saw their position being slowly but surely eroded away during the twentieth century. They saw their place in the industry being taken by another, essentially *semi*-skilled sector — the cigarette machinists — and their standing in the labour force as a whole considerably lowered. How they and other workers in the industry were to be affected by this and other great changes, the sort of feelings aroused in them, and the ways in which they tried to fight against what was happening to them, we are about to see.

PART THREE

Tobacco, nation and class

9

Militancy and the growth of the unions

That the tobacco industry should stand out for its militancy in the nineteenth century is hardly surprising. Nineteenth-century Cuba was a predominantly agricultural, slave society until the 1880s; and tobacco, Cuba's second most valuable agricultural product and only large-scale industry, tied up the livelihood of thousands of men, women and children. Precisely because of this, unrest in the tobacco sector was a very serious affair.

Widespread agricultural unrest dating back to the early eighteenth century[1] had its parallel in nineteenth-century industrial unrest as large concentrations of wage labourers came together to take strong collective action. At the same time, there were strong countervailing forces to early forms of class solidarity: the heterogeneous, fluctuating and irregular nature of the labour force, the decline and instability of the industry, bringing with it a decline in numbers and changing composition in the overall labour force from the late nineteenth century on – including changes in race, gender and skill – the high proportion of outwork, and increasing periods of chronic un- and under-employment are some of them.

Mutual aid societies in predominantly tobacco neighbourhoods were forerunners to craft guilds as such, the first Asociación de Tabaqueros de La Habana being set up in 1865. Guilds based on other trades in the industry came with the Havana Gremio de Escogedores (1872), Unión de Rezagadores (1880) and Gremio de Fileteadores (1886). Records of guilds in major provincial tobacco towns around Havana were to be found from the late 1860s on, further afield in the late eighties as in the case of the Gremio de Tabaqueros de Cienfuegos and Gremio de Tabaqueros de Santa Clara (1888).

No recorded membership has been found for any of these early organizations, but most were highly exclusive and local in nature. They were not vastly different thirty or forty years later, when the first attempts were made to set up regional, provincial, and national craft unions, and these were little more than a name for a loose amalgam of autonomous local organizations. Only top cigar makers in the large shops and factories formed a stable enough nucleus of workers to form a viable labour organization. With the possible exception of the eight-hour day, before 1914 there was really no question of trying to establish standard wage rates and work conditions throughout the island. This was true up until the 1930s and still a great drawback to union organization throughout the forties. After the very short-lived Gremio de Despalilladores of 1878, there was no other recorded attempt to unionize the women stemmers, even those in Havana's factories, until the twentieth century. It would seem that seasonal rural and semi-rural labour in the sorting and stemming sheds went on completely non-unionized well into the century. Similarly, the first known Gremio de Dependientes de Tabaco – comprising those engaged in receiving, wetting, preparing, blending, and drying the tobacco – was as late as 1912. In the cigarette industry, the first recorded organization of any importance was the Unión de Obreros de la Industria de Cigarrería en General in 1918, and until the thirties this, too, was much smaller than its name might suggest. Only in the late thirties and early forties were the big national craft and industrial unions formed and consolidated with mass membership throughout the country, among all sectors of workers, and even this was considerably limited.[2]

Now, if over a relatively long period of time the labour movement was so limited, whence the reputation for militancy among these workers? The fact was that organized workers, from an early date, formed strong pockets for industrial bargaining. The very strength of the early guilds of master cigar makers and sorters over the years 1860–90, and of Havana's cigarette workers from the 1920s on, in no small way helps account for increased wage differentials between these and other workers over the two periods.

There was, moreover, strong periodic worker unrest in the industry around wage demands, protests against wage cuts and the like, but also against discrimination and victimization of workers, against the cigar machine, and around other highly political issues. This unrest went far beyond the confines of existing worker organizations and could easily paralyse one of the most sensitive nerve centres of the Cuban economy.

For much of the nineteenth century it was centred around the large concentrations of workers in Havana's factories who were on the margin of the guilds and who challenged both their existence and their ideology. In the early twentieth century, it involved large numbers of unemployed cigar makers returning from Tampa and Key West after independence. By the third decade of the century, it had spread to all sectors of tobacco workers in Havana and the provinces and constituted the basis for the growth of new unions and a new-found radicalism in this sector. It took the form of strikes (the greatest of which were not over straight wage demands), boycotts, occupation of factories and, in the provinces, the total disruption of whole towns, which could amount to a quasi-insurrectional state.

It has long been noted that explosions of labour activity and labour organization do not always go hand in hand, and this was particularly true of the Cuban tobacco industry. Widespread unrest inevitably affected union structure but with a tremendous time-lag. The very nature of the labour force as a whole and general conditions prevalent in the industry meant that well into the twentieth century only the older, more entrenched groups of cigar makers and the like were able to maintain unions with strong local bargaining powers. There were sudden and sharp variations in the amount of labour activity. The outbreak of strikes over the periods 1886–91, 1902–8, and 1931–3 – all of which were concentrated in Havana and, with the exception of 1931–3, around cigar makers and sorters in the export factories – and prolonged industrial action over the years 1925–7 and 1947–8, in both Havana and the provinces, are the better known.

The specific periods of large-scale expansion in labour organization did not – with the possible exception of the 1880s – coincide with the former. The most important of these periods were 1914–25 and 1936–44. Both, especially the latter, involved expansion into new grades of skill, new geographical areas and new ideas, mainly anarcho-syndicalist during the first (though this remained weak) and communist during the second.

Neither kind of explosion can be explained simply in terms of slump periods, rising cost of living, and the like, but must be seen in the context of particular changes taking place in the industry. The jumps in labour activity of 1886–91 and 1902–8 occurred in times of expansion for the industry and have their origins in the extreme concentration of production taking place over these two periods. That of 1925–7 was a direct response to attempted technological change under extremely adverse conditions, that of 1931–3 to economic depression sparked off by wage-cuts, and that of 1947–8 to both technological change and political repression of established unions. In terms of the growth of labour organization as opposed to activity, the 1914–20 period was one of both economic setback and post-war prosperity for the industry and 1936–44 on the up-swing of a trade cycle. Of course, the further the twentieth century progressed, the greater the overall decline of the industry and the increase in unemployment, and, hence, a generally inflammable situation, favourable to trade union militancy and defensive radicalism. This could have been sparked off equally well by attempts to increase productivity or undermine seniority rights, by the machine, redundancy, wage cuts, or straight worker demands for wage increases.

The reaction of workers was not all that predictable. Certain well-established social and cultural traditions combined to make this so. The early cigar makers' guilds were instrumental in establishing that to be one of the privileged stratum of cigar rollers was to be one of a community and, despite strong political, economic, and social upheavals, certain ideas and patterns of behaviour were carried over from this. The fact that work was handed down from generation to generation, that there were tobacco areas and towns, the important tradition of reading in the factories,[3] and the emphasis of early union activity on worker education, all played a part in consolidating this sense of community.

It is interesting to note that over 90% of cigar makers in Havana, some 70% in Las Villas, knew how to read and write in 1899 – in an age when the great majority of the population was illiterate.[4] As 'intellectuals of the proletariat', cigar makers have been described as having the almost inherent trait of vacillating before a social problem. One-time cigar maker Gaspar Jorge García Galló in 1936 described their condition as follows:

The cigar maker is a worker who, through his tradition of struggle, his discussion on the shop floor, the daily readings of the press and literary works, and radio broadcasts, has a cultural veneer which makes him feel superior in this respect to other workers. Because of this he speaks and gives his opinion on everything. He generally takes up theatrical poses and oratory style which make him stand out in any meeting or assembly. If he is on the platform, or writes for any paper, he uses flowery and metaphorical language, even if this means that the thread is lost in the exuberance of form . . .

The cigar maker is a sworn polemicist. He loves discussions and this can be explained in terms of the way he works and his wide knowledge. There are daily debates in and out of work and there are times when they gain such impetus that the whole gallery takes part. When a debate reaches that point, those taking part have recourse to dictionaries, scientific works, newspapers and journals, and experts on the matter . . . Years ago there was the famous case of a law-court judge in Havana city who seemed to know cigar makers well, but bore them no good-will. He was called Marcos García. And when a cigar maker came before him in court, he used to say: 'Are you a cigar maker? Ah, then you're a lawyer. Defend yourself!'

One of our closest friends, on referring to the cigar maker, throws out the following: 'He has cultural indigestion', he says, and he's not mistaken. He attributes that indigestion to the quantity and quality of the things that are read to him and that he himself reads. And it's true, the cause is to be found in the lack of method in reading in the shops. Nonetheless, workers in the industry must, at the same time, be seen as the most educated nucleus of workers. From the tobacco industry have come public officials, teachers, artists, professionals, members of congress, and intellectuals, and their first steps were always taken in the galleries of the cigar factory.[5]

What García Galló quoted so eloquently as 'cultural indigestion' made for two almost contradictory trends within this group of workers. The first was a revolutionary romanticism which made many of them staunch supporters of José Martí and the independence movement, and of anarchist, anarcho-syndicalist and early socialist ideas. The second was a well-imbued sense of order and discipline, a sense of what was right and proper, even in the most turbulent of periods, and an underlying reformism of the older and more en-trenched groups which pervaded others as well.

Those who emerged to become strong working-class leaders were of both political trends. On the one hand were men of reformist ideas, such as Spanish cigar maker Saturnino Martínez, who formed the first cigar makers' association, edited the first worker review and was largely responsible for starting the tradition of reading. Martínez was a man of collectivist ideas who strongly believed in the harmony between labour and capital. His trend of thought was reflected decades later in José Bravo, the man who most built up the Havana cigar makers' union in the early twentieth century; Andrés Santana, president of that union in the late twenties; José Cossío, president of the sorters; and many others around that time. In a more corrupt form, it produced men like Luis Serrano Tamayo and Manuel Campanería in the fifties.

On the other hand, from the ranks of the cigar makers came some of Cuba's most outstanding radical working-class leaders. The three best-known are Enrique Roig San Martín, reader in the cigar factories who, in the 1880s, attempted to organize all those workers in the industry on the margin of the old guilds along anarcho-syndicalist lines; Carlos Baliño, exiled cigar maker of firm socialist beliefs who for long years struggled to lay the foundations for a genuinely worker party; and Lazaro Peña, a communist who built up not only Cuba's first strong industrial union, the 1936 Federación Tabacalera Nacional (FTN) but also the first Confederación de Trabajadores de Cuba (CTC) in 1939, becoming general secretary of both. Each, in his time, was one of a strong group with similar ideas. Around Roig were Enrique Messonier, Sandalio Romäelle, Sabino Muñiz and Valeriano Rodríguez. With Baliño in exile, and back in Cuba with him after independence, were Ramón Rivero and others of more anarchist leanings, like Rivera and Cendoya. Lazaro Peña worked closely with communists Inocencia Valdés of the stemmers, Luis Pérez Rey of the cigarette workers, Havana cigar makers' president Evelio Lugo de la Cruz, and their lesser known counterparts in the provinces: Faustino Calcines, Manuel Duke Linero and Diego León (Las Villas), Alejandro Reyes and Vicente Avelado (Placetas), Pedro Arboláez (Santa Clara), Manuel Cárceres (Cabaiguán), Ángel Rodríguez Vásquez (Caibarién), plus a host of others.

Restricted along colour and gender lines, early guilds were exclusively white, male, and urban. Their leaders, whether reformist, anarchist, or anarcho-syndicalist, were white, a good number of them the sons of teachers, small shopkeepers and the like. Challenges to exclusivism along race lines from the late 1880s on, and along gender lines from the 1920s on, produced some outstanding communist leaders who were black, often from poor tobacco families and not all male – Lazaro Peña, of the cigar makers, and Inocencia Valdés, of the women stemmers, are cases in point. In the context of change in the industry, this in itself was significant.

Interestingly, all shared a sense of the justness of tobacco workers' demands and the orderly fashion in which to conduct strikes and industrial action. This won them considerable support from small shopkeepers, traders and general public alike. There is considerable evidence that tobacco workers, right up until the late forties, accepted traditional symbols of stable hierarchy. Since their demands were just, they were lawful, and many were their petitions addressed to pillars of authority in this vein.

Fierce repression, as of the 1892 Congress, the 1902 strike, and the occupation of Havana factories in 1947–8, was precisely due to the fact that these coincided with acute crises in national affairs, in both economic and political terms. 1892 was only three years before the outbreak of the Second War of Independence. Worker support for the independence cause, expressed at the Congress, was something Spanish colonial rule wished to avoid at all costs. In 1902 there was grave doubt as to whether Cuba could make it as an independent nation, and the new national government of Estrada Palma was in no way ready to tolerate large-scale worker unrest. In 1947–8, the effect of US Cold War policy was making itself heavily felt on nations such as Cuba. Significantly, communist-led unions were to be smashed. Trained gunmen were sent into the factories, and troops into whole towns in the provinces. 1902 and 1947–8 were clear cases in which workers had considerable public sympathy, and the government was far from ignorant of this. Their backing of the tobacco manufacturers at this time stemmed as much from political reasons as from the economic reasons which provoked manufacturers themselves.

On all of these occasions there was a significant radicalization of the workers. Conversely, it is also significant that the great expansion and radicalization of trade union organization as such (1938–44) – among tobacco workers and the Cuban working class in general – and the renewed strength of certain reformist elements in the 1950s, came precisely over periods in which there was considerable government patronage.

Both repression by force and government patronage during the twentieth century stemmed from one thing: the weakness of the national bourgeoisie in a neo-colonial country like Cuba. Tobacco manufacturers, landowners, and leaf dealers, who together formed one of the strongest sectors – in the late nineteenth century possibly *the* strongest – bore eloquent testimony to this. Relatively limited in their political power in the face of strong pockets of workers, manufacturers and government were early compelled to play a double-edged game, using force but at the same time buying a certain amount of social stability.

Both manufacturers and government (including the Spanish colonial authorities) had been tolerant toward early elite organizations which they could contain. The 1887–8, 1902, 1907–8 and 1931–3 strikes, however, went outside the bounds of this. And the very crisis of the post-1925 economy in general, that of the tobacco industry in particular, created a wave of unrest which could not be contained.

Labour was a key element in the 1933 revolution, and after the overthrow of Machado, the new and short-lived government of Grau San Martín had to be both nationalist and labour-oriented. There was a tremendous burst of labour activity. Soviets were set up, and much social and labour legislation passed. By 1934, a fourth national workers' congress claimed to represent over 400,000 workers, including some 61,000 in tobacco. Anti-imperialist and socialist feelings were running high.

The only way for the traditional bourgeoisie to regain a hold of the situation was by a military coup, with US backing. At the same time, the strength of labour was such that some sort of class collaboration had to be on the cards. Batista's military regime legitimized its rule through mock elections for puppet presidents, recognized and even fostered the trade union movement, legalized the Communist Party and promoted considerable social and labour legislation, in an attempt to recruit the support of labour. The year 1940, with the passing of about the most progressive constitution in the whole of Latin America and with six communist deputies, became a sort of landmark in class collaboration in Cuba.

This was obviously a period of both advances and setbacks for the labour movement. Class collaboration allowed for the building up of strong unions on a scale hitherto unknown, with tobacco workers' unions very much in the lead, for some tangible gains in terms of income distribution and for the radicalization of the movement with a strong communist leadership. Class collaboration also led to a certain embourgeoisement of union structure in comparison with the pre-1933 period. But much social legislation inevitably remained unfulfilled in practice and the ministry of labour became a device for channelling labour disputes into a bureaucratic network which failed to resolve anything. For this reason the web of conciliation and collaboration, though elaborate, went far less deep than imagined. Unions may have been forced to work through it but workers were never really taken in.

The extent to which the labour movement was able to retain its integrity over this period is shown by the fact that, from 1944 on, the national government was out to curb the power of the unions, its attack culminating in an all-out war in 1947–8. This was particularly concentrated on the tobacco unions because of the mass support for outstanding communist leaders and because of mechanization. The newly established official tobacco unions of the post-1948 period became little more than an instrument of state policy, increasingly divorced from the rank and file. Because of this, great care needs to be exercised when talking of the post-1948 labour movement.

To recapitulate, it can tentatively be said there were three main phases in the growth of the labour movement in the tobacco industry and that these, by and large, coincided with the growth of the labour movement as a whole in Cuba. Indeed, for the first two, the Cuban labour movement was very much centred around tobacco workers' unions as such.

The first phase was brief and essentially covered the years 1865-8, when it was prematurely cut short by the First War of Independence. It corresponded to the small movement of craft-based, friendly-type societies and the like, geographically limited to Havana and surrounding districts. These societies had two main purposes: through them artisans were able to band together in sickness and death, and they served as a social and educational centre providing libraries and schools. Aristocrats of labour, many Spanish in origin, these artisans were inclined to accept their employers' views and to be reformist in their political attitudes.

The second phase was one of transition, extending from 1878 to 1914. Although largely craft-based in nature, the labour movement in this period went through a series of expansions which set in motion changes in both its scale and its nature. During the war, small but newly expanding sectors of Havana's industry – sorters and box decorators – first founded their craft guilds and were joined by master cigar makers after the war. These were largely reformist organizations. Over the late 1880s, the ideas and position of these guilds was challenged as industrial concentration in tobacco created the conditions for labour activity on a new scale and paved the way for conflicts between older reformist and new, more radical ideologies. The concentration of workers in factories coincided with the abolition of slavery and an influx of Spanish immigrants into the large factories at a time when anarcho-syndicalist ideas were prevalent in the Spanish labour movement.

The period as a whole was interrupted by the Second War of Independence of 1895-8, in which tobacco workers were considerably involved. The outcome was to usher in the imperialist phase of Cuba's historical development and, correspondingly, a new type of labour movement. The virtual state of ruin facing much of the industry had as its corollary the disarray of worker organizations. And yet 1900 was something of a watershed, creating the conditions for widespread discontent, which, as in the 1880s, was centred around Havana's export factories and especially the new and enormous Trust factory. A new kind of revolutionary nationalism was born, which was the prelude to early, abortive attempts to set up socialist groupings and an independent socialist party.

Not until after 1914 (more specifically after 1933) did the unions change in any radical way. This third and last phase corresponded to the setting up of large national craft and industrial unions. The first step was the consolidation of strong craft associations of Havana's cigar and cigarette makers. These were followed by regional craft organizations: the bi-provincial federation of cigar makers of Havana and Pinar del Río and its weaker counterparts, such as the Las Villas federation, formed in 1920. Finally, in 1926, came the first national cigar makers' federation. All were moderate and essentially reformist in their aims, so they were among the few unions untouched by Machado over the late twenties. The national federation was extremely effective in mobilizing cigar makers throughout the country against the cigar machine but lacked any strong directive power when it came to establishing standard wage rates and the like. It was this kind of weakness that led to the failure of strike movements and other industrial action over the late twenties and early thirties both in the provinces and Havana.

The year 1933 was again something of a watershed. It was only after the depression years – which were decisive in teaching tobacco workers throughout the island that they needed to fight united – and the culminating 1933 revolution that there was any possibility of real expansion of unionism into new areas and new sectors. Under the national tobacco federation of 1936, cigar and cigarette workers in the provinces, women stemmers, and leaf sorters were organized for the first time on anything like a large scale. Out of a defensive radicalism were born new socialist and communist ideologies, such that tobacco workers were among the last to hold out against the implantation of official unions and some Las Villas towns were never forced to acquiesce. Only among the last watered-down cigar aristocrats and the new cigar and cigarette machinists was there at least tacit acceptance.

And yet serious limitations to the spread of union organization were manifested in several ways. The success of strong local cigar and cigarette unions rested largely on militants at the shop level. Workers in the provinces, particularly stemmers and leaf sorters, were at a distinct disadvantage: hence the drop in their wages and the worsening of conditions when national unions were waging and winning considerable battles. At the same time, the overall situation was to some extent complicated by general unions, such as the Unión de Camioneros y Carreros, which cut right across the industrial union.

This is not the place to consider in detail the nature of trade unionism in general in Cuba, but it would seem that tobacco workers' unions remained among the largest, strongest, and most effective of the whole labour movement right up until the time of the 1959 revolution and that they were also among the most radical. Back in the late nineteenth and early twentieth centuries, there had been craft guilds of artisans such as cobblers, bricklayers, cabinet makers, blacksmiths, bakers, and the like, largely in Havana but also in the provinces. With the growth of the docks and railways in the twentieth century and, later, expansion in sugar and the new light consumer and service industries, new unions were formed by workers in those sectors. Dockers' and railwaymen's unions rose to importance over the twenties, sugar and other workers' unions over the thirties, giving rise to great industrial and general unions, loosely organized into the national workers' federation of 1939.

This growth was necessarily slow during the twenties – the Federación Obrera de la Habana (FOH) of 1920 and the Confederación Nacional Obrera de Cuba (CNOC) of 1925 lacking any widespread union organization at the base – and cut short over the depression years. After the 1933 revolution, however, it was clearly the national tobacco workers' union that was giving the main push to a well-structured national confederation of labour, such that by the late forties no sector of workers was technically left unorganized.

In this context, three points must be borne in mind if we are to assess correctly the growth of unionism among the tobacco workers. First, the particular nature of industrial development in Cuba and its lateness meant that, although the new working class destroyed much of the unity of the older proletariat and changed the character of the labour movement, the older groups of workers, with their tradition of militancy, were already well-organized and continued to be so as opposed to newcomers on the industrial scene. Thus, besides being the most numerous sector of the working class, tobacco workers also appear to have been the most unionized. According to CTC figures for 1944, some 75% of maritime workers, 58% of transport workers, belonged to unions, as against 27% in textiles (largely women workers) and 17% in mining (an old but revitalized industry). The 39% unionization reported for tobacco workers was low because it included field labour and sorters. Excluding field labour alone, the figure shoots up to 80%, more than any other single industry.

Second, the extensive patronage role of the government over the early forties and the fostering of a mass labour organization regulated by the Ministry of Labour, with communist leadership excluded in the fifties, made it increasingly difficult to assess the role of workers and their ideologies as opposed to those of official union leaders. Not the benevolent gift of a paternalist regime, social and labour legislation had been fought for by the workers, especially in the years leading up to and after the 1933 revolution. Having fought so hard and so long, these workers were not going to allow the government to take over their unions so easily. That there were great fights over this among older sectors of workers, as in tobacco, was no coincidence.

Third, colonial history and the later struggles against American involvement in the Cuban economy gave to the movement at an early stage a feeling of nationalism and anti-imperialism, both of which were superimposed on anarcho-syndicalist, communist and other ideologies, so that these were significantly different from those known in Europe, where they originated. In tobacco, this was particularly marked and helped create the conditions for converting tobacco workers as a whole into one of the most radical groups of Cuban workers in both national and class terms.

10

Early reformism and anarcho-syndicalism

The first signs of worker consciousness in the tobacco industry were becoming apparent in the late 1850s, when mutual aid societies were established in white, artisan, predominantly tobacco neighbourhoods. A typical example was the Sociedad de Socorros Mutuos del Barrio del Pilar in 1857, which admitted '. . . any white person of education by virtue of being a neighbour of the parish . . . and whom it deems will serve its worthy purpose.' By the mid 1860s, there were general craft guilds with wider geographical pretensions – La Sociedad de Artesanos de La Habana (1865), La Fraternidad de Santiago de las Vegas and La Sociedad de Trabajadores de San Antonio de los Baños (1866). There was also the first exclusively tobacco craft guild, La Asociación de Tabaqueros de La Habana (1865).

There are specific reasons as to why mutual aid societies and craft guilds should have emerged in these areas over the late 1850s and 1860s. First, the large tobacco factories were by this time growing up there. Second, the industry had come through the considerable upheavals of the mid-fifties, increased US tariffs having put one-third of Havana's cigar makers out of work. Despite recovery in the sixties, the threat of mass unemployment can but have taught these stable workers to band together in a specifically craft guild as a buffer against losing their jobs. Third, the skilled nature of quality cigar rolling was by then clearly established. There was a growing training school for apprentices under the auspices of the Sociedad Económica de Amigos del País, and many more served as such in the factories.[1] To become a master cigar maker, an apprenticeship of three to four years was necessary. Skilled artisans, such cigar makers were concerned with their mutual well-being and the provision of some sort of education for themselves and their sons.

The most prominent of them was Saturnino Martínez, a Spanish cigar maker in the great Partagás factory, then studying at the Liceo de

Guanabacoa and influenced by its director, Nicolás Azcarate. Azcarate believed that a way of alleviating the monotonous nature of the work, and giving men a moral education, would be to read out loud to them while they laboured. He was largely responsible for the custom of *la lectura*, or reading, being introduced in two of the long prison galleries of the Arsenal del Apostadero in Havana, where prisoners rolled cigarettes. Martínez worked towards its introduction in the cigar factories, thus helping found what was to become perhaps one of the most important institutions in the development of labour organization and ideology among tobacco workers.[2]

Martínez – a founder member of the Asociación de Tabaqueros de La Habana and active in propagating craft societies whose main purpose he regarded as cultural advancement – saw reading as an ideal way of fostering worker education. The very nature of cigar rolling, quiet, monotonous, individual work, allowed for reading and conversation. Thus, Martínez was initially involved in opening a school for the primary instruction of artisans and founding the first worker weekly, *La Aurora*, in early 1866.[3] Through the tobacco section of that paper he was able to spread his ideas on reading, which that same year was introduced into the Viñas factory in Bejucal, El Figaro and Partagás in Havana, and soon spread to other Havana factories. For an hour or so every morning and afternoon, workers would listen to news, novels, philosophy and politics, read aloud to them by a special reader whom they paid and for whom they selected what was to be read.

While it is not clear how widespread reading was, the result was electric. The original ideas of Azcarate and Martínez may have been far from subversive: Martínez advocated a form of harmony between worker, employer, and Spanish government. And yet, if neither Azcarate nor Martínez realized the tremendous implications of such an institution, both manufacturers and government surely did. With independence feelings running high, at a time when industry was emigrating to beat overseas tariffs and Spanish colonial restrictions, reading could scarcely be viewed as anything but potentially explosive. Jaime Partagás was somewhat of an exception in so favouring it that he provided a special wooden reading desk. The owners of Henry Clay, Cabañas, La Intimidad, and El Designio strongly opposed its introduction in their factories. 'The shops were for working, not reading; and reading desks were for schools, not cigar factories', declared Ramón Allones, of El Designio.[4]

By May 1866, a decree had been passed which prohibited reading.

'The reading aloud of papers in public in some shops of different trades, mainly directed toward those working in them', declared the Spanish colonial authorities, 'is wont to produce frequent enmity of serious consequences.' On the 14th of that month, Cipriano de Mazo, governor of Havana, wrote to the chief of police that it was prohibited to 'distract workers in cigar factories, workshops, and all kinds of establishments in Havana with the reading of books and newspapers, and discussions alien to the tasks that those workers perform'. No matter how the workers fought – and the first recorded strike was over this question in the Cabañas factory – prohibition was enforced within a year and the protagonists of reading persecuted. Similarly, *La Aurora* was attacked and transformed into a purely literary magazine.

With the premature death of both reading in the factories and the weekly paper, and with the onset of war, a great blow was struck to the incipient labour movement. The classical reformist period was, in a sense, brought to a close. The first attempts at worker collectives had been not only small-scale but also, because of the prevailing political climate, short-lived.

Reading was to be re-introduced as new craft associations sprang up at the end of the war in 1878, in the form of the Junta Central de Artesanos and the Gremio del Ramo de Tabaquerías.[5] Martínez re-emerged to edit the latter's weekly paper *La Razón*, which continued much in the vein of its predecessor *La Aurora*. The initial aftermath of war could only serve to consolidate a certain reformism. Within ten years, however, the *gremio* was dissolved and the old ideas were being seriously challenged.

Anarchist ideas in Cuba have been traced back to 1872, when cigar maker Enrique Roig San Martín, Enrique Messonier and others set up the Centro de Instrucción y Recreo in Santiago de las Vegas, and the new worker paper *El Obrero* in the following year. Little importance can be attributed to these ideas until at least around 1885, with a re-organized Junta Central de Artesanos aimed at all workers, and more probably until 1887, with the publication of *El Productor*, edited by Roig. Their growing importance was such that the decade of the eighties is usually depicted as a political battleground between reformists and anarchists, a struggle which, in terms of personalities, was centred around Martínez and Roig. Spanish immigrants brought with them anarchist ideas, it is argued, which subsequently pervaded the Cuban movement. And yet, some prominent new leaders – Roig included – were not first-generation immigrants, and those that were did not come from particularly anarchist strongholds.[6] The real questions to be asked are just how widespread either reformism or anarchism was, which workers were turning to them, and why.

Looking to Spain for a moment, there were strong divisions among anarchists between professional revolutionaries, terrorists, and later anarcho-syndicalists, and also tactical divergencies within socialism. Andalusia, with its mass of day labourers produced by large-scale migration from the countryside, was the land of terrorist anarchism. The messianic traditions of peasant society combined with new revolutionary energy to make terrorism particularly attractive. The Andalusian labourer did not see social war as a long struggle but as a sudden triumph of truths learned from the Apostles: the strike was a moment of exhortation as well as one of demands for better conditions. Catalonia, Spain's most advanced industrial region, produced a different kind of anarchism. Worker conversion was a long process, worker leaders producing a remarkable amalgam of the early associationism of the 1840s and 1850s and the newer anarcho-syndicalism. Catalan employers reacted strongly to the early, respectable unionism, insisting on absolute freedom of contract in labour relations. Denied the legal outlets of associationism and bargaining, some workers turned to more terrorist tactics. Eventually, although purists of individual action remained, the Catalan workers turned to anarcho-syndicalism with a strong revolutionary union, using the instrument of the general strike, along the lines of the French syndicalist organization. The Socialist Party had its main support in the aristocracy of Madrid's proletariat, the printers, who were nearly always to the fore of working-class radicalism.

In Cuba, as in Catalonia, the strength of respectable associationism among a stable nucleus of workers was already so great that the terrorist variant was never a viable form. And, although favoured by certain factors, such as the break-up of the old guilds during the wars, the exclusion of many workers from the new ones, and the weakness of formal religion (early tobacco workers had a reputation for atheism), anarcho-syndicalism was never completely incompatible with the old reformism and was to merge over certain periods with more orthodox socialism. During the 1880s, manufacturers were in some respects less intransigent than their Spanish counterparts and opted more for favouring organizations which were amenable to their own ends rather than denying all form of organization, thus splitting the worker movement. At the same time, the whole question of labour became merged with the abolition of slavery and Cuba's political independence from Spain. This gave a highly political content to worker organization, also paving the way for socialist ideas growing strong among Cuban émigré workers in Key West and Florida.

The tobacco industry was inevitably the main ground for new ideas over these years and witness to a most extraordinary jump in labour activity. Abolition swelled the ranks of wage labour and meant these workers were for the first time free to participate in worker action. Precisely over these years, concentration of production on an unprecedented scale was creating the conditions for a new worker consciousness. The very size of the new factories was conducive to strike movements and meant a far greater separation between worker (including top cigarman and sorter) and employer. Manufacturers were far more definitely a class apart. They obviously identified themselves as such, for the first Gremio de Fabricantes de Tabacos was set up in 1880, its successor the Unión de Fabricantes de Tabacos de La Habana in 1881, and in 1884 the more ambitiously titled Unión de Fabricantes de Tabacos y Cigarros de la Isla de Cuba. Workers were able to see, on the one hand, the enrichment of the manufacturers and, on the other, their increasing indifference to even the most respected of workers like the sorters and the kind of conditions under which tobacco workers as a whole laboured. Injustices to which they were victim were clearly set in a wider context than that of the individual factory.

The strikes of the late 1880s were unprecedented. Estimates run to 15,000 participants in the great 1866 *huelga de partido*[7] (the name given the second- and third-class factories) over the demand for higher and standardized wage scales for those rolling the inferior cigars. The strike broke out in four third-class factories: Flor de Nogueiras, La Victoriana, Béjar y Álvarez, and B. Suárez, which paid cigar rollers some two to three pesos a thousand less than others. Béjar y Álvarez eventually agreed to increase their rate by one peso a thousand but by then workers in other factories were out. The situation became complicated as the year wore on: some manufacturers gave in and splits formed among cigar makers that led to the dissolution of the cigar makers' guild.

In late 1887 came what the workers called the *huelga de los fabricantes*, (manufacturers' strike). In October a worker of La Belinda factory 'whose only crime was that of not wishing to work where he felt he had been offended'[8] was dismissed and put on the manufacturers' black list. The rest of the workers came out on his behalf. Before a rumoured lock-out on the part of the manufacturers, workers of La Intimidad factory demanded that the leaf be prepared for the following day's work. When this was refused, they too walked out. By mid-November no solution had been reached, and the Unión de Fabricantes sent a private letter to all its members calling on them to close ranks if they were not to be 'knocked down by the impetuous attack of the workers' who were causing them 'difficulties and hindrances of all kinds'. A lock-out was declared, which the manufacturers justified in terms of 'the existing disorganization among the ranks of the workers' which did not permit an agreement to be reached.

A second manufacturers' circular of that month, this time published in the press, touched on a concern coming from another quarter: the sorters. 'The increasing demands of these workers', manufacturers cried, 'have a marked stamp of imposition, and have reached the extreme of intending that the owners of a factory do not enter into the same and that in each one of these there should be no more than one apprentice in the sorting department.' Sorters were airing a very different grievance, which was the alarming increase in the number of sorter apprentices. There were only enough jobs, when the factories were working to capacity, for some 400 sorters, the sorters claimed. There were already 600 trained in this skill and a further 300 finishing their apprenticeship. There would soon, then, be some 900 sorters for 400 jobs. In good times, 500 would be out of work; in bad times, which the industry had been known to suffer, a further 200. What they wanted was a limited apprenticeship of 2%. They were quick to defend themselves in an open letter to *El Productor* on 30 November, quoting the main objective of their guild as that of

protecting the workers . . . against the unjust demands of the manufacturers, always striving to maintain the best rates possible for the work, to see that the workers find jobs quickly if for any just motive they leave or lose the one they had, and to help them while they find that work in order that their lack of funds is not taken advantage of, always having recourse to conciliatory measures between capital and labour.

On analysing the surplus of skilled men and apprentices in the trade, they argued:

this surplus will be of grave consequence, not only to those depending on this craft for a living but also to society in general, because those without work will be in the greatest misery, and misery is always the cause of crime; why should not the Society, then, exercising the right which has been granted to it and the common sense with which its members are vested, formulate a project to regulate apprenticeship, if it judges this to be opportune?

Not only the rules and regulations of our society, but also our condition as free workers, give us the power to formulate and carry out such a project. It is our understanding that from the moment in which we are called upon to work and we accept the neutral and natural condition of giving an amount of work for a quantity of money, there exists a contract or understanding between the employer and the employee, which only binds us to the duty of fulfilling that condition. If the employer wishes us to teach our craft to any other person that he chooses to send, it is clear that since this duty is not in our contract on entering the factory, which is, we repeat, in our condition as free men, we have every right to accept or refuse according to our particular convenience.

Those manufacturers of the Union may well call this unjust demands with a marked stamp of imposition; do you, comrade editor, believe that in this there is anything of an imposition? Yes, there is, in effect, but not on the part of the worker toward the manufacturer, as they say, but on the part of the manufacturer toward the worker, the former wanting to impose on the latter duties which he did not contract on entering the factory.

They still stressed the conciliatory nature of their guild and appealed to manufacturers, some of whom they still regarded as former fellow workers. Yet, at a meeting called by the civil authorities, Segundo Álvarez, president of the manufacturers' union, admitted that 98% of the workers were for the 2% restriction but claimed 'there was something that could not be pinpointed, but the effects of which were being felt, and that something should be cast out from among the workers'. He was shouted down by sorters who asserted 'that something' was simply the way in which manufacturers were acting. But there was more to it than that. Accustomed as they were to being treated as aristocrats, sorters were reacting by closing ranks and becoming very defensive. The disrespect and intransigence of their employers was turning that defensiveness into a radicalism that could find a perfect outlet in anarcho-syndicalism. The fact that the majority of them were Spanish was important but secondary to this.

Both sorters and cigar makers were again under attack in the aftermath of the 1888 cigar makers' strike. This was sparked off in the Henry Clay factory, which had fast concentrated one-tenth of Havana's cigar makers and was notorious for paying less than the older, more established, and smaller factories. There cigar makers working the particularly low-paid 'Alvas' kind claimed an increase. Henry Clay's owner, Segundo Álvarez, granted them this, only to dismiss all 30 'Alvas' workers a few days later. Again their fellow workers came out on their behalf. Similar situations developed in La Legitimidad and Aguila de Oro over low-paying cigars, and in La

Diligencia, where all workers were out over a peso increase on all cigars. As president of the manufacturers' union, Álvarez took advantage of the strikes in other factories to press the union to declare another lock-out. This time the motives were clearly specified:

Turbulent, noisy strikes yet again, provoked and stirred up by a tiny group of workers, obstruct work in several shops. An insignificant minority seeks to obstruct if not block the just, honorable, and legal working of the industry by men whose work, thrift, activity, and aptitude gave it a name, credit, and fortune . . . without stopping to consider that the methods employed punish with privation and hunger the very working class whose name they have taken up . . . When the limit has been reached in the price of work, they aspire to regulate it to their taste, set the conditions of the same, and demand that no more apprentices be taught, that the shop owner cannot check over the work, that the manufacturer employ the number of workers they stipulate, and that a certain employee or other who jealously guards the interests of the firm be dismissed. And when their aspirations are not met, they declare the shop on strike . . .

The lie was given to their declarations when only a handful of workers had voted against coming out on strike, none at all in some of the factories.

Upheavals in the sorting sector on the one hand, and a tremendous explosion of labour activity in general, is evident. And yet, just how much did this affect labour organization? There was, without doubt, a strong body of agitators who were actively working with the classic anarcho-syndicalist concept of a strong revolutionary union and the general strike as its weapon against the manufacturing bourgeoisie. This was clear at the so-called first worker congress held in October 1887; Roig was largely responsible for a resolution declaring 'the need to give a new form of organization to the collectives, abolishing all trace of authority' along the lines of Spanish worker federation of 1882. Points 5 and 6 of the congress resolution read:

5. That all political and religious doctrines should be prohibited from all worker collectives and from the Federation, leaving only the universal principle of social and economic emancipation and the fraternity under the principle of all producers that inhabit the land.
6. That solidarity should preside over all strikes to which worker collectives are forced by the extreme tyranny and shameless impositions of those who still, at the end of the nineteenth century, consider the worker as a vile being, born to support in silence all kind of privation and insult.

According to reports of the time, the Resolution was carried with great enthusiasm. Roig, then a reader, had ample chance to expound his ideas on the old reformist organizations, and *El Productor* was recorded as having considerable circulation. Significantly, the sorters chose to address manufacturers through his paper; in March 1888 it became the official organ of the Junta Central de Artesanos; and it became the cigar makers' mouthpiece in the July 1888 strike. Roig's Alianza Obrera of late 1888 appears to have won considerably more support than its reformist counterpart, Martínez' Unión Obrera – which, to all intents and purposes, grew out of the manufacturers' refusal to enter into dealings with the Alianza and their invitation for a new worker commission to be set up.[9] Manufacturers blamed the agitators and, faced with the disintegration of old guilds, denied the existence of any other. On the founding of Unión Obrera, Roig claimed it was 'nothing but a small number of dissidents who carry no prestige among their fellow workers'. He may have exaggerated, but over 1,000 workers signed a protest against the Unión in *El Productor* and two contingents of cigar makers sailed for Tampa rather than call off the strike.

Cigarmen in the older, smaller and better-paying factories such as Villar y Villar and La Carolina formed the strongholds of La Unión (*unionistas* were nicknamed *Carolinas*). Of them, it could be written in 1890:

The cigar makers have comfort, space and relative cleanliness . . . the consideration of the owners: indeed, because nobody more than they stand to profit from harmony . . . Competition between manufacturers has reached the shop floor and one thing is most evident as regards the social question: he who most accommodates himself to harmony between capital and labour is he who is most considered and left alone.[10]

La Alianza had its support in Henry Clay and the whole spectrum of middling to small factories working cheaper cigars. It also attracted many former free coloureds and slaves, excluded from earlier white artisan societies, on the margin of existing guilds yet lacking the necessary experience to create a viable alternative.

Remarkably, there appears to have been not one incident of disorder on the part of strikers. On the contrary, there is considerable evidence of their sense of order and discipline. In the 1887 strikes, they were praised as having given unmistakable proof of their 'wisdom, sense and sound thinking'.[11] A noted lawyer by the name of Pedro González Llorente, who had taken up their defence, was given a rally of honour outside his home in March 1899. Symbolically, on that occasion he applauded 'the peaceful attitude of the workers in past strikes', encouraging them 'to always use the force of reason and not reason by force' and exhorting that 'always as until now they should fight for their rights without violent tumult'.[12] Roig himself wrote of the 1888 strike, 'We applaud the peaceful attitude workers have adopted', urging them to use 'all legal means available.'

In conclusion, there appear to have been three marked trends. The first was that growing among sorters who still stood apart from the majority of workers and whose material conditions had not been affected greatly. Threatened by the widening gap between them and their employers, however, they turned to anarcho-syndicalism to regain customary rights of an earlier Golden Age. The second was that growing among cigar makers, especially in the newer factories and among those working inferior cigars, for whom anarcho-syndicalism represented a more radical form of action under new industrial conditions. The third was the continuation of the older craft guilds among top cigarmen and the like, along reformist lines. Only the second could aspire to becoming a mass movement and yet, by virtue of the very nature of the workers supporting it, was foredoomed as such. It was one thing that in strikes the mass of workers should adopt the stance taken by the Alianza as against the Unión, it was another to attribute to them fully developed ideas and full union activity.

Roig himself was well aware that such times had not come. What he could not foresee was the form in which they would. The anarcho-syndicalist in him meant that he failed to relate to the national independence movement. And yet, it was only when worker organizations embraced the cause for independence that the great mass of workers were involved. Despite their good intentions as to treating all workers equally, regardless of colour, race and nationality, and possibly because of this, it was easy to point to many Spanish supporters of anarcho-syndicalism who were against the national independence movement and accuse them of being anti-Cuban.[13]

Political events then took over. Spain's complete disregard for the aspirations of Cuba's landed and manufacturing oligarchy and the strangulation of Cuba's economy, especially the tobacco industry, which was then also facing falling US markets, combined to produce an independence movement which this time had far more popular support. In 1892, what is most commonly referred to as the Primer Congreso Obrero was held in Havana; over 1,000 delegates were present at it. The premature death of Roig in 1889 did not mean the death of his ideas. A strong anarcho-syndicalist current was to remain. But the simple solidarity pacts which he advocated were finally rejected. In this sense, the congress almost appears to have been a victory for the socialists, who also defined the strike as a fundamental weapon for the workers but saw a strong organizational form as the necessary structure of the workers' federation.

On this, documentation is weak. The socialist nature of the proposals may have been overstated. The victory for socialism was in any case temporary; after independence, reformism and anarcho-syndicalism were to gain new strength. It is significant, however, that anarcho-syndicalist thought had itself become early infused with socialist ideas.

This can be seen in Roig's writings in particular. His early campaigns were strictly centred around strike activities and union organization, and against any sort of worker party. '. . . The microscopic worker parties that are supposedly organized only aspire to the conquest of political power with the aim of themselves becoming bourgeois and exercising over the masses a much more odious form of authority and exploitation than the one at present in existence', he wrote in 1887. In his articles 'Realidad y Utopia' (1888) his ideas were beginning to change and in 'O pan o plomo!', written shortly before his death, he was as good as advocating just such a party.

Most significant of all was that the 1892 congress did come out in support of the independence movement.

11

Revolutionary nationalism of the 1900s

With the dissolution of the 1892 worker congress and the imprison-ment of labour leaders by the Spanish colonial authorities, labour activity as such was again brought to a halt. Mass unemployment during the 1890s, partly for economic reasons – by 1895, the year war broke out, half of Havana's cigar makers were out of work – and partly for political ones, meant that more workers went to swell the ranks of the already well-established strong nucleus of Cuban émigrés.[1] Labour issues almost exclusively gave way to the political issue of independence.

During the 1880s guilds had grown up in Tampa, Key West, and Florida; there had been a wave of strikes in 'Cuban' factories and close contact had been maintained between émigré workers such as Carlos Baliño and Ramón Rivero and those back home. Shortly after a January 1877 strike over wage demands in Martínez Ibor's Príncipe de Gales factory – in which one worker was killed, five injured, and 75 driven from the locality – cigarman Rivero founded the Federación Cubana de Obreros to oppose the reformist International Cigar Makers' Union, affiliated to the American Federation of Labour. Baliño, a sorter in the Hidalgo Gato factory in Key West, was early active in the sorters' guild and in 1892 was on the editorial board of the paper *La Tribuna del Trabajo*.

Both had great respect for Roig and helped encourage support for the Alianza and the strikes back home. Baliño was a contributor to *El Productor*, denouncing Hidalgo Gato and Martínez Ibor, who 'despite their revolutionary affiliation, do not hesitate to exploit the workers'. In October 1894, he wrote: 'The relationship between manufacturers and workers is that of master and slave no matter how laced it may be with mutual courtesies.' His ability to read English meant that the classics, and especially the works of Marx and Engels, were available to him. His experience of the United States and his readings had made him far more of a socialist than Roig could ever be and also made him particularly aware of Cuba's need for independence.

The first revolutionary club of Cuban émigrés, the Patriotic Association of Key West, had been set up as early as 1869, the year in which Martínez Ibor had transferred his factory and workers to the region. Over the next twenty-five years, 46 small organizations of this type grew up in Florida; and wherever there were émigré communities, as far north as Philadelphia and New York, recreational centres, schools and revolutionary clubs were formed. There was little coordination between them until the 1890s, when José Martí, a Cuban intellectual exiled for his outspoken criticism of the Spanish government and involvement in the independence cause, founded the Partido Revolucionario Cubano. There is no doubt that he did so – becoming Cuba's great independence leader, alongside men like Antonio Maceo and Máximo Gómez back in Cuba – with the support of the tobacco workers and their leaders Baliño and Rivero.

Rivero had been instrumental in founding the Liga Patriótica, the paper *Cuba*, and the Flor de Crombet revolutionary club in Tampa in 1889. In 1890, the Príncipe de Gales factory in Ibor City became the birthplace of the Cuban Liceo, or Casa del Pueblo as Martí was to call it. In 1892, Baliño personally accompanied Martí to Tampa to win support for the Partido Revolucionario and in 1893 helped found the Enrique Roig (in posthumous tribute) and 10 de Abril Clubs there. Many émigré workers never lost hope of returning to an independent Cuba (favourite readings in factories were the events of the Ten Years' War and exploits of the early independence leaders), and they supplied money for arms and provisions for expeditions to Cuba.

Among the anarcho-syndicalist followers of Roig who had been forced into exile, however, there were those like Enrique Messonier, Ramón Rivera and Manuel Cendoya, who were convinced neither by socialist nor independence ideas. On coming back to Cuba after independence they were able to iron out some differences, but others were only heightened. Conditions prevalent in Cuba for the workers, especially the repatriate Cuban workers, were hardly those for which the émigrés had fought so long.

The outcome of the 1895–8 war was to give formal political independence to Cuba. In the process, the Cuban people lost two great leaders, Martí and Maceo, both of whom had been astute enough to foresee the dangers of future dependence on the United States. Twentieth-century Cuba, and especially the tobacco industry, became economically – and hence in the final analysis politically – dependent on its great neighbour to the north. The particular importance of tobacco to the Cuban economy at the time, the fact that virtually the whole export sector fell into American hands, at a time of great post-independence political euphoria, especially that of returning workers, while the island was under US military occupation (1899–1902) combined to produce a particularly explosive situation. The independence struggle over, the class struggle was renewed with a vengeance. Six months after the end of war there were disputes, and within three years (soon after the 1902 Republic was founded) the industry was torn apart by a strike that was to paralyse much of Havana.

'Having arrived in Havana, cigar makers – as almost all the repatriates were – found they were without work and with no means on which to live', wrote Felipe Zapata in his labour history notes:

Bitter reality shattered in a day the enchanted castle that political work had built up over long, difficult, and bloody years of struggle. Cigar makers had nothing to live on in their own land. The factories, yes, they were working to capacity. The industry was prosperous. There was great demand. There were many empty benches in the cigar rolling departments. There was a demand for workers. There was good pay. Children and young men were sought after as apprentices because the future for tobacco was bright.

There was all this; but nothing for the returning Cubans. When the cigar makers, some years earlier, left for the North, *de facto* they gave up the jobs they had in the factories. During their absence these jobs were taken by foreign hands. The managers and foremen, also foreigners, began to call on children and young men of their own nationality to take up the positions vacant for apprentices.[2]

While something of an exaggeration – the industry as a whole was far from prosperous and Spaniards had a monopoly only of the more elite Havana factory jobs – his remarks are worth analysing. They clearly did apply to the large Havana factory sector around which the labour movement was concentrated. Rivero Muñiz was more explicit on this:

The managers and foremen of those Trust factories, all Spaniards, continued since their new owners considered them the most able, given the time they had been doing the job, to direct work. It almost goes without saying, then, that the already existent discrimination was to continue unaltered and Cuba youth were to be excluded from the better jobs . . .[3]

In March 1899, 95 cigar makers in the Henry Clay factory addressed a letter to the Trust demanding that Spanish foremen be removed. The letter went unheeded, but the call was then taken up more widely. That same month Baliño, Rivero and others recently back from

Florida attempted to organize the Partido Socialista Cubano and, in the months that followed, the labour weekly *Alerta* and (with Messonier) the Liga General de Trabajadores Cubanos.

Alerta published the news of a Cuban boy who had applied for apprenticeship as a leaf selecter in the Flor del Todo factory and whom, a Spanish head of department had replied, 'would be a bishop first'. Despite the provisional US government's admonitions to workers not to make untimely demands,[4] a whole campaign for accepting Cubans and Cuban apprentices grew out of this. The right to work, 75% of all jobs for Cubans, became the cry. The league's five-point programme was:

First: That Cuban workers in general should enjoy the same advantages and guarantees enjoyed by foreigners in different industries in this country.

Second: To strive by all means possible to achieve employment in all shops for Cuban émigrés to be repatriated.

Third: To initiate a campaign on behalf of the moral and material interests of Cuban women workers.

Fourth: To make all possible provision for the welfare of all orphans, whether or not they are children of liberators, who are roaming our streets.

Fifth: To be prepared, to defend ourselves against all harmful elements which, for reasons whatsoever, aim to impede the advance of the future Cuban Republic.[5]

There were evidently going to be great splits among the workers over this. Rivera organized the Sociedad de la Tranca (literally, 'Society of the Stick') to go around enforcing the 75%. However, the more anarchist wing also accused the league of being nationalist in its objectives. Already existing, predominantly Spanish-run worker organizations continued to defend vigorously their right to control entry into their trade.

The Sociedad de Escogedores de La Habana felt it was being wrongly accused of being exclusively Spanish and was on repeated occasions to make this clear. In February 1900, a meeting took place between the two worker organizations at which the sorters manifested their moral support for league resolutions. Their continued restrictionism was not based on race or nationality, they maintained, but on the acute shortage of jobs.

In June 1902, the sorters put out a manifesto explaining 'how the numbers of apprentices had grown so alarmingly that a limit was needed:

in order that the excessively high number of sorters in the future should not have as its outcome that relatively lucrative work become one of the many that give rise to just protest on the part of clear-thinking and honourable workers for the exploitation to which they are victims. For this, there was a strike of nearly three months in the year 1887 . . . which ended in the dissolution of the Gremio de Escogedores. Re-organized years later, it directed its attention again to establishing the conditions whereby the craft would suffer no damage and be remunerated as was only right and proper, in the interests of all sorters of today and logically tomorrow.

The manifesto came in response to a league meeting in which it was agreed to put an official demand before manufacturers that Cuban apprentices be accepted for all departments. A league letter to the sorters asked what their position would be on this and, in the event of their being in agreement, what kind of support they would give the league.[6]

Despite the protests of sorters to the contrary, it was clear that Cuban children would continue having difficulty entering such a restricted trade. At the end of their manifesto, the sorters claimed that 80 of the 350 members of their organization, 49 of the 110 apprentices, were in fact Cuban. These may well have been Spaniards who had opted for Cuban citizenship or Cuban-born sons of Spanish descent.

The apprenticeship question was but one factor in the situation at the time and yet, given independence ideals, one of the most irritating politically as well as materially. American owners were already concentrating production, undercutting established manufacturing practices, and curtailing unionization. Their attitude in favouring Spaniards was more than Cubans had bargained for.

It was no coincidence, then, that the large Trust factories should again be the centre of violent struggles at a very early date. Already in 1902 the league was preparing for a confrontation with manufacturers over the apprenticeship question, during the September–December months of peak Christmas demand, when cigar makers in the Cabañas factory came out demanding better leaf. The Trust had embarked on its policy of squeezing labour, one of the ways being to expect first-rate workmanship from second-rate leaf. Since poor leaf could easily crumble, extra time and care was needed on each cigar, hence lowering wages. The demand for higher wage scales went up in this and then other Trust factories. About the strike in Villar y Villar, Zapata wrote:

The immediate causes were none too clear. Charges were made against the foremen . . . against one because he was Spanish, another because he was American. They were not duly respectful to workers of this country. The tobacco was not wetted as it should be. They wasted workers' time. The Trust was a pack of imperialist US millionaires who exploited the workers and oppressed Cuba. Conclusion: workers found this intolerable and were ready to fight until 'victory or death'.[7]

A Trust strike committee was set up on 8 November and formulated the demands: (1) that Cubans be admitted to all departments; (2) that apprenticeship be limited to 5%; (3) that there be seniority rights; (4) standardized wage agreements; and (5) a recognized worker committee in each factory department. The Trust rejected the whole petition and the strike was on. Almost simultaneously with the Trust, workers in independent factories came out on these demands, especially that for standardized wages, since theirs were on the whole lower. One strike anecdote is that the Aguila de Oro factory opened its doors to Cuban apprentices, whereupon it was decided to continue work, the feeling being that a general strike favoured the Trust by eliminating competition. Some 500 marched on the factory, clamouring for it to join the strike movement. On 11 November, a bill went before the Senate's agriculture, industry and trade committee regarding the employment of Cubans, only to be lost in government machinery.[8] On 20 November many small shops and businesses did not open, and the docks were paralysed. It was estimated on the 21st that strikers numbered some 30,000 in all.

From Tampa and Key West, supplies of money were collected and food bought to distribute to the most needy. The Trust and other manufacturers threatened to move their factories out of Havana to places where they would have no labour problems. The order went out from the Estrada Palma government for severe measures to be taken to secure law and order. The strike was then brutally put down as troops were sent in and strikers imprisoned.

Only in the aftermath of repression did the founding fathers of the Republic – Máximo Gómez, Juan Gualberto, Sanguily and others – begin their conciliatory gestures. They who had qualified strikers as 'ones who disturb the peace, enemies of public order influenced by Spanish anarchists whose aim was to impede the setting up of the Republic' were to implore, 'Cubans . . . you're destroying the homeland. Independence is endangered by your violence. It is essential that this state of revolutionary strike end immediately. What is it you want, if not to abort the Republic?' Their hostility clearly sprang from US pressure, economic dependence on tobacco and their own extremely delicate situation, but grievances smouldered on. The poor harvest of 1906 sparked off another major strike. Poor quality leaf meant working more slowly at a time when real wages – paid in Spanish or Cuban currency – were falling as more goods were priced in the more highly valued American currency.

The Trust was back under attack. In February 1907, at the height of the second (1906–8) US military occupation, Cabañas cigar makers demanded better leaf and payment in dollars. Trust manager Bock promised the first but not the second. With Cabañas workers out, a so-called 'American money strike' soon spread to other Trust factories. Bock used his powers to 'persuade' independent manufacturers to declare a lock-out. But the ones whom he couldn't control were the small *chinchaleros* and private rollers.[9] They thrived on having the local market to themselves and, we are led to believe, it was this competition which helped break the lock-out and force the Trust to accede to workers' demands. Independent factories were left to reach individual agreements with their workers. On the strength of these gains, a further strike of Trust workers was sparked off by threatened redundancy in January 1908. It lasted six weeks, but ended in total failure.[10]

The failure was significant and points to very serious limitations on worker activity during this early period. In 1902, large factory, and especially Trust, workers had been the centre of the strike movement, but for both economic and political reasons the issues had wider relevance. The 1907 strike was initially confined to the large factories – others only being effected by a lock-out on the part of manufacturers. *Chinchaleros* and other independent manufacturers who later broke the lock-out had no trouble finding workers. In 1908, not only was the strike limited but blacklegs ensured its extinction.

It can in no way be thought that the strikes indicated any strong worker organization that could channel strike activity. After the long years of independence struggles, few guilds were worthy of the name. Those that were – the cigar sorters are a case in point – were often grouped around the much-disputed Spanish workers and for that reason very much turned in on themselves. Attempts to reorganize the labour movement in the form of the league and a revolutionary nationalism had broad appeal, but could scarcely, at this stage, be lasting in any tangible form. The great mass of unemployed in whom it originated remained unemployed, and hence impotent in terms of direct industrial action. Those who had jobs, especially in the face of those who hadn't, became more concerned with keeping them. Only those in Trust factories, subjected to a particularly new form of both political and economic exploitation, remained at all vociferous in their demands. They were consistently refused the right to worker committees until 1907, when manufacturers made sure they were limited on a factory-to-factory basis.

Baliño and Rivero made successive attempts to found a socialist workers' party – the Partido Obrero de la Isla de Cuba (1904) and the Agrupación Socialista Internacional (1906) – but found little concrete support for such moves. Baliño in particular was always on the alert to explain that 'Without economic freedom, political freedom is no more than a treacherous mirage.'[10] The fierce reprisals of strikers and the hardships to which they and their families were subjected – such, indeed, that there was a return move to Tampa and Key West – had subdued the great majority of workers. Baliño tried to counteract this, explaining in 1905:

. . . the aim of the socialists is to equalize while at the same time raising standards; to make extensive to all the well-being and pleasures that are today the privilege of the few.

For this it is necessary in the first place that the mass of the workers, who comprise the great majority of mankind, become convinced that hunger, destitution, insecurity, excess work or enforced idleness, endless anxiety . . . are not to be justified by the laws of evolution.[11]

As a socialist, he strongly opposed the anarchists in the Agrupación who did not take up the struggle against privileged groups of workers. In a February 1909 letter to Agrupación president Benigno Miranda, he wrote:

Where there are privileges there can be no union, and without this socialism is not possible . . . In all countries workers are moving toward social fraternity, realizing that among workers there can be no distinction of race or nationality . . . but here there are guilds where work is so monopolized by Spanish workers that few Cubans work in the trade and *not one negro*. For such controllers of the job market, who so deeply divide the workers here, the Agrupación Socialista has not one word of reproach, not one exhortation to Social Fraternity . . . Those Spanish workers who consider themselves to be politically aware, who are grouped under the red flag of International Socialism, who come here with the word of redemption on their lips to be the guides and spokesmen of the mass of workers, who proclaim the brotherhood of all men throughout the world, must take up the hard but necessary task, the essential preparatory work of ending those iniquitous privileges. They should take upon themselves this task because they themselves do not experience the pain and oppression of such disregard and can therefore work without the anger of those obliged to act in self-defence. And only when they take up this task will the people have trust in them and listen without misgivings . . .[12]

It was over this question that Baliño finally left the organization, though not abandoning his belief in socialism. In a subsequent letter to Miranda that same month, he declared:

While the workers are content to simply follow the bourgeois parties, asking for more from governments that are no more than, in Marx's words, the administrative committees of the bourgeoisie; while they spend their lives on their knees begging, accustomed to disdain as Diogenes before the Statue, they will receive but the bone which is thrown to the masses, unaware that they act with no direction or ideal in an endless night of misery.

Throughout the world the proletariat today builds up two simultaneous movements, each essential to carry it to victory. One is the organization of resistance for the economic struggle, and in this there should be no privilege or caste. The other is the political action of its class party which has as its objective the socialization of industry. Only through the carrying out of this ideal can a seat be prepared for all at the banquet of life, and all exclusive privileges which hinder the fraternity of man be erased.[13]

A man with great insight, Baliño was in a sense far ahead of his times. His great ideal was far from realization. Workers – those in the tobacco industry included – barely formed a class capable of mass organization at this point.

12

Cigar makers on the defensive

The year 1914 appears to mark a turning point in the history of the labour movement in the tobacco industry. After a complete lull in labour activity following the 1908 strike and due to the limited nature of worker organization, from 1914 on came the first moves to build up regional and later national craft and general unions, incorporating workers of all areas of skill and industry. And yet the extent and nature of the involvement of cigar makers point to how the newness of these movements can easily be overemphasized.

The new moves in 1914 were largely in response to three factors. The first was the rapidly increasing cost of living (especially reflected in food prices), which was causing a drop in real wages in all sectors. The second was the worsening economic situation particularly of the Havana and surrounding tobacco industry, hit by blockages on the export market at the outbreak of World War I. Factories were cutting back on production and workers – over 7,000 Havana cigar makers, 2,000 in nearby San Antonio de los Baños, and some 6,000–7,000 stemmers were reported out of work in 1914. In August, a central aid committee was set up by and for cigar makers and annexed crafts; and, at the insistence of Partagás workers, a demonstration was organized to demand 100,000 pesos credit from the government. On the eve of the National Worker Congress, held on 28–30 August, it was cigar makers and their families who made up the greater part of a hunger strike in Güines.

In the wake of the great tobacco strikes and the death in 1910 of Havana Trust President Gustav Bock, American Tobacco's G.W. Hill and Edgar Ware personally journeyed to Havana to inspect Trust factories and evaluate the local situation. The benevolent Bock, it was claimed, 'had kept useless workers on, paying the hospital costs of tubercular cigar workers, subsidizing the upkeep of their families suddenly left with no means of support.'[1] Economies on personnel were in no mean measure connected with an unstated awareness that cheap docile labour was not exactly one of Cuba's advantages. Significantly, worker societies of Trust factories like La Corona and Cabañas were to be in the forefront in pressing for new union organization.

The third factor was the changing stance of manufacturers and government. Active government intervention before 1914 appears to have been confined mainly to occasional interference and repressive police or troop action in large disputes. This had been enforced in the case of the cigar makers, given their numerical strength, the serious implications of the strike of these workers, and the particular political context of strike action and moves to worker organization: hence the public meeting between civil authorities, manufacturers and workers in 1887, the repression of the 1892 congress, and the sending in of troops to quash the 1902 strike.

By 1909 (after the 'stabilizing' period of the 1906–8 military intervention), there were signs of change. The commission which drew up the 1909 report on the industry claimed it had not had sufficient time to study the 'labour problem' but did include in the questionnaire 'one particular universal truth . . . related to the discord between the essential factors of production: labour and capital, represented by the worker and the manufacturer . . .'[2] It also recommended that the government devote special attention to labour matters and considered that arbitration courts 'with proportional representation of both elements, and the intervention of one person neutral to both, as moderator'[3] could be set up, thus reducing or possibly completely avoiding disturbances in the industry. Arbitration courts were not actually set up until much later, but it is significant that they were already being considered. In December 1913 a committee for social affairs was created, its brief being part of:

a scientific movement of social reform, to which Governments now need to give attention, not only for reasons of justice and humanity but also in order to procure . . . social normality and an adequate solution to collective problems, avoiding, by means of opportune measures, conflict between the different social classes . . .[4]

Hope was expressed that labour codes and social provisions would soon follow, and in February 1914 came the first known project for a secretariat of labour, forerunner to the later ministry.

It was against the background of hardship and within the framework of a kind of class collaboration, then, that the (third) First National Worker Congress of August 1914 took place.

The 1914 congress was considerably limited in scope. Delegates came largely from the tobacco industry and from traditional artisan groups such as tailors, painters and carpenters, who were also finding times hard and whose guilds had also set up their aid committees. By sheer strength of numbers, the cigar makers' aid committee was inevitably the stronger and more financially solvent, although at the same time struggling to cover the needs of all cigar makers affected by closures. It was understandable that this sector of workers should be seen to be turning in on themselves, thus losing a certain prestige they had among other groups. '. . . The cigar makers, who had always marched at the head of the workers, had this time closed the doors of charity to those who were not cigar or related workers', declared a delegate of the painters' guild, to which Ramiro Neyra, secretary of the cigar makers' central aid committee replied that 'cigar workers cared about other workers but could not include the other guilds while they were still a cigar makers' committee'.[5]

The great majority of the delegates to the congress from the tobacco industry represented individual factory guilds or aid committees for each craft and necessarily came preoccupied with the specific problems of each. Nonetheless, the fact that the industry as a whole and other sectors of the economy were affected by the war had the consequence of widening the workers' horizons again. It was, significantly, the Sociedad de Resistencia 'La Corona' which submitted the winning essay to the congress on 'Resistence Societies in Cuba, the Need for Reorganization'. Among their suggestions was that a committee be set up for the rest of the workers; and they, along with delegates from other sectors, founded a central aid committee for the unemployed. Only the leaf selecters' guild withdrew its delegates to set up a separate federation of leaf selecters, cigar sorters and box decorators.

The congress was, then, a tentative step toward a more unified worker organization. The fact that this could not yet materialize was a reflection of diverse developments over the next years. Cigar makers still formed the only strong nucleus of the *industrial* working class. At the same time, their strongest unions were still dominated by the more skilled groups, whose experience of violent conflict had taught them a moderation not common to other sectors. The fact that in periods when the factories were working to full capacity, as with the abnormally high post-war demand in 1918, these groups enjoyed relatively high wages and better conditions, only contributed to this even more.

Thus it was not tobacco workers but new and growing sectors of workers who were to become the centre of a wave of strikes which broke out in Cuba from 1917 on – stevedores and dock workers in general, railwaymen, machinists, and to a lesser extent workers in the sugar mills. The semi-skilled nature of much of their work and the sort of conditions under which they laboured attracted many to more radical ideas that were anarchist, anarcho-syndicalist, and similar in nature. Although cigar makers were to take the lead in forming a provincial and then national craft union and in organizing the Second Worker Congress and the first general union in 1920, their ideas were hotly challenged by both older artisan and newer industrial groups and their leaders.

The year 1918 witnessed strikes on an unprecedented scale. Aside from the many small local strikes, there were 20 large-scale ones in 1918, 28 in 1919, centred around demands for wage increases and the eight-hour day. Even Beck, military attaché of the US legation, was to report after the March 1919 general strike:

I have tried to ascertain the causes of the strike and I have reached the following conclusions: the basic cause is that salaries have not increased as much as the cost of living. In each strike the workers have deep down had legitimate cause.[6]

Nonetheless, the authorities were quick to locate and arrest or deport strike leaders and decry the Spanish anarchists who were arriving every day. While it was clear, on the one hand, that new immigrants from Spain were bringing new strength to anarcho-syndicalism, at the same time the 1917 October Revolution had its effect. 'Down with the Kaiser of Cuba', shouted workers in the November 1918 strike of dock, rail and other transport workers.

This was the background against which new moves were made to unite the working class in local and provincial unions.

The year 1920 opened with the Cigar Makers' Congress in January. While strikes and ideological divisions were splitting apart other sectors, the cigar makers of Havana and surrounding districts had been quietly building up their union organization. By 1920 all the local craft guilds were loosely united in the bi-provincial Federación de Torcedores de La Habana y Pinar del Río, under cigar maker José Bravo. A man of reformist ideas in the tradition of his great American counterpart Sam Gompers, Bravo had worked to build up the Havana cigar makers' union and to obtain better wages and work conditions. Sufficient funds had also been raised to construct a school, library, printing shop, and social centre – some $70,000 in all. The printing shop was completed and turning out the *Boletín del Torcedor* by 1920. More remarkable is that (so the story goes) when the financial crash of 1920 ate away funds and when Bravo finally absconded with the tidy sum of $39,000, cigar makers got the money together again and a construction plan to the tune of $85,000 was completed.

It was Bravo who, together with Carlos Baliño, chaired the January congress and it was largely his ideas which influenced the agreement to call for a national labour congress in which workers from all sectors were to participate to send a delegate to a Pan-American Congress of the Federation of Labour. One of the central issues motivating the holding of the Second National Worker Congress of that year, it was no less one that was hotly disputed. *Nueva Aurora*, a paper of anarchist leanings, had the following to say:

The cigar makers, having put themselves to resolving international questions as well as those related to their own trade and workers in general, can find no better solution than that of recognizing the American Cigar Makers' International, deciding to send representatives to the Cleveland Convention, and advising Cuban workers to send delegates to the Pan-American Congress of the American Federation of Labour.

With what authority and in the name of what kind of logic did these pseudo-congressmen agree to send their representatives . . . to the Cigar Makers' International and through that to the American Federation of Labour? Who is to gain from such an arbitrary measure? . . . Not the workers, though perhaps those who stood to gain from the Cuban worker movement being affiliated to that inspired by Mr Gompers, Holland, Morrison and a hundred other such bandits.

And with what reasons did they justify their invitation, their recommendation to attend the Pan-American Congress in Mexico, while omitting to even mention the other Congress, that of the Third International?

The Federation of Labour? . . . The Pan-American Federation? Its men? The first, a big labour trust, an immense monopoly acting against those who do not belong to it and a shackle to the aspirations of those who are members; the second, a trap laid by the government and American capitalists to guarantee control over Spanish-speaking America; and the last, a heap of wretches only worth lynching by the workers. And this is where the representatives of the cigar makers wish to take us.[7]

There are reputed to have been delegates from 128 different organizations, representing 200,000 workers, at this second and much more important national congress. The more reformist cigar makers would seem to have been outvoted this time. Craft groups came out in strong opposition. The printers' vote had gone to Antonio Penichet and Alfredo López, 'who carry the brief to vote against sending delegates to the Pan-American Congress and for sending them to the

Latin American, which represents the Third International of Moscow'. Proposals were made to send fraternal greetings to comrades who founded the Soviet Republic. Criticism of cigar maker Sam Gompers, 'a blustering and swaggering bourgeois',[8] and his union was so strong that the final resolution was to send delegates to the Latin American Congress.

The congress ended with the setting up of committees which included Penichet, López, and Bravo to consider the organization of a central worker organization. This fell through when Penichet, López and other anarchist leaders were arrested. Bravo, taking advantage of the situation, held a congress of Havana and Pinar del Río cigar makers at which, going against the final decisions of the national congress, it was agreed to recognize the International Cigar Makers' Union and send delegates to the Mexico congress.

In the absence of exact figures on unionization, the two early congresses give very definite clues as to the nature of worker organization over this period. Although Havana cigar makers were significantly voted down in 1920, other groups were isolated and weak, and no alternative organization was yet viable. Thus it was that during the twenties cigar makers' unions were to be consolidated along much the same lines as before.

There were strong local craft unions in towns like San Antonio de los Baños and Bejucal, and in some towns of Las Villas province. Bravo devoted considerable time and effort to the latter, drawing them into regional craft organizations. Many old tobacco workers throughout that province tell of personal visits from Bravo and, indeed, the Federación de Torcedores de Santa Clara (province) was also set up in 1920. However, the strength of the local tobacco oligarchy and the utter dependence of the workers on them meant that unions were to make little headway. Ranchuelo was an extreme example of this. Octavio Mesa, a founder member of the cigar makers' guild in those days, remembers:

In Ranchuelo, the most powerful economically were the Trinidad family and, consequently, they also dominated the economic and political life of the town. In those days there was no national police, it was municipal, under the direct orders of the mayor and, moreover, the Trinidad family had their lackeys ready to do whatever they wished. They also belonged to the president's [conservative] party and because of this had great political influence . . . [when we set up the first unions] they sacked us from work . . . some were driven from town on foot, women and children along with them . . . In 1920 their agents visited cigar makers with forms for them to sign saying that to work they must keep out of the union.[9]

The very pattern of events such as these also meant that, when they did get off the ground later, unions were to be far more radical than their earlier Havana counterparts. At the same time, there were also signs of change among Havana's cigar makers. Anarcho-syndicalist ideas seem not to have been that strong among the rank and file although there was support for the 1917 Russian Revolution. *Justicia*, the paper first edited by José Bravo, was reputed to have been in the hands of the anarcho-syndicalist element of the Agrupación Socialista de la Habana by late December. That same year the Agrupación put out a manifesto calling for the support of the workers for the 1917 Revolution (this being published in the *Boletín del Torcedor*). Within a couple of years, Baliño had formed a new Agrupación Comunista, forerunner to the Cuban Communist Party founded in 1925. And *Justicia* was being put out by Gregorio Marrero and Joaquín Valdés, both Communist Party founder members. It was also in 1925 that a new general union – the Confederación Nacional de Obreros de Cuba (CNOC) – was formed, soon to be of strong communist leanings. And over the years the confederation was to become important not only among newly unionized groups such as sugar and dock workers but also traditional groups such as cigar makers and the like.

13

The sleeping lion awakes

The machine throughout history has brought with it serious confrontations. Opposition to the machine has often taken the form of hostility but this has not always been so specifically directed against the machine as has been assumed. Classical Luddism in England has been shown to be a considerably sophisticated movement. Machine breaking was used as a valuable technique of workers in pre-industrial society, was often highly political in content, and had the support of many manufacturers and public opinion in general. In France, there was less agitation of workers and more competition between manufacturers. And, for long after the initial industrial revolution, in many industries the machine brought with it long-drawn-out struggles of this broad nature.

The cigar industry was particularly outstanding for such struggles. The fact that the cigar machine came into use at a relatively late date and that there was a particularly strong tradition of hand rolling meant that in the United States, for example, only a handful of manufacturers introduced the machine, often only managing to do so by moving production to other areas and employing women machinists to break the hold of the unions. In Cuba, the land of the best hand-rolled cigars in the world, where development of the industry had been so held back that both manufacturers and workers were scattered over 1,000 odd shops and factories, it was inevitable that the issue of the machine should extend far beyond the workers and employers and assume proportions which were national in scope and political in content.

In the late twenties, when Por Larrañaga installed the US-invented cigar machine, other manufacturers were quick to realize that sooner or later they would be run out of business. Because of this, the anti-machine movement was quickly converted into a broadly based movement of workers and manufacturers which swayed opinion and eventually secured government resolutions that were prohibitive to its introduction into the industry.

The initial struggle was largely confined to Havana's workers. In 1925, all but eight of Por Larrañaga's workers came out on a strike that was to last until 1930. Por Larrañaga continued with blackleg labour during that period but under heavy opposition from the newly formed Federación Nacional de Torcedores (FNT).

This first national craft union was set up at a special cigar makers' congress held in Santa Clara in 1926. It comprised resistance societies and craft guilds from all over the island, grouped into three bi-provincial federations, and was a clear response to the attempted introduction of the cigar machine in the Por Larrañaga factory. It signified an attempt to mobilize cigar makers throughout Cuba against the machine. It's leaders travelled the country – especially Las Villas province, where numbers of cigar makers catering to the local market had increased significantly over the past two decades – speaking to mass demonstrations.

The unity and morale of the cigar makers and their organizations were high over this question and a successful boycott of Por Larrañaga cigars was early infused with no small measure of nationalism and patriotism.

Moreover, there was an almost total coincidence of views between opposing workers and manufacturers. The 1926 FNT report differed little from that drawn up by the manufacturers. It, too, was addressed to the President of the Republic, laying great emphasis on how hand-rolled cigars accounted for the prestigious export market and how this would be destroyed by the machine. The whole life-line of thousands of men, women, and children would be cut off, concentrating production and wealth in the hands of the unpatriotic few, it was stated.

By 1928 the anti-machine movement was widespread. An article in the daily *El Mundo* of 26 August ran:

Remedios. Representatives from the National Cigar Makers' Federation of Cuba, headed by its president Juan Abelardo Mujica, arrived here at twelve noon today. There to welcome them at an early hour were representatives of guilds throughout the province and they also attended a meeting of the provincial committee. In honour of the visitors a banquet was held, at which more than two hundred were present, including the local authorities and the press . . .

In Santa Clara thousands marched through the city to a meeting at which the mayors as well as delegates from the different tobacco towns were present. Similar scenes were repeated in Cienfuegos, Cárdenas,

Matanzas, Pinar del Río. A great demonstration organized in Havana
on 11 November had the participation of

... veterans from the Independence War, patriotic institutions, masonic
lodges, cultural societies, the Federation of Stemmers and annexed guilds, a
musical band, different local authorities, the press, the Union of Cigar and
Cigarette Manufacturers of the Island, the National Committee for the
Propaganda and Defence of the Havana Cigar, the national executive of the
Cigar Makers' Federation, the executive committees of the cigar makers in
the different provinces, worker collectives, the Society of Federated Cigar
Makers of the Republic, and other institutions of the interior.[1]

President Machado received a delegation of the cigar makers with
promises of doing what he could in their favour.

When Por Larrañaga finally came to terms with the workers, those
terms were based, significantly, on the fact that 'the firm POR
LARRAÑAGA, S.A., used for mechanized production the brand
name "POR LARRAÑAGA" which has earned prestige through the
craftsmanship of the cigar makers, thus usurping a legitimate
right . . .' The agreement signed between the FNT and Por
Larrañaga stipulated that neither this nor any other company could
machine-produce any famous Havana cigar 'which owes its fame to
craftsmanship'. The FNT sanctioned blacklegs 'who committed a
manifest violation of proletarian ethic' and Por Larrañaga agreed to
dismiss all those who had worked for them over the past four years.
Their dismissal was of great significance for the national federation. It
meant control was re-affirmed over all members and the central
committee could state, not a little pompously:

The Central Committee . . . giving proof of its generosity and noble nature,
will, when it is esteemed opportune and in the form considered to be most
viable, concede the necessary rehabilitation of those who one day left its
ranks, such that federated cigar makers will admit them again in their midst,
and thus the Committee ends its role as arbiter on this question, in which the
sole inspiration for imparting this pronouncement has been one of justice,
well-being and, to complete the trilogy, the love that goes with this final
pardon.[2]

The attempt to mechanize had come at a time when conditions in
the industry were such that wages and piece-rates were being beaten
down and unemployment was on the increase. Because of this,
mechanization and redundancy were to permeate all aspects of the
labour situation, breaking down the earlier strength of the Havana
unions and, in the long term, paving the way for a radicalization of
both union structure and ideology.

In 1925 President Gerardo Machado had come to power. Initially elected on a quasi-populist base, he and his government advanced a form of nationalism that corresponded most to the interests of the more conservative elements of the national bourgeoisie, which had been shaken by the 1920–1 crisis. The Machado government was largely an attempt to boost their flagging position and took a hard anti-worker line. This was tempered somewhat, especially in the early years, as far as the moderate unions went; and many of the cigar makers' unions, including the FNT, went untouched for several years. This was pinpointed by Zapata in his work on the labour movement:

In reality, the situation created by that government became notorious. Worker organizations of a moderate, legalistic nature could subsist. The gastronomical workers' unions with the moderate spirit traditional to them, subsisted without difficulty. The old dockers' guilds, many of which were equally moderate, also went unhurt. The recently founded Federación Nacional de Torcedores carried on as normal. La Hermandad Ferroviaria, with the new executive that emerged after the last strike, continued peacefully. Many old and respectable institutions with an orderly and fruitful existence, like the Unión de Conductores de Carros y Camiones, and all those which remained free from anarchist or communist contamination, continued to be equally well respected by the new government. On the other hand, all the unions that dared to challenge the force of public power were eliminated rapidly and drastically.[3]

In the last analysis, it was the evident inability of the Machado government to counter the oncoming 1930s depression which provoked widespread opposition and a very strong movement of anti-imperialist feeling. As the economic crisis came to a head, producing a crisis in the affairs of national government, even established unions and official policy toward them changed drastically.

By 1929 the Federación Nacional de Torcedores might have been nearing success over the machine but it was also at a critical point in its short history. This was reflected in the new-style *Boletín del Torcedor* brought out in June that year, with the quite considerable circulation of 10,000. The *Boletín* ran informed articles about mechanization. One was penned by Eduardo Plochet, a cigar maker who had once worked in the United States:

I'm no old fool who passes his time thinking back on his youth. I am an old man who breathes innovation and sighs decadence. I am a man of today . . . and the cigar machine doesn't worry me. I know it and fought it back in 1900 as secretary of the Cigar Makers' Union of New York. I fought it convinced that sooner or later it would invade the cigar shops and wipe out the cigar maker's work, and if we did not then manage to suppress its use completely, we at least blocked it from being installed in the shops where cigars were hand made by Cubans and Spaniards. That was how we maintained the prestige of the industry and our unequalled superiority of craft. I never thought then that this inartistic inhuman artefact would be installed in Cuba, where we must of necessity each day exalt the dexterity and art of the Cuban cigar maker and reward his artistic endeavour, his striving to produce the best cigar in the world.[4]

Plochet described the machine as inhumane. It had not been perfected and could use only the best leaf. For Plochet, it was clear that the manufacturers would then maintain a labour force whose whole job would be to work the inferior leaf, 'eking out a daily wage and breaking its back for the benefit of the manufacturer'. The overall thrust of the *Boletín*'s position on the anti-machine campaign was summed up in a 1 December editorial which concluded it was 'the protest of a people tired of suffering the oppression of the cruellest capitalism of all, that of the US'.

At the same time, early *Boletín* issues heavily denounced existing apathy and division among cigar makers. The old bulletin had hardly been read, it was claimed. The Havana cigar makers' union was so dormant that average attendance at meetings had fallen to 60–80 when in the past over 1,000 had not been uncommon. This was an echo of earlier complaints: at the height of the anti-machine protest, a 1927 *Boletín* cartoon had depicted the strong but sluggish Havana union as a huge sleeping lion being prodded by smaller fry.

Also included in its pages were reports on abuses by manufacturers and cigar makers and certain 'bad practices' growing up among the workers themselves (including *el garoto* whereby workers would deliberately incur debts to a key man in the factory, that way buying their job security) and on the state – or non-existent state – of unions throughout the island. 'We can say', wrote the FNT reorganization committee of Matanzas province, 'that in all the towns we visited we found that fellow cigar makers wished to uphold the organization but that over and above those wishes was the shortage of work.'[5] In Las Villas province the situation was not much better. Some local unions managed to defend certain rights and keep up wages and conditions but often only by insisting that manufacturers employ only local labour. This made for strong localism, which the FNT found difficult to combat.

Strong political differences were reflected in the *Boletín*. Much emphasis was placed on worker education. 'We must show that we are educated', wrote Juan Lara, who had a regular bulletin column. There was an element of traditional distrust for politics. 'My humble opinion is,' wrote cigar maker Eusebio Sandarán in the June 1930 issue, 'that the worker should keep away from politics, whether of the bourgeoisie or of the working class.' A rousing May Day march, written in 1919, was reprinted in its splendour:

> Capital and Labour is the theme
> Of a thousand struggles and agony,
> That is the lifeblood of vile tyranny;
> – To defend our honour is our duty.
>
> That the years of living toil
> Spur us on to triumphal glory,
> The time has come for final victory;
> – To defend our honour is our duty.
>
> The host of workers already united
> Are the legions of redemption,
> Socialism is the faith of salvation;
> – To defend our honour is our duty.
>
> Socialism, fighting and conscious,
> Which makes man live as man should,
> Shakes the centuries with its justice;
> – To defend our honour is our duty.
>
> That an end is brought to cruel villainy,
> And the strong chains are broken,
> How many years of hard labour;
> – To defend our honour is our duty.
>
> That we march forever united,
> Sharing grief and pain;
> And we shall at last triumph;
> – To defend our honour is our duty.

The FNT was by this time adhering to the principles of the CNOC, publishing them in the *Boletín*. The January 1931 issue carried on the cover a figure of Marx with the call 'Workers of the world unite!' Finally, the great tobacco workers' strikes of 1931–3 – comparable only with those of the 1880s and 1900s – shook both the industry and reformist and anarchist ideas among the workers. The appeal for a strong class organization such as the CNOC and a unified, truly national union became much stronger.

There is evidence of strikes by tobacco workers throughout the island over these years but most is known about those in Havana. Once again they were centred on the Trust and other large export factories. The ones in the cigar industry rocketed the already critical state of the export industry and were, hence, the particular object of attention. The first, however, was in the cigarette, not the cigar, sector.

The world economic depression of the late twenties and early thirties hit the tobacco industry with great force. Closures, redundancy, wage cuts became the order of the day as manufacturers tried to hold out. Falling profits caused manufacturers to turn to a union war and, in that war, Trust factories were to take the lead. In December 1930, the Trust carried out a study on the wages paid in different factories in Cuba and compared them with those in the Durham branch of the American Tobacco Company in the United States. The conclusion was that higher wages were paid in Cuban factories when, paradoxically, there was greater prosperity in the US industry. The study explained the lower wages in the majority of Cuban factories in terms of the fact that few of the workers, especially outside Havana, were unionized.[6] It was during the post-war boom in the industry that the first Unión de Obreros de la Industria de Cigarrería en General had been founded and wage agreements reached. Given the competition of factories with non-unionized labour, Havana manufacturers in 1921 had unsuccessfully demanded lower wage scales. In 1926, however, Havana cigarette workers had been forced to accept a 20% reduction in wage rates in return for a minimum eight-hour day with overtime and an agreement to employ only unionized labour.

As a prominent member of the Unión de Fabricantes de Tabacos y Cigarros de la Isla de Cuba, the Trust in late 1930 was instrumental in persuading all manufacturers to form a united front against the workers, so as to enforce significant wage cuts and break the power of the unions. On 11 December 1930, the manufacturers' union wrote to the secretary for agriculture, labour and trade, explaining that special circumstances in the industry meant manufacturers were unable to afford to pay the wages they had been paying over past years. They proposed a standardized wage scale for the whole of Cuba based on those being paid currently in the non-unionized factories.

In March 1931, a dispute broke out in the Henry Clay factory over the interpretation of a collective labour agreement of 1926. In May a strike broke out in La Competidora Gaditana over an attempted 27% reduction in wages. And the cigarette workers' union began the struggle to unionize workers in factories where unions did not as yet exist.

In mid-September the Trust proposed a reduction of wages in the Siboney factory. On September 30, men refused to load or unload any cigarettes because an employee had been fired and the Trust closed the factory down. On October 14, the cigarette workers' union declared an official strike. Non-unionized blackleg labour was brought in[7] for production to continue as normal. And a huge boycott was mounted against the Trust, organized by the cigarette makers' union but almost certainly with the support of many of the other manufacturers. Coupons were reported inside packs of other brands of cigarettes, and Havana manufacturers began to claim in their advertisements: 'This is a Cuban factory.'[8] With allies such as these and the support of other sectors of workers – the CNOC made a considerable issue of the 'La Corona case' of imperialist penetration and oppression – cigarette workers of the Trust held out for almost two years. Their bargaining power was not sufficient, however, to either stop production or prevent blackleg labour during that time. It was only the more general political climate of 1933 which lent added support to the strikers and led the company eventually to cease production and come to terms with the old workers.

The terms of the agreement reached were: 1. dismissal of all personnel that had worked in the factory during the strike period; 2. re-instatement of unionized workers; 3. re-opening of the factory with an eight-hour day; 4. seniority rights; 5. union-recognized wage rates. 'Suffice it to say for the moment', Havana Trust man Hernández wrote to Cuban Tobacco's vice-president Gregg, 'that we were placed in a position in which we had absolutely no other course to pursue than to effect a settlement with the strikers. The lives of all the employees of the Company and its properties were in great danger.' In a letter the following day to Cuban Tobacco president Houston, he added: '. . . . our jubilation at the fall of the "tyrant" was a bitter one due to the dangerous situation as regards the cigarette factory. Thank God we have been able to put an end to an absolutely untenable situation, and we can now breathe in a more tranquil, if none too optimistic atmosphere.'[9]

Two days before the Trust capitulated, the manufacturers' union as a whole had reached an agreement with the cigarette workers' union. Wage rates were to be standardized and unions recognized in factories where they had not been so far. The agreement was, with few exceptions, accepted by manufacturers in the provinces. Casas, Ravelo y Cía protested that there should be some compensation for small factories. Trinidad y Hnos cautiously stated that they would agree when the rest of the factories were seen to put the plan into practice.

The situation in Havana began to calm down. On the 29th

Hernández wrote a final note to Gregg: 'Police agents that had been engaged in the custody of the factory and to protect some of us have all been dismissed', he reported. 'We are no longer carrying guns on our hips and we can now use our minds freely for the good of the business.'[10]

If the outcome of the cigarette workers' strike was eventually a favourable one for the workers, the same cannot be said for the great 1932 cigar makers' strike. To quote from *Fortune* magazine's ironic, and devastatingly disdainful account of the build-up to that strike:

The two negroes strolling down the street are workers in a cigar factory. They were, of course, sure to be that or workers in a sugar cane field. A cockfight might have detained them, as might the ball game which these have eschewed. They are paid piece by piece, not day by day or week by week, so whether or not they go to the factory they are acting according to choice, and it is pleasant. At the factory their deft fingers will smooth tobacco leaves, twirl amazingly, somehow fashion Cuban cigars. It is monotonous work and they know it and to pass the time they choose one of their members, pay him from their own money to read to them. He starts with the newspapers. Then it is magazines or a novel, often Victor Hugo. Thus they have worked and they once believed their Cuban sons would work after them. But somebody in the United States invented a machine.

Cuba is too pleasant an island for an industrial revolution. And yet, since somebody did invent a cigar-making machine and since a good half of Cuba's working population is engaged in the making of cigars by hand, a revolution of some kind was inevitable. Cuba's, bloodless, like England's, was no less bitter. There were meetings in the unions and shakings of fists and scowls in the factories in the mornings. There were no strikes, because striking would have made no sense. If the worker went on strike, he was merely helping the machine. This much anybody could apprehend, though when the first machines entered Cuba nobody knew what they would do and nobody seemed to care. Only when the first were installed and the cigars rolled out, one after the other, did the people realise.

The unions were outraged, the battle was on and inevitably went to the public, becoming 'social and epicurean', claimed *Fortune*:

It became the mark of the knowing smoker not to smoke anything other than the hand-made cigar. The epicurean boycott might have had the effect, and won the battle for the unions, were Cuba the greatest consumer of its own cigars, or even the greatest manufacturer of cigars made of Cuban tobacco. But Cuba is neither of these. And, in the U.S., the machines were fast monopolising the process of manufacture. In Cuba it became evident that the handsome cigar was destined to no brilliant industrial future, that its niche in the world was among esoteric luxuries, that the hand-manufacturer ironically must maintain the desirability of his product by the very same quality which ensures the fact that it will never make very much money, its rarity.

To a degree, therefore, the Cuban unions won their battle. The prestige of the handsome cigar is still assured. Of Cuba's many cigar factories, today only one, the Larrañaga, fifth largest, uses machines and does not use them exclusively. But, if G.W. Hill should persuade the world that even the great luxury, the Havana hand-made cigar, is better and more sanitary when made by machine – well, on that day, the picturesque Cuban will have lost finally and forever.[11]

G.W. Hill did not actually convince the world of that. Havana cigars still remained a prized and highly priced luxury on the world market. He did, however, convince the majority of smokers that machine-made cigars were as good, if not better, than the greater part of those that were hand-rolled. This in itself was to have great repercussions on the Havana industry, one of which was the Trust's transfer of all export production from Cuba to Trenton, New Jersey. A decision argued on the basis of reducing import duties, taxes and general production costs, it was also linked to the machine.

Hill never considered making top Coronas by machine. Machine production did, however, teach him the economies of employing women as opposed to men in cigar manufacturing. 'Female labour' had the advantages of costing less, being 'less troublesome', and not expecting that daily quota of free cigars – *la fuma*. American Cigar had already met with 'labour difficulties' among Cuban workers in bonded factories for the manufacture of Antonio y Cleopatra and Flor de Cuba cigars in Tampa and subsequently moved the rolling plant to Trenton, employing women to do the work for which Cuban men had previously been considered essential. And in 1932 veteran cigarman Albert Gold, 40 years in the trade, began to train New Jersey women on La Corona.

Meantime in Cuba, Hill launched his offensive on Havana workers and their union. *Fortune* succinctly recounted its version of the story:

Mr. Hill was in favour of delivering an ultimatum to the Cubans. Stuart Houston, President of Cuban Tobacco, Albert Gregg, vice-president (and president of American Cigar), tobaccomen both who had known Cuba ever since George Hill was a youngster, were a little worried at the prospect. They knew how easily the Cuban tobacco workers could tie up the entire production of fine cigars. Hill, thinking of the great surplus stock of La Coronas in the old Palace warehouse, was not worried. He resolved to go ahead and, if he met with difficulties, to move all his fine cigar manufacturing to the U.S.

Houston conferred with the Unión de Fabricantes de Tabacos y Cigarros. He found the other manufacturers who had no association with Mr Hill's Trust quite willing to co-operate in testing the power of the cigar makers' federation.

In January 1932, the Federation was told that its members would have to accept a 12% wage cut, and a strict limitation of the number of cigars allowed a worker to eight per day. The war was on. The labour union was given to understand that any victory it might win would be a Pyrrhic victory for, unless the manufacturers won, Mr Hill would move his rolling activities out of Cuba for good. The Federación Nacional answered this threat with a strike. For five months not a cigar was made in Havana. In May, at the instance of President Gerardo Machado, the manufacturers agreed to compromise on a 10% wage cut. The Federación refused to accept, and the strike went on. Tobacco workers, deprived of even their free cigars, lounged around on street corners smoking cheap cigarettes, confident that the manufacturers would have to come to terms. They did not realize the stock of La Coronas which Mr Hill's old palace contained. In New York and London silk-hatted smokers were getting their Coronas as usual – from the stock of 13,000,000 left over from 1931. On 1 June 1932, the cigar city of Havana learned that it had lost most of its cigar factories. The workers, too late, accepted the 10% cut, but all but two of the independent manufacturers moved away from Havana, fearing further trouble.[12]

The 12% wage cut originally proposed signified a return to the wage scale of 1917 and naturally met with opposition on the part of the workers. 'There is already talk', reported *El Mundo*, 'of violent attitudes and of a strike that will affect five to six thousand families, just at the time when peace of the spirits is most necessary and when the domestic economy, unfortunately already affected in all spheres, can least stand disruption of any kind.'[13] The Henry Clay factory was the first to come out on January 14. Houston wrote to Gregg the following day: 'The action of the workers is more in keeping with the untoward attitude which was normally the mode twenty-five to thirty years ago among this labour element.' On 18 January the manufacturers' union took several decisions: to pay half the month's wages and declare redundant those who came out in solidarity with Henry Clay operatives; to publish no reply to the workers, 'our position being clear and measured'; to send a cable to the London Importers' Association notifying them of the workers' attitude; and to declare a stop-work until further notice. Significantly the only company which broke ranks was Por Larrañaga and the manufacturers pressured for it to join them.

In March the Camacho plan was formulated to reduce wages by 10% and was accepted by cigar makers in Güines, Bejucal, Guanajay, Artemisa, and other localities. The national federation and some local unions like San Antonio de los Baños stood their ground, even though manufacturers proved intransigent. On 13 April Houston wrote to Gregg: 'A complete surrender of the manufacturers would not only result in our failure to accomplish the economies which we had every reason to demand from the labourers but it would make the operation of our factories almost impossible from a moral standpoint. You are sufficiently acquainted with our labour conditions here to judge for yourself what would be the frame of mind of our cigar makers if they should go back to work after obtaining such a victory.'[14]

On the 23rd, the FNT met with President Machado, who proposed that an arbitration committee be set up between strike leaders and manufacturers. That same week the chief of police, Alfonso Fors, who had been appointed as mediator in the situation, proposed a new Fors Plan of lowering the rate per thousand cigars by 1, 2 and 3 pesos according to the *vitola*. Substantially no different from the Camacho Plan, it was rejected by the workers and the Trust then announced its decision to transfer export production. Months earlier, the US magazine *Tobacco* had warned: 'Cuban cigar makers are still out – and out's the word . . . Henry Clay and Bock and some of the other manufacturers are slipping across the water to Tampa and to old Key West, having their goods made there – and at a lower cost.' In his 2 June statement to the CNPDTH, informing of the company decision to 'abandon' manufacturing in Cuba, Houston declared: 'It is evident that the cigar export industry in Cuba can only be maintained by the closest, most sincere and intelligent cooperation between manufacturers and workers. The possibility of achieving this cooperation took on crisis proportions in January last.'

While Havana's male cigar makers were left to fight their struggle, La Coronas were being made under more harmonious conditions in Trenton: 'During the rolling, weighing and inspecting, from a platform above each of the great sunny floors, come the strains of piano playing to entertain the girls at their work', wrote *Fortune*:

The calming element of music is substituted for the more dangerous one of public reading to which Havana cigar makers are accustomed and into which the Cuban readers, hired by the workers themselves, often injected comment on and criticism of labour conditions. In Trenton, the music is supplied by the Company and if the player avoids such things as Chopin's Revolutionary Etude, it is not likely to cause much unrest. And it is very picturesque.[15]

In Havana the newly formed Tabacalera Cubana announced that the company factory would work with a reduced number of workers – possibly 150 (as against the 590 prior to the strike), paying wages according to the Fors Plan; that the company might or might not open the Havana factory according to whether or not the FNT accepted these conditions.

By July, the Partagás factory had already re-opened in Bejucal; Tabacalera Cubana and others followed suit in Santiago de las Vegas. In moving to depressed outlying towns, they tapped a very considerable reserve of cheap, largely non-unionized labour all too willing to work for less than their Havana counterparts. The ground was cut from under the feet of Havana workers and their union. They were 'left entirely in the air', as Trust man Gregg put it; and by September they had been forced to give in.

The workers came to the negotiating table with varying shades of expectations. José Huerta, president of the box decorators, expressed the feeling of his union that if there were to be more work and those at present unemployed were to be re-instated, then they would consider the sacrifice of a wage cut. Cossío spoke for the leaf selectors, saying that his union was prepared to accept if the manufacturers could prove with facts and figures the need for such cuts. The stemmers and cigar makers took a firmer line. Inocencia Valdés, of the stemmers, affirmed that if this could not be proved the stemmers would be the last back. FNT President Irurzún argued that if, as the manufacturers said, the basis for the cuts was insufficient demand, then it was better to face the end of the industry than accept reductions. Houston came for the manufacturers 'with soft words and a smile on his lips' to offer a concessionary lower reduction. And, in an FNT referendum, the majority of workers – 1,173 to 570 – accepted. Henry Clay workers still held out but the FNT abided by the majority decision.

And so a devastating blow was dealt. Throughout the strike, the morale of Havana workers had been strong, but this had been of little avail when other workers were not with them and manufacturers were free to take production elsewhere. And yet, important lessons were also learned. Over the next few years, a new-found radicalism, while still essentially defensive in nature, was to put the tobacco workers as a whole, cigar makers in particular, once again in a vanguard position as regards the Cuban working class. The sleeping lion had awakened; it had yet to find its strategy of attack.

14

The big tobacco unions of 1936–48

The thirties in Cuba and Latin America as a whole were years of labour struggles: the fight for labour legislation, the fight for its enactment, and a tremendous growth in the labour movement. In Cuba, labour was to no mean extent responsible for Machado's downfall and accounted for the efforts of post-1933 governments, alongside employers, to define codes of social and labour legislation which were especially directed toward industries such as tobacco, where labour was strong. Clearly, the hopes of labour in the 1933 Revolution were dashed in the repressive aftermath. At the same time, labour was split between those who had supported the new Grau San Martín government (still representing conservative elements of the national bourgeoisie but more progressive in nature) and those in opposition. Anti-imperialist feeling was running high as the CNOC and member unions, fighting to change the old union structure which had ensured the ultimate weakness of labour in the events of 1933, denounced Grau as 'social fascist'.

At the same time, the reforms undertaken by Grau were none too pleasing to the US government which intervened by backing the military coup of the young Fulgencio Batista. Despite the brief nature of the period in which Grau was in power, it was nonetheless in this period that the lines were drawn of the political rivalry which was to dominate the labour movement through the thirties and forties – that is, between Grau's Partido Auténtico followers and the more communist wing. The years 1934–44 witnessed the predominance of communist leadership of the unions on a scale hitherto unknown. The years 1944–8 saw Grau and then Prío Socarrás in power and the destruction of those unions. In both periods, tobacco workers were very much to the fore in building and subsequently defending what they viewed as their 'legitimate' union organization.

The March 1935 general strike was actually sparked off by workers in the tobacco industry who were on strike in Havana. Early that month the government offered military protection to blacklegs loading tobacco for shipment to the United States. The indignation of the tobacco workers was shared by dock workers and later workers in the electricity and printing industries, lorry and bus drivers, chemical workers, nurses and hospital employees, bread, milk and ice distributors, and many others. Under the leadership of the CNOC, whose general secretary was at that point cigar maker Lazaro Peña, over 200,000 workers came out. The repression unleashed on them was such that the strike was soon over, union leaders were persecuted, and the union movement temporarily forced underground. Nonetheless, much of the hard, uphill work of the late twenties and early thirties was far from lost, especially in tobacco.

It will be remembered that the national executive of the Federación Nacional de Torcedores had travelled the country attempting to reorganize local union structure. It had found that in many towns four or five cigar makers were struggling to keep the local guild functioning, that many cigar makers were working only two or three days a week, more often than not for less than the established piece rate, and that many were simply unable to pay their dues. There were reports of 'those who made a cigar or two' to try 'to barter for foodstuffs'.[1] Many were the areas where only the direct mediation of the National Committee ensured local success in disputes, whether it be against attempts to reduce the piece rate or 'the incorrect attitude of foremen' or the sacking of a union delegate for attempting 'to harmonize the two parties . . . as befitted his post and in the most correct way.'[2]

Local union insistence on only local labour being employed had been heavily criticized by the FNT, and the Unión de Torcedores de Camagüey was actually expelled because of it. Such localism divided the workers, it was declared; 'one town will be pitted against another, there will be everlasting struggle among us . . . and when the manufacturers realize what is happening, down will come the piece rates . . .'[3] Havana leaflets of 1930 demanded consumption of cigars made in Havana factories only. Again the FNT battled to maintain 'principles and ideals that do not define workers according to nationality, province, town or race', declaring such a campaign to be against 'doctrines being put into practice to achieve the true emancipation of the workers . . .'[4]

The new *Boletín del Torcedor* had tried to bring together political divergencies, while at the same time allowing a wide range of political expression in its pages. The great thrust of early issues was characteristically cultural: 'We must be educated; that is the weapon we must wield, because the more knowledgable we are, the less ready will we be slaves', was the cry. Editor Pablo Palenzuela wrote: '. . . the cultured nature of our readers demands that the sciences, the arts and literature be expressed in our paper . . . [as] the endeavour of a class conscious of rendering tribute to culture and progress.'[5]

The new *Boletín* brought information on union activities, plus short stories, poetry, articles on theory, philosophy, and the history of the tobacco industry and its workers. Guillermo Gener, of the executive committee of the Santiago de las Vegas Sociedad de Torcedores, captured the new feeling when he wrote in the opening issue:

The *Boletín de Torcedor* will be so much more than it has been so far; it will be like flashes of light to illuminate the night and dissipate the obscure mind; it will be like the voice of thunder, to carry to the most remote parts our cry of emancipation and cultural betterment . . .[6]

Guillermo Gener wrote plays which were a great success in the social centre of the unions. When one of his plays, *Dolor* – 'a day in the life of a cigar maker in particular, of workers in general', as one critic put it – was performed in Santiago de Las Vegas, it received an ovation from the workers and a glowing review in the *Boletín*:

. . . it unfurls as naturally as real-life events. It is a work that exalts and brings out the merits and noble sentiments of the suffering working class that so effectively contributed to the independence of Cuba and today, despite its precarious situation, works quietly for cultural betterment and to uphold our prestige. A work of which the Federación Nacional de Torcedores must be proud . . .[7]

That noble sentiment of day-to-day sacrifice and suffering was clearly finding new outlets of political militancy and the FNT adhered to the CNOC and embarked on its major 1932 strike. This renewed militancy was in turn finding renewed rivalry from a more defensive Alianza Tabacalera, formed in 1930 by the Unión de Dependientes, Sociedad de Escogedores, Sociedad de Fileteadores, and Unión de Rezagadores and joined in 1932 by the Sociedad de Anilladoras y Envolvedoras de la Habana. A 1933 Alianza manifesto vented singular grievances. 'We have to put an end to cheap one-cent cigars . . . We have to avert the danger that the manufacture of poor quality products at rock-bottom prices represents for the industry and those of us who depend on it.' The same manifesto attacked a boycott declared on Partagás and H. Upmann factories in Bejucal for working with blackleg labour:

That boycott, whose sole purpose is the destruction of our guilds and the annihilation of the tobacco industry, must be rejected and fought by the organizations of the Alianza because, in addition to being an arbitrary and illegal measure, it sets the terrible precedent of subjecting the legitimate interests of a majority to the dastardly machinations of unscrupulous elements . . . We do not want a deplorable repeat of what happened in our industry not long ago when a certain firm that accounted for 30% of Cuban production withdrew, leaving hundreds of households in poverty and hunger . . .[8]

This viewpoint was echoed in a 1933 'Tribuna Obrera' column of *Tabaco*, recalling how after the 1932 strike the workers

went back to work like an army in disarray . . . Everybody was out for himself . . . The sole concern was to find work. Since there wasn't enough to go round, many were left on the streets in hopes of better times to come. Nobody protested . . . offering to do work under much more onerous conditions than before . . .[9]

The group that had led workers into the 1932 strike and therefore to the withdrawal of Henry Clay, it was claimed, were now leading to a situation in which other factories might well follow suit. And yet it was the Alianza that was to fall into disarray and dissolution that same year, and other organizations that were to be consolidated.

Little by little, the call to more militant union organization was to make its mark in the provinces and for the first time not only cigar makers but seasonal tobacco workers, sorters, and stemmers began to band together in any systematic way to demand certain basic conditions. Old trade unionists of this period, many of them still working today, talk of how communist leaders would come out from Havana and the larger towns to explain the real causes for their suffering and discuss ways in which they could begin to fight back. Recounting a 1929 strike in the Placetas Pascual factory, José Alejandro Reyes spoke of how early actions had taken place 'under a guild system which acted as a brake on worker demands, sometimes because of a sell-out leadership, others because of police or Rural Guard intervention. So the old rotten union structure had to be broken and the conditions created for a body able to defend the aspirations of the working class.'[10]

Pedro Arboláez, who formed the Carlos Baliño circle in Santa Clara in 1933, explained: 'In those days the worker leadership was in reformist hands – they were practically bosses' agents, always ready to accept lower piece rates for workers to be exploited more.'[11] Manuel Cáceres remembers how in the Cabaiguán sorters' guild those with revolutionary ideas 'had to struggle against the aggression of the bosses and the attitude of leaders serving the latter's interests'.

Stemmers had the edge over sorters in that there was a national federation of stemmers under the militant leadership of Inocencia Valdés. Between militant stemmers and cigar makers a close identity of struggle was to grow up. In Havana, the cigar makers' building was open to the stemmers for their meetings, and the *Boletín del Torcedor* began to direct considerable attention to the need for organizing this highly exploited sector. The late twenties were, of course, the years of women's organizations and the stemmers – the largest and, despite all shortcomings, one of the most militant sectors of women workers – were the object of considerable propaganda both from the more bourgeois women's movement for the sexual and social emancipation of women and from their fellow workers.

Thus it was that strong radical movements were building up in the tobacco sector. There are few records of the newly formed Sindicato Nacional de Obreros de la Industria Tabacalera, affiliated to the CNOC after 1933. A couple of early manifestos, however, testify to its radical nature and strong opposition to the newly formed government:

From the stemmers of Cumanayagua:
　　To all men and women workers of Cumanayagua, Manicaragua, Cienfuegos, etc.
　　From the second [of this month] we, the stemmers of Cumanayagua, have maintained a militant strike movement for tobacco to be weighed before being worked and that we be paid 5c. per pound of tobacco worked. Despite the justice of our demands, the imperialist monster Kaffemburgh aims to continue to submit us to the most terrible exploitation, paying miserable rates, as in last year's harvest, when we were organized into guilds led by reformists who accepted low rates from the bosses. Today, organized in an industrial union on a national scale, like the rest of the Cuban proletariat, we take up the flag of combat for the immediate and lasting improvement of the conditions under which we labour, in order to sweep away the rule of hunger and misery and unemployment. Our strike has the support of all sectors of workers in the area . . . [and yet we were] attacked by the so-called democratic government which professes to be giving ample democratic freedoms to the workers [but is] hindering their development and openly supporting exploitation by imperialist companies . . .[12]

From the Cienfuegos tobacco workers' regional committee:
　　. . . against the military dictatorship and for the immediate withdrawal of troops from places of work, the withdrawal of Yankee boats from Cuban waters, the upholding of all gains won; for a government of workers and

peasants supported by committees of soldiers and marines, which will guarantee the eight-hour day, a minimum daily wage of one peso, unemployment benefits, and all the economic and political demands of the proletariat . . .

Long live the general strike of the tobacco workers!
Long live the general political strike!
Long live the Confederación Nacional Obrera de Cuba![13]

Clearly militant organizations of this nature aroused great opposition and were almost all stamped out in the repression of 1934–5. However, the strength shown by labour in the thirties meant that sooner or later, if only to stabilize their position, post-1933 governments would have to work within some sort of class collaboration. In effect, conditions were ripe for strong union organization although new moves had equally to be couched within such a framework. This helps explain the highly effective if moderate call put out by former CNOC general secretary Lazaro Peña for 'the enforcement of social legislation' and a new Confederación de Trabajadores de Cuba in 1939.

Significantly, the prelude to the new CTC was the Federación Tabacalera Nacional, the first of the new industrial unions, and the first Congreso Nacional de Tabaqueros in 1938, at which such leading government figures as the secretary for agriculture and the secretary and assistant secretary for labour were present.

From the outset, the congress stressed the continuing worker tradition of the tobacco sector:

. . . with legitimate pride but without vanity, its leaders are guided by the principle of showing the Cuban proletariat, that is, our brothers in struggle and suffering, the actions of tobacco workers – those who yesterday struggled for a free and sovereign homeland and today uphold democratic institutions, who are ready at all times to give their solidarity to any fellow worker in misfortune, or any worker collective fighting for moral or material betterment, always heeding all that affects the prestige and furthering of the tobacco industry and, last but not least, the happiness and well-being of the people of whom they constitute an important part.

'The moment in history has arrived for the great family of workers to occupy a worthy place . . . as a principal factor in the course of national affairs', declared Alivio Riveira Vidal, secretary for reorganization and propaganda. This was further spelt out by Lázaro Peña, then general secretary of the FTN:

We are ready from this forum to defend our industrial activity, the defence of which is not only the concern of industrialists but also of the working class which desires economic redemption, in accordance with the most elementary sacred rights of workers, which gives them direct participation and responsibility in the destiny of all people who are proud to be progressive, liberal, and democratic.

It was indicative of the times that he was to add:

It has been said that we are trying or that we would like to unite the forces of the workers so as to put them at the service of subversive action against the present regime. Nothing could be further from the truth; we are not working to set up a Soviet Cuba, we are working solely for the restructuring of all our national institutions and to offer our firm, cordial and brotherly aid to the peasant who demands land, asking for low rents for the industrialist who wishes to further his activities in an upright way and along patriotic lines and who always comes up against the obstacle that our national economy is being gradually absorbed by the imperialist monopolies to which we are subject and from which it is essential that we free ourselves.[14]

As a leading communist, Lazaro Peña was expressing popular front policy, and there can be little doubt that in Cuba this was highly successful in union terms. From an initial FTN membership of 15 unions in 1936, there were by 1938 no less than 72 main affiliate organizations, claiming a total membership of 80,000, some 30,000 in Santa Clara province alone.

This growing tobacco movement had its wider national parallel. In 1939 the Primer Congreso Nacional de Trabajadores was held in Havana, the Confederación de Trabajadores de Cuba set up and Lazaro Peña elected its first general secretary. Among major congress resolutions were a negotiated government agreement on minimum wages, the removal of prohibitions on union organization, strong government action against the transfer of factories, a pension scheme, defence of national industry and peasant farmers, more social services and amenities for working people, and an end to sexual and racial discrimination. These demands were reaffirmed at subsequent congresses held in 1940 and 1942. Over these years, major sectors of workers gained substantial monetary wage increases and CTC activities extended in scope to a programme to combat poverty and inflationary prices that were undercutting real wage increases, advocating a price freeze at the March 1942 level.

Over these years, tobacco, sugar, railway, maritime, and metallurgy workers, bank clerks, civil service workers, and the like were all organized. National unions were formed in 30 industries in all, and major local labour organizations in the six provinces and most important cities. A total of 567 unions sent delegates to the first congress, 592 to the second, the latter representing 218,000 members. To the third congress came representatives of 973 organizations representing a total of 407,000 members. Collective labour contracts became widespread. And it was in no small part due to the very active labour movement that the 1940 Constitution of the Republic was the most advanced in the hemisphere and that that year saw two prominent communist ministers without portfolio, namely Juan Marinello and Carlos Rafael Rodríguez.

The strength this kind of movement gave to the workers can be seen in the gains made in the tobacco industry over this period. Collective labour contracts and considerable piece-rate increases were achieved for all sectors and a pension scheme and other welfare measures introduced. Growers, agricultural labourers, sorters, stemmers, and cigarette makers throughout the island were brought into the union movement on a big scale. In 1942 unionization was made compulsory for manufacturers, growers and workers. Nonetheless, the considerable variations in figures are still sufficient to indicate certain trends. CTC figures for 1944 – a year of high unemployment, especially in Havana – give a figure of approximately 66,000, over 35,000 in Santa Clara (in comparison with the 1938 figures of 80,000 and 30,000 respectively). Excluding field labour, there was 80% unionization in the industry as a whole: 100% of cigar makers throughout the island, 58% of cigarette workers, 94% of stemmers and 66% of sorters (33% in Pinar del Río and Havana but over 90% in Santa Clara).

The FTN had from the start directed activities to lesser unionized sectors. In June 1939 the first national conference of stemmers was held, with the presence of Lazaro Peña and the executive FTN committee. Great emphasis was laid on the importance of demands for rigorous inspection and study of piece rates in stemming and sorting and standardized wages in cigarette manufacturing, in a national commission for minimum wages.

This was backed by long years of struggle at the base. Reinaldo Fundora, active in the movement at the time, recounts:

From 1938 on, each sorting season had before it a strong strike movement, [the declaration of] 'dead towns' in which the whole population took part, and on many occasions we even had the support of councillors who were supposed to represent the people in the municipalities.[15]

Cigarette workers in the provinces had been fighting throughout the thirties to establish minimum wages and the right to unionize. The Trinidad factory at Ranchuelo, it may be remembered, was one that had been consolidated on the strength of hold-ups in Havana production during the 1920s and 1930s depression and cheap local labour. It was not until August 1933 that a cigarette workers' union – affiliated to the CNOC – was set up in the factory. In less than two years (with the failure of the March 1935 strike) this was destroyed and all strikers, almost half the total number of active workers had been laid off. Nonetheless, during that short period, the eight-hour day, the first collective labour contract, and a strong nucleus of labour militants had been established. Thus it was that a highly successful boycott and 'sabotage including [putting] non-smokable materials in cigarettes and setting fire to distribution vans' was organized against the factory until all the workers were reinstated in 1940. That year, communists Wilfredo de Armas and Faustino Calcines were elected to the executive committee of the union and the workers secured a 20% wage increase, a union building and a life insurance scheme. By 1946 successive wage claims had raised wages fivefold.

The Ranchuelo union obviously derived added strength from wider union backing but its success was largely due to strong local bargaining power and militant leadership. Other workers did not always have that local strength and the fluctuating and irregular nature of their work militated against them. National and provincial unions tried to lend as much support as possible to local unions, but this was all too often, in the last analysis, dependent on the limited local holding power of workers themselves. And so, for the great majority – whether cigar or cigarette makers, stemmers or sorters – resolutions and legislation passed at the national level remained little more than a yardstick for ideal conditions which unions could fight to attain. The time and energy national unions spent pressuring for the implementation of such legislation is but further testimony of the weakness of union organization at the base. Paradoxically, the fact that legislation could only really be enforced in the large factories and shops and certain key localities not only created a certain added disparity but also in turn gave greater strength to the bargaining power of the shop floor in the factory sector.

Even the great *industrial* tobacco union, then, tended to be more dependent than statistics might suggest on the increasingly reduced numbers of factory workers in Havana, along with those of certain other major tobacco centres. This did not make them any the less militant, but did make for a certain defensive radicalism. Rank-and-file support for a restructuring of the industry so as to guarantee wages and conditions sprang from not a little hostility and fear among factory workers that work would be taken from them by that increasingly large outwork sector. In the provinces, where workers quite literally had nothing to lose, movements were markedly less defensive, whole towns becoming involved in violent clashes over what were strictly labour issues. Whether more or less defensive, however, there can be no doubting that by the mid-forties the tobacco workers, banded together under the watchword 'In the union lies our strength', had built up a movement that was a force to be reckoned with on the national scene.

15

The machine and the anti-union war

The 1947–8 'purging' of the communist trade union leadership, and in the process the division and very destruction of many unions, was part of Cold War policy emanating from the United States. In national terms, it corresponded to a shift in the position of the national bourgeoisie away from class collaboration with what were increasingly powerful labour unions, as Partido Auténtico leader Grau and subsequently Prío Socarrás came to power. In the case of the tobacco industry in particular it served a double purpose. It meant that large Havana manufacturers would undermine some substantial worker gains and FTN opposition to renewed attempts to introduce the cigar machine.

It will be remembered that in the late twenties only one large manufacturer, Por Larrañaga, had attempted to install the cigar machine. It met with opposition from all the other manufacturers, workers, and general public opinion, and an eventual government prohibition on mechanized production. By the late forties, there were some six to eight Havana manufacturers ready to install the machine, advocating the need for government approval to do so in order for Cuba to compete again on the world market, thereby regaining overseas markets which had been shown to be there during World War II. Cigar workers were themselves concerned over ways of maintaining the abnormal conditions of wartime prosperity in times of peace. As the cut-back in demand was already felt in 1945 (with over one-fifth of Havana cigar makers out of work), workers were pressing for government action in finding a solution to the new crisis affecting the industry.

In September 1945 some 8,000 workers responded to an FTN demonstration in Havana over precisely this question. Within a month, a special commission had been set up comprising representatives of the CNPDTH, the growers' association, the manufacturers' association, and the FTN to study the situation of the industry in general and the introduction of the cigar machine in particular. From the beginning, it was clear that there was much hostility to the machine. The initial reaction of many Havana factory worker committees was one of outright rejection, as in the late twenties. The FTN, however, stressed that the question was not so much the machine in itself as the conditions under which it was to be introduced and the workers' share in the benefits of economic progress. Those representing the FTN on the new commission were Lucas Pino and Evelio Lugo de la Cruz, communist general secretary of the Havana cigar makers' union since 1940. They went with very strong ideas as to the conditions under which the tobacco workers' federation would accept.

Two questionnaires were formulated. The first was aimed at generally determining the manufacturers' position as to why and how the machine was to be introduced. The second was more in the form of the necessary conditions the workers laid down for mechanization. Five basic points were: (1) redundancy payments; (2) a general census of workers in the factories from December 1944, when production was at its height, to the end of 1945; (3) seniority rights; (4) preference for redundant workers entering machine departments; (5) machine-made cigars for the export market only. Manufacturers left their position vague on points 3 and 4 but insisted that they could not foot redundancy payments, that it was illogical to take a census of 1944 and not of the moment when the machines were introduced, and that any limitations on machine production would be 'uneconomic'. The FTN stuck to its demands that redundancy payments were imperative; that the domestic market had to be left alone for the well-being of 'the thousands who depend on [it] and who would be right away condemned to misery . . .'[1] An FTN manifesto drawn up by Evelio Lugo ran:

We know that the cause of the negative aspects of progress is the system which gives the monopoly of those mechanical artefacts to a limited number of persons who use them to accumulate wealth, without taking into consideration the needs of the rest. That is why we said before and we say again today that progress interests us as much as the employers but we also have the right to benefit from it and therefore the formula has to be found that allows us all to contribute to the growth of the cigar industry with neither heroic attitudes nor vain sacrifice.[2]

It was in this context that a government offensive on the labour movement was particularly attractive to Havana manufacturers in their attempt to undermine the FTN (and CTC-supported) position on machines. From 1945 on, there had been evident signs of attempts to oust communist leaders from the unions. CTC general secretary Lazaro Peña had countered with threats of a general strike if Grau so much as tried to touch the labour movement. Meanwhile, in September 1945 and again in January 1946, Auténtico supporters Juan Arévalo and Francisco Aguirre, both on the CTC executive council, travelled to the United States to confer with Association of Free Labour (AFL) leaders. Auténtico factions were formed within the CTC, such as the Comisión Obrera Nacional (CON) and the later Comisión Obrera Nacional Independiente (CONI), under electrical workers' leader Ángel Cofiño. Government funds were found for both under clause K of the national budget. In April 1947, CON and CONI used their funds to attempt to gain a majority at the fifth CTC Congress. Gunmen were infiltrated, operating labour protection rackets which built up into an intra-union war waged by assassins. Lazaro Peña was threatened with his life if he insisted on re-election as general secretary of the CTC. The Auténticos' failure to get a majority in the labour movement was such that their only recourse was for the congress to be officially suspended on the charge of public disorder. When it finally did take place in May, Lazaro Peña was again re-elected, congress agreements were accorded no official recognition, and manoeuvring at a new congress in July resulted in Ángel Cofiño's being elected general secretary of what become nicknamed the CTK (after the famous clause K funds).[3]

As support continued for the old CTC and Lazaro Peña, there was an October attack by gunmen on the old CTC building. Indignation was so great among the workers that a four-hour stop-work was held, after which hundreds of workers were detained on returning to the factories. In December, Aguirre was designated to take over from the minister of labour, Prío Socarrás, who later successfully ran for the presidency. The old CTC and its leaders put up a good fight but, during 1948, Jesús Menéndez of the sugar workers' union, Aracelio Iglesias of the dock workers' union, and Miguel Fernández Roig of the Havana cigar makers' union were all assassinated and others eventually forced out or underground.

The seeds of division had been sown, although the new 'official' labour movement was often never much more than a paper union.[4] A good number of the new leaders were at worst corrupt, at best divorced from the masses, especially among older sectors like the tobacco workers who had fought hard and long to establish not only their own but also general unions. Because of this, and because of the machine, struggles in the tobacco sector were to be particularly violent.

While publicly attempting to veil their political sympathies, manufacturers were privately closing ranks to counteract the power wielded by labour unions. Thus a TCSA announcement of mid-1947 to workers, employees, and the general public ran: '. . . the Company is a private entity with no connections to any political party and with no interest in backing one candidate or another, each being free to defend the candidate of his preference . . .'[5] A June 1947 manufacturers' association circular read:

Every day one of our members complains of exorbitant labour unions, of the influence they have in official circles and of the disdain with which manufacturers are treated. Occasionally the voice of the more serious, alarmed by the prevailing anarchy of production and the reversal of economic values and categories, can be heard dramatically appealing for common sense in the place of unchecked demagogy.

The danger has been comprehended, the way of averting it should be obvious to all. None can fail to see that at this time the solution lies in establishing social equilibrium by means of coordinated manufacturers' action to countervail the growing power of the unions. No amount of lamenting or complaining will ever produce this equilibrium. Only force can neutralize force, and this holds for Cuba as much as the rest of the universe.[6]

Closing ranks and using force inevitably entailed political and governmental action.

Early evidence of government–manufacturer collaboration – and not in the healthiest of ways – came in the cigarette industry. On 26 September the Criminal Section of the Supreme Court passed sentence on minister of labour Francisco Aguirre and other labour department officials, together with Martín Dosal, owner of the La Competidora Gaditana cigarette factory, 'as guilty of the crimes of betrayal of trust, bribery, coercion, committing grievous afflictions against the carrying out of work, against the rights of union and others in an attempt to destroy worker organizations and impose government leaders in the same. . . .'[7] Ministry officials had received 100,000 pesos from Dosal to destroy cigarette unions.

Two lengthy 1948 memos from TCSA lawyer Felipe Silva to Trust directors gave the background to a build-up of government–manufacturer action in the industry.[8] An initial memo in January explained how the Auténtico government had 'started a campaign to substitute the old leaders in the local labour organizations . . .'

Both opposing groups ask the employer in each case to transact labour matters with it, advising at the same time that dealing with each other would be an act of aggression to it.

The matter is further complicated by the fact that the Labour Department is the one that rules which leaders are legally elected but all such resolutions are subject to administrative and judicial appeals. Therefore, the losing party (Communist) always claims that the matter is not settled yet, that the Government is merely trying to introduce members of its political party in the labour organizations and that it is a temporary situation because they really continue to have the support of the majority of labourers.

The new leaders claim that the Labour Department has recognised them (often elected in very dubious procedures) as the legal representatives of the workers and that the employer must not deal with the old leaders any longer.

Felipe Silva ventured the opinion:

It is unknown as yet what the final attitude of the non-political labourers will be, but it is evident that many continue to support the old leaders, taking the action of the Government as a direct attack on labour. It is important to point out that these controversies are going on continuously with short interruptions, even if there are no great issues to solve between employers and employees. It is something that comes up in connection with any minor matter that has to be discussed between the management and the labourers of the factory.

The March memorandum was specifically over how things had come to a head in the company's cigarette factory 'between the old communist leadership with majority support and the new Auténtico leadership with official recognition'. Important production had been lost when delegates of both groups insisted on being the customary ones to do the roll-call for overtime. The matter was taken to the manufacturers' union – 'where it was found that other manufacturers had similar problems but that in no other factories were they as difficult as in ours' – and by the manufacturers' union to the minister of labour. The minister's response was that the change in the leadership of the labour unions had to be carried on and that the manufacturers could not take an unbiased stand in the situation because it represented a fight against communism. His idea of the industry taking on new personnel, 'men with new ideas', was rejected as unfeasible; but his offer to appoint a labour department official in each factory 'as an immediate step to relieve manufacturers from the great responsibility they were facing . . . to intervene in the existing conflicts' went down well.

In the next week labour department officials went into the factories and proceeded to notify employers of the names of the new labour delegates with whom they must deal. This went ahead not without opposition and some ugly incidents in the factories.

The FTN, the Comité Conjunto de Obreros de la Industria de Cigarrería en General, Unión de Vendedores de La Habana, Unión de Obreros de la Industria de Cigarrería en General, and Unión de Dependientes del Ramo del Tabaco jointly considered this the most serious act of aggression against the workers since the repression of the 1935 general strike. A joint press release published in the Communist Party paper *Hoy* ran:

This naming of 'union dictators' for the factories only has its precedent in Hitler's Labour Code, in Mussolini's Italy and in Franco's Spain . . . the minister of labour has become the head of all industry in Cuba, ignoring our rights as workers to organize freely and our freedom to belong to a union or not, as is laid down clearly in Decree 2605.

We announce that we will have no dealings with union dictators of the ministry of labour, that we will behave with dignity and decency in the face of such attempts. We draw the attention of the manufacturers to such extreme actions, since the intervention of outsiders can only be a source of constant unrest and will be of the gravest consequence to all.[9]

Within a matter of days, La Corona workers were out demonstrating against police terror in the factory designed to force workers into supporting the CTK and the old CTC declared a boycott against La Corona products.

In March 1948 Felipe Silva was reporting: 'The cigar factory is quiet for the time being but we are afraid that trouble may arise any day because the cigar makers are still supporting their old leaders. The new group is small and has not been very active as yet.' By the previous October Auténtico leaders Manuel Campanería and Julio Suárez had emerged for the Havana cigar makers and the FTN, respectively, and yet worker delegates of 73% of the island's cigar makers had attended an extraordinary congress ratifying FTN general secretary González Collado and Evelio Lugo. When in early 1948 the government had attempted to introduce a decree on mechanization without consulting the old unions, a National Cigar Makers' Conference declared 10 February a Day of Struggle. On 18 February, a great convention of thousands of workers from Las Villas, Matanzas, Pinar del Río, and Havana provinces was held in Havana's Central Park.

On 1 April, an attack was made on the cigar makers' building but was frustrated by cigar makers and stemmers present. The following day saw the attack on the La Corona factory in which Miguel Fernández Roig, organization secretary of the Havana cigar makers' union and secretary of La Corona union, was assassinated by Campanería and his men. Police immediately occupied the factory and the assassins escaped. La Corona, 'traditional enemy of Cuba and of Cuban workers who have been struggling against it since the famous "currency strike" of 1907,' had been transformed into 'a concentration camp', its workers were to claim.[10]

Meantime, the TCSA El Siboney stemmery was fighting closure. Isaac Martínez Muniains (dubbed 'Von Muniains') was heavily attacked for large-scale sackings and police methods in the factory. The FTN and CTC organized a whole support campaign for La Corona workers, with telegrams coming in from all sectors of workers throughout the island. On 19 April work was stopped in the stemmery on the grounds of disorder. On the 20th, many workers refused to return. The CTC supported the stemmers financially on their strike, while Muniains was reported as claiming 'the need for a bloody purge' and 'for those black women to be seen to'. What was needed 'was a death as in La Corona cigar factory'.[11]

In September, further clashes were sparked off by the refusal of manufacturers to meet wage increases put forward by cigar makers and ancillary workers in both the cigar and cigarette industries, demanding a 40% wage increase. The arguments put forward by the Havana cigar makers', union were:

This union considers that the present high cost of living and the insufficient wages now being earned by cigar makers makes it quite impossible to defray the economic demands that such a high cost of living requires.

This union considers that the presidential decrees in effect, . . . which were issued to regulate the cigar industry, have been ignored or boldly violated by all parties connected with the industry that are under obligation to comply with them and to see that they are complied with, in the best interests of the Cuban tobacco industry and of the general well-being of the nation. The ignoring or violating has reached breaking point from the viewpoint of those honestly interested in the development and functioning of the second of the nation's industries.[12]

The manufacturers' refusal to comply led to the occupation of several factories and the arrest of 600 workers. In November new elections were held for the Havana cigar makers' union and some 90% of the vote went to Evelio Lugo. When the cigar makers' building was taken by CTK leaders five days later, cigar makers and stemmers came out on strike until it should be returned. This time over 900 workers were reported in jail. On their release it was decided workers should go back and fight in the factories.

By late 1949, the decree on mechanization was imminent and a great campaign was organized throughout the country to pressure the government to accept worker demands. Only continued repression proved divisive enough to enforce any tacit acceptance of the new unions in the factories and of the final 1950 mechanization decree, which paid no more than lip-service to the workers' demands. The machine was to be introduced for the export market and 20% of the home one, a proportional quota for the latter being assigned to each of the export factories with machines installed. A subsidy of $40 per month was introduced for workers directly affected by the machine and those laid off from the factories since December 1946. The subsidy was to be temporary and gradually diminishing until its suspension.

The decree, naturally enough, was strongly denounced by both workers and small manufacturers. Two coherent critiques came from Evelio Lugo and Jacinto Torras in the Communist Party journal *Fundamentos*. The latter in particular reiterated:

. . . it would not be right for it to be a struggle against the machine but against the form in which it is to be employed against the interests of the workers and the country as a whole. The machine should be a tool for freeing the workers from the toil of labour; an element that multiplies production capacity and which, correctly applied, should increase the products of work available for consumption, for the satisfaction of human needs. This can only happen integrally in a socialist system of production where there is no contradiction between the social nature of production and the collective appropriation of the means of production and product of work.[13]

In the provinces, Las Villas in particular, the fight was on against Decree 1073 and the 20% home production clause. 'You have to remember that the economic situation in our country at the time was such that national cigar sales were really down. Cigar makers would work for 15 days, be out for a week, go back . . . Annual wages were scarcely sufficient to keep a family. Only in the export factories would there be any regular work. If, on top of that, machines were introduced it could only have brought more hunger and more misery', was Manuel Duke Linero's comment as former general secretary of the Las Villas tobacco workers' federation at that time.[14] 'If the government desires the well-being of the country why does it not mechanize the export cigar industry at its own cost and risk?'

demanded the joint manufacturers' committee of Matanzas in 1950.
'Why not nationalize the industry for profits to be channelled to the
benefit of the public and not four or five men?'[15] As whole provincial
tobacco towns saw the possibility of their principal means of
subsistence being taken away from them, small manufacturers, cigar
makers, stemmers and their families were united in a movement which
acquired a quasi-insurrectional nature.

The antecedents to this were largely unsuccessful attempts to
replace local union leaders which had led to repeated assaults on
existing union buildings. Vicente Avelado, of the Placetas cigar
makers, for example, recalls a meeting held at which the labour
department official Rómulo del Rey showed up with an ultimatum

in which they were ordered to surrender the union executive, since they were
considered by the government to be subversives, communists and agitators,
and being threatened moreover with repressive action on the part of BRAC
[Buró para la Represión de las Actividades Comunistas].

When the leaders addressed the mass of workers present, these again
ratified their true leaders, who were then arrested. This was registered in the
minutes of the meeting. They were soon released, due to pressure from the
masses and the people. Five days later, Rey and his henchmen turned up again
with a new, sold-out executive, specially picked to take over the union. This
was again rejected as before.

That night, at around three in the morning, the Rural Guard broke down
the door of the union building and went inside. The workers mobilized
against this . . . more than 200 met outside the union determined to continue
paying their dues to their legitimate union organization.[16]

By June 1951 resistance to new unions and Decree 1073 was such
that old unions had succeeded in establishing joint committees with
tradesmen and small shopkeepers and manufacturers. On 2 July, town
after town in Las Villas – Guayos, Sancti Spíritus, Zaza del Medio,
Camajuaní, Cienfuegos, Manicaragua, Caibarién, Cabaiguán, Santa
Clara – were declared 'dead towns' as life ground to a halt. In Santa
Clara bottles, nails, tins, and the like stopped traffic on the central
highway and other main roads. Shops, roads, and railways were closed
and the town hall occupied in Cabaiguán, where over 3,000 congre-
gated in the park. Many were hurt and a young boy of seventeen shot
in clashes with troops.

Thus it was that in July 1951 the government was forced to suspend
the quota of machine-made cigars for the home market. With the
repeal of the clause, the industry quietened down considerably,
though was not without its sporadic clashes. Machinists formed their

own Sindicato de Obreros de Maquinas Elaboradoras de Tabacos y sus Conexos de La Habana, which broke away from the Havana cigar makers' union, complaining:

. . . the cigar makers of Havana, those who work in factories that are union-organized and demagogically oriented (completely disoriented we would argue), do not on the whole realize the gravity of the situation which cannot fail to end up with them all working in the non-organized sweatshop sector . . .

We bear no grudge against the cigar makers but rather the fraternal esteem that comes of our condition as workers. We are breaking away from the union because we were an isolated group in that union, which saw us an enemy trying to eliminate the other workers. What is certain is that the interests of the cigar makers and ours conflict. But it is no less certain that we are not trying to eliminate anybody because the introduction of the machines cannot be attributed to those of us who work them. They are part of progress, which nobody, to the present day, has been able to stop in any civilized land . . .[17]

There were also new seeds of division being sown with the relative prosperity of certain cigar and cigarette factories (sometimes with substantial wage increases) during the trade up-swing of the fifties, and some former militancy was lost. The case of the Trinidad factory, though exceptional, is also illustrative. The leadership of the old cigarette workers' union in the factory was ousted with considerable difficulty, but over the years the Trinidad policy of harmonious relations, combined with high wages and general prosperity, meant that the 1952 *Libro de Cuba* had cause to comment that the factory was 'a model in the labour world. Social conflict is unknown there.' It continued:

Some reference will be of help in understanding just how normal is this abnormal case.

In the firm Trinidad y Hermanos the week's work is forty hours with forty-eight hours' pay, the only case in Cuba in the cigarette industry. Workers are paid during any illness that might befall them, over days, weeks, months. There have even been cases of workers receiving their full salary over years . . . And because this is known and experienced; because they and the firm Trinidad y Hermanos live in harmony and mutual understanding . . . Trinidad y Hermanos, in addition to being the most important cigarette factory in Cuba, is an example that should become the norm in establishing a lasting and beneficial way of good work and discipline. Both aware of what is needed for social equilibrium and for a better world, they live united, pooling their efforts, directed toward the same end.[18]

The power of this sort of philosophy was that behind the new unions, consolidated in the fifties with former labour department official Eusebio Mujal taking over from Cofiño as 'CTC' general secretary. The two main tobacco workers' journals, *El Tabacalero* and *El Cigarrero*, especially the latter, came to read like glossy publicity magazines, testifying to harmony and well-being in the industry. This was belied, however, by the constant denunciations from their very pages of 'the communists and their allies, the demagogues and fanatics' and by the fact that one of the main tasks of new labour leaders was to report 'communists' to the labour ministry and the Bureau for the Repression of Communist Activities (BRAC).[19]

In this respect, there was much continuity between the period before and after Fulgencio Batista took power in 1952 by means of a military coup. And yet, while it is difficult to speak of a legitimate labour movement as such in tobacco in the fifties, strong opposition to the payment of compulsory union dues to official unions continued in both Havana and the provinces. As late as September 1958, hundreds of workers in the H. Upmann and Partagás factories were reported to have been laid off and/or arrested for refusing to pay their dues.[20] Even that aura of harmonious relations at the Trinidad factory was broken with militant demands for a 20% wage increase. These were signs indeed that what was happening at the base was not all it would seem from official union positions and pronouncements.

Epilogue: a new twist

In April 1953, Lazaro Peña wrote, 'Mujal and his CTK officials . . . in their role as imperialist and bourgeois agents in the ranks of the working class, maintain division, make a mockery of trade union democracy and the wider wage struggle, acting at the service of manufacturers and government in implementing a reactionary, anti-worker policy.'

One of the effects of that anti-worker policy and repression of any radical trade union challenge to it was to channel worker militancy out of the factories and the labour movement as such into the wider revolutionary movement, including guerrilla struggle. Directed against the Batista dictatorship, it was a struggle for deep-rooted socio-economic and political change, which involved breaking away from dependence on the US. The Revolution of 1 January 1959 was in a very real sense a successful culmination to struggles dating back to the last century. It was also only the beginning of a process that was not without its difficulties and upheavals. The tobacco sector was no exception on either count.

The full story of Cuban tobacco in the twenty-five years since then merits a study unto itself, but this history would be incomplete without reference at least to some of its more salient characteristics.

Agrarian reform and the nationalization of industry were two key elements of the revolutionary programme. Neither was an easy measure, and they were born in the heat of national and class struggle. Both the US and Cuban large landowning and industrial bourgeoisie quickly proved hostile to what was at that point a populist revolution. Their action ranged from spreading rumours and pessimism to withdrawing capital and allowing property and production to run down prior to leaving the country. To this there is peasant and worker testimony demanding revolutionary government action on their behalf.

The First Agrarian Reform Law was in May 1959. Generally

speaking, large plantation administration land farmed by wage labour continued to be run that way but under state ownership, while plantation land that had been parcelled out under the various farming systems was turned over to the tenant and subtenant farmers and sharecroppers, allowing former owners to keep up to approximately 400 hectares. Given the complexities of land tenure and farming practices, the reform was not easy to carry out and all too often meant that former owners kept the best lands, on which agricultural machinery and servicing depots were also located. The withholding of machinery and services was one of the reasons for the early proliferation of peasant societies, credit and service co-operatives, and finally the Asociación Nacional de Agricultores Pequeños (ANAP), set up in May 1961.

A month earlier, the socialist nature of the Revolution had been proclaimed and from that point on there was an accelerated rundown of production, property, capital, and services – as well as overt political hostility – on the part of the middle agrarian bourgeoisie. This largely motivated the Second Agrarian Reform Law of October 1963, according to which a ceiling of 67 hectares per holding was left in private hands. Overall the first law had affected some 70% of agricultural land, of which 40% became state-controlled and some 30% was placed in the hands of the small peasantry, leaving a further 30% in the hands of the middle peasantry. This last was eliminated under the Second Agrarian Reform Law. By 1977 the proportion of the state-held to private-sector agricultural land was roughly 80% to 20%, and has remained more or less the same since.

The vast majority of state land was in the sugar sector, which had overwhelmingly been a plantation economy. In other branches of agriculture, where this had been less so, the proportion held by the state was markedly less. It was at its lowest in tobacco: exactly the inverse of national figures, with 20% of land state-owned and 80% private in 1977. The pre-revolutionary agrarian structure in tobacco, with its prevalence of sharecropping and small tenant and subtenant farming, was the reason for that.

Tobacco growers were prime beneficiaries of agrarian reform, so also they pioneered peasant societies and credit and service co-operatives in the early months after the Revolution. In Pinar del Río alone, there were by 1962 over 280 credit and service co-operatives and over 100 societies.[1] Credit facilities came from the new DECAI (Departamento de Crédito Agrícola Industrial) which incorporated the former BANFAIC and was set up in 1960 by the Instituto Nacional de Reforma Agraria (INRA).

By the 1963 Second ANAP Congress, 345 agricultural societies had been formed, in addition to 587 credit and service co-operatives. The latter were largely in tobacco in Pinar del Río and Las Villas, grouping 46,133 peasant farmers for the collective use of curing sheds, irrigation and machinery, credit, and supplies. The overall number of societies had dropped by 1967 to 136, by 1971 to 41, although the number of credit and service co-operatives had grown to 1,119 in all.

The drop in the number of societies was but one indication of problems besetting tobacco that can only be understood in the national developmental context. It was a logical reaction that in early post-revolutionary years there should have been a 'flight' from sugar cane and tobacco and attempted diversification and industrialization. This programme proved ambitious and costly in terms of imported capital goods and raw materials, while returns on industrial investment rates were low. Moreover, the relative collapse of sugar-product exports and the sharp fall in quantity and quality of tobacco exports meant a steep drop in foreign exchange earnings to finance such a programme, in addition to financing overall education, health, general welfare, and housing schemes of the Revolution.

From 1963, the underlying logic of the new development strategy was that industrial investment was to be reduced while export capacity was restored and further expanded. Renewed emphasis on industrial growth was to await the building up of a necessary infrastructure and to be financed by an increased foreign exchange earning sector, primarily sugar but also tobacco, livestock, citrus fruits, mining, and so on. The major pre-revolutionary trading partner, the US (which had placed a total trade embargo on Cuba in 1960), was to be replaced by more diversified markets, including new index-linked markets in the socialist bloc.[2]

Within this programme, the sugar sector was again accorded priority, and correspondingly the state farm was seen as the 'model' of socialist agriculture, allowing the application of technology and mechanization. Many agricultural societies died out in the sixties, not least because direct attachment of private lands to state enterprises (by sale, rent, or other arrangements) was given greater government priority. An all-out effort for a record sugar harvest in 1970 had the effect of channelling major resources into the sugar sector, exacerbating the already growing problem of non-prioritization of credit and other facilities to the private sector, which was that much larger in other branches, especially tobacco. The 1969–70 tobacco harvest was only 44% of the 1965–6 harvest, and in itself pointed to the need for a re-evaluation of agricultural policy and small farming.

The 1971 ANAP Congress was outspoken in this respect, and a channelling of resources to other branches and especially the private sector from then on resulted in an overall increase in output. The years 1971–6 were defined as a period of tobacco recuperation. This included greater state attention to small growers, greater land area planted to tobacco, higher-quality and higher-yield strains, and bigger price incentives. Investment in fertilizers, hydraulic equipment, repair work on curing sheds, and general research work paid off with a 100% increase in the tobacco crop over this period. In 1975–6 the total crop area harvested for marketing was some 52,000 hectares (over 44,000 in the private sector), in comparison with just under 24,000 in 1970–1 (20,000 private), approximately 46,000 (40,000 private) in 1967–8 and 44,000 (39,000 private) in 1963–4.

The 1977 Fifth ANAP Congress came out strongly for a pronounced co-operative movement in the private sector.[3] In effect, the new agricultural production co-operatives were a more carefully organized variant of the earlier move to pool private holdings in collective production units owned and managed by farmers forming their membership. Stress was put on the voluntary nature of the process, with an independent valuation of contribution in terms of land and other means of production of individual members for each to be reimbursed from common funds. The rudiments of financial accounting were required, and co-operatives received low interest rates on credits and preferential treatment in allocation of agricultural machinery and equipment. Their success was much publicized over the following years and explained largely in terms of the co-operatives' more advanced division of labour, combined with more technically advanced means of production. Their social advantages were also highlighted: there were electricity, running water and other amenities in the new co-operative villages, social isolation, especially of women, was broken down and their contribution to production and income grew as labour was organized collectively with related child-care facilities.

Although the state farm was still seen as the 'highest form of production', the co-operative movement reflected a major shift in the model for the private sector. Political considerations aside, the main advantage of state farms, as a corollary of industry with high mechanization and technology, had not held in the Cuba of the sixties and seventies, not even in sugar, where only in the eighties are conditions becoming fully propitious. In other sectors, state farms were all too often seen as a waste of resources that could have been used more effectively in private hands. The new co-operatives are more modest in scale and technology, controlled by the growers themselves in tune with national agrarian needs. As such they show every sign of appearing more relevant as institutions and more promising in terms of productive and social advance at this period in time.

In tobacco, the record has been exceptional, as yields have in some cases been more than doubled and picturesque co-operative villages have grown up in lush tobacco areas. By May 1983, in Pinar del Río province, some 40% of private tobacco land – 5,381 *caballerías* – was pooled in 166 co-operatives, with an average of 32 *caballerías* of land and 52 full members per co-operative, the overall number of co-operative farmers totalling 9,466. Similar figures were reported for Villa Clara and Sancti Spíritus provinces (corresponding to the former Las Villas province). Villa Clara boasted 49% of private tobacco land – 2,816 *caballerías* – in 60 co-operatives, averaging 46 *caballerías* and 62 members, with a total number of 3,788 members. Sancti Spíritus reported 41% (2,358 *caballerías*) in 51 co-operatives, averaging 46 *caballerías* and 63 members, for a total of 3,217.[4]

A parallel process of industrial reorganization started after the initial agrarian reform but events then moved quickly. By December 1959, there were increasing factory-level tobacco worker demands, as well as FTN demands, for the revolutionary government to intercede in industry. Indeed, workers were instrumental in detecting anomalies such as cut-backs in production and withdrawal of capital on the part of foreign and Cuban firms.

One of the many case files from the ministry of labour in this early period was that of General Cigar. From February to May 1960, letters from workers in various company stemming and sorting sheds were coming into the ministry. A final letter was from Lucilo Vásquez Molina, president of the Unión de Empleados de Tabaco de Las Villas, and Josefa Pozo, president of the Asociación de Despalilladoras y Ripiadoras de Santa Clara, formally requesting that official action be taken in the case of General Cigar's Santa Clara stemmery and its sorting sheds in Placetas, Báez, Fomento, Zaza del Medio, and Cabaiguán, on the grounds that the company was 'employing the reactionary imperialist tactic of declaring it would withdraw business from the Republic of Cuba, making redundant more than 1,500 workers'.[5] Among the points made were that the company had threatened to send all the books – including pension books – to Havana; had justified stopping work on the pretext that no stocks of leaf were forthcoming; and was exporting the leaf unstemmed, leaving stemmers and other employees without work. On 23 May 1960, General Cigar formally requested legal authorization to close down its subsidiary in Cuba, given US exchange controls which meant it had no capital for buying and operational costs.

In July 1960 all US firms in Cuba were nationalized. In the case of the tobacco sector, Ministry of Labour Resolution 20260 of 15 September decreed wider government intervention on grounds explicitly set out in its preamble:

WHEREAS: The legal representation of the Federación Tabacalera Nacional has exposed before this Ministry the crisis in the tobacco sector which is a consequence of the policy being carried out by cigar and cigarette manufacturers and leaf dealers, which has produced a considerable drop in production, and the laying off of a great number of workers which has adversely affected the national economy;

WHEREAS: It is evident that manufacturing interests in the tobacco sector have taken a selfish stand, one that is overtly hostile to the economic development of the nation, their narrow trading policy being directed solely towards the aim of obtaining greater profits and personal wealth, thus effecting an extraordinary drop in production for both home consumption and in export for Cuba's overseas markets, a decrease which surpasses 15 million cigars in the first six months of this year . . .

WHEREAS: The self-centred attitude, contrary to the interests of the national economy and of the workers has borne no limits and has been manifest in all aspects of production, from the sale of raw material which should be in stock in order to produce the correct blends, and the refusal to buy leaf of this year's harvest to the neglect of certain departments of the factories, has brought as a consequence a lowering of the quality of the product, which has thus lost prestige and customary markets;

WHEREAS: The withdrawal of capital . . . has contributed, moreover, to the ostensible cutting back of production, this being carried out almost exclusively on the basis of state loans, which in itself shows that the attitude of tobacco interests is consciously directed toward provoking a situation of disorganization and paralysis of the industry . . .

WHEREAS: Some have already abandoned their businesses and left the country, leaving behind them considerable debts and many unemployed, creating an increase in unemployment which the Revolutionary Government and especially this Ministry must avoid;

WHEREAS: It is necessary to guarantee supplies to Cuba's overseas markets, producing cigars of the quality that has always been characteristic of the Havana Cigar, for all these reasons the Revolutionary Government adopts the measure necessary for restoring the situation created in the cigar and cigarette industry back to normal, guaranteeing work stability for those in the industry and output, decreeing intervention in work places in which the above-mentioned has occurred . . .[6]

This was a prelude to the wider nationalization law of October 1960, which affected most significant private enterprise. Tobacco was first put under INRA and then under the newly created ministries of industry and agriculture. What had been set up in 1961 as the Cubatabaco export enterprise was broadened in scope in 1966 as the state tobacco enterprise unifying under one body all agricultural and industrial planning, production, distribution and export. Large-scale re-organization concentrated production and some 60,000 workers in 402 sorting sheds, 30 stemmeries, 6 cigarette factories and 95 cigar factories throughout the island. This structure remains largely unchanged to date, although under the institutional re-organization of government in the seventies the agricultural side of tobacco fell under the ministry of agriculture, the industrial side under the ministry of food, and the export side under the ministry of foreign trade. This would seem to have created a certain amount of confusion but has not been a major drawback to development.

Hand-rolling continued to predominate in the cigar sector, though machines were also seen in a different light. With a diverse programme of national socio-economic development, they no longer signified mass unemployment and misery but the freeing of hands much needed in other sectors of a newly diversifying economy. The general shortage of labour felt throughout Cuba by the mid-sixties had its corollary in the tobacco industry, which was a campaign to train women cigar makers. Today any cigar factory gallery has a strong section of women in its ranks.

The industrial re-organization of the sixties must be seen as an attempt to rationalize production, eliminating the small sweatshop and outwork sector that had become so prevalent in the cigar sector prior to the revolution, and thereby improving conditions and standardizing wage rates. Internal demand that had been created by a general re-distribution of societal resources meant that although by 1966 home consumption of cigars and cigarettes had respectively tripled and doubled their 1958 figures, supplies were never enough. Moreover, as the quality and volume of the tobacco crop was hard hit in the late sixties, so also was the quality and volume of industrial production.

The seventies saw the gradual introduction of the new national economic planning and management system. Broadly speaking, while the emphasis continued to be on centralized national planning, the key to the system was a certain degree of administrative autonomy, with factories run along the principles of economic accounting and profitability, increased worker participation in management, and material as well as moral incentives for worker collectives. End-of-year profits were to be proportionally given over to the state to finance wider development programmes, ploughed back into factory re-investment, and given over to workers in the form of premiums or bonuses or collective facilities ranging from housing to social clubs. The system went hand in hand with a national wage and social security reform and a strengthening of the mass organizations, particularly the trade union movement. The trade union was seen as both counterpart and counterbalance to management, in the quest for greater productivity and higher quality production, greater administrative efficiency, and greater social and material benefits for workers and the wider population.[7]

The spin-off in tobacco was a return to quality leaf and cigar export production; and quality hand-rolling of cigars truly came into its own again. The cigar export industry had been particularly badly hit by the US embargo, given that (on 1958 figures) over two-thirds of the volume of leaf exports, half the volume of cigar exports – even higher proportions in terms of value – were accounted for by the US market. Cuba's problem was to expand other existing markets and find new smaller ones, in some cases offering a lower-priced cigar. Militating against this was the early drive to diversify the economy and lessen dependence on cash crops such as tobacco and sugar, only to be modified in sugar in the late sixties and in tobacco in the early seventies.

Subject to natural fluctuations in a product of this nature, export figures are a reflection of this process. Cigar exports dropped from 79,000,000 in 1958 to 55,000,000 in 1970, but were up again to 120,000,000 by 1976.[8] A determined effort to promote long-standing quality cigars in six Havana export factories – four of which were the traditional Romeo y Julieta, Partagás, La Corona, and H. Upmann – had upped sales, especially in traditional Western European markets such as Spain, the United Kingdom, France, Switzerland, Belgium, and Holland. There smokers were receiving their usual Montecristo, Romeo y Julieta, Partagás, H. Upmann, Por Larrañaga, Bolívar, and the like, along with the newer Davidoff. Simultaneously, markets had been opened up in the socialist countries, the GDR and USSR in particular. By the early eighties, Cuba had diversified its markets to over 90 countries, and demand still far exceeded supply. In the case of the Spanish importer Tabacalera S.A., imports stood around the 40,000,000 mark while sales potential was felt to be around 68,000,000.[9] Meanwhile, there had been an opening up of cigarette markets in the socialist community, major importers being the USSR and Czechoslovakia.

Leaf exports dropped from 58,000,000 lb in 1958 to 31,000,000 in 1970, to climb again to just over 33,000,000 in 1976, the principal markets being Spain, Holland, and the USSR (and there were also many others). More significant was that while in 1970 the value of leaf exports was half as great again as the value of cigar exports, by 1976 it was only two-thirds that of cigar exports. The elimination of the US market on the one hand and a controlled export policy on the other had produced the reversal of a century-old trend. While fluctuating, the ratio of leaf to manufactured tobacco exports has since remained a favourable one, to the extent that when the 1979–80 harvest was decimated by blue mould, leaf export commitments were not met in order to guarantee at least minimum supplies to home industry. In 1980, cigar exports were almost 60,000,000 units, leaf exports less than 7,000,000 lb, only one-sixth of the value of cigar exports.

Such was the national effort that went into redressing the 1979–80 blue mould that the next year's harvest proved to be a record (over 121,000,000 lb), with record export levels of 40,000,000 lb. The quality was such as to cause one UK importer to comment, 'The Cubans look after their tobacco as the British look after their gardens!'[10] Cigar exports that year were over 75,000,000 units, and in export value, cigars still exceeeded leaf by some 20%.

The 1981–2 harvest was affected by heavy rains and flooding, and marginally down to 111,000,000 lb, export levels dropping accordingly. Natural fluctuations of this nature are impossible to regulate. Most important of all, however, is that the burden of such fluctuations no longer falls on the individual grower or workers. When blue mould struck, state farms, co-operatives and private growers benefitted from agricultural and crop insurance, and from 8.2 million pesos in national bank loans, as well as the channelling of material and human resources into tobacco. They were also more collectively prepared to cope. Factories affected by lack of leaf supplies were forced to close down but industrial workers were either provided with alternate employment or kept on 70% salary until production could be resumed.

Key figures in peasant and worker struggles of the past have taken an active part in tobacco re-organization, whether it be on the payroll of state farms or in ANAP – where former Pinar del Río sharecropper Adelfo Martín is currently head of the co-operative programme – or in charge of factories or in Cubatabaco – where Havana cigar makers' Evelio Lugo was for many years industrial chief. This in itself has ensured that worker and peasant interests have been uppermost, within Cuba's national and international limitations.

This does not mean to say that those interests have always been uniform or uniformly met, nor does it mean there has not been a great deal of trial and error in practice. Attempts to over-standardize cultivation, production, and wages acted as a disincentive to quality output. Workers guaranteed stable, regular employment on a traditional piece-rate system did not necessarily reflect on the need to meet production targets, nor were those targets necessarily realistically assessed.

It was not until the early seventies that the trade union movement as such came into its own again. In the strengthening of the mass union base in those years, one of the key meetings was that held in the Old La Corona – today Miguel Fernández Roig – factory. Lazaro Peña, then 70 years of age, himself the man most responsible for organizing the November 1973 workers' congress (carrying on the enumeration left off in 1947), was an obvious choice in elections for the post of general secretary of the new revolutionary CTC.

For a nation of producers and smokers, there can be no entertaining thoughts of eliminating tobacco, not even on health grounds! Continued low-priced rationing of many staple items, to guarantee minimum supplies to a maximum number of people, includes that of low-priced cigars (to one per adult male per week) and cigarettes (to one pack per adult per week). There is also a parallel state market on which any amount can be bought at a much higher price. In contrast to export production, however, the quality of domestic output still leaves a lot to be desired. This may be cause for complaint but, coupled with the current campaign on the harmful effects of smoking, it does keep the habit within reason.

The overall world structure of tobacco production, distribution, consumption and export might not have changed very much over the last twenty-five years, but in Cuba it certainly has. No longer is that burden of dependence passed ruthlessly on down the line. Conditions may be far from optimal, as Cubans will be the first to admit. However, there is no doubt that Cuban tobacco at least approaches a 'realm peopled by congenial spirits and . . . kindlier human emotions' in a way Karl Avery Werner can scarcely have anticipated.[11]

Appendix

Figures given in tables are often the only ones available and have to be taken largely at face value. Where the figures appear odd, I have endeavoured to point out possible reasons as to why this should be so. Figures do not always add up correctly, but in the absence of other sources it has been impossible to judge which figures are wrong. They have therefore been left as given in the original source.

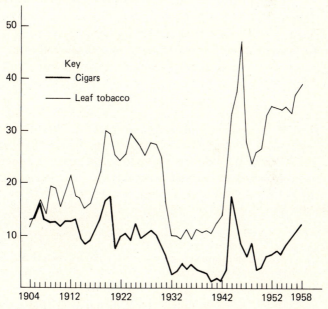

Tobacco exports from Cuba, 1904–58 (millions of pesos)

Table 1. *Selected occupations 1899–1943*[a]

Occupation	1899	1907	1919	1943
Total active population	602,113	772,502	948,846	1,520,851
Bricklayers	6,557	12,163	14,025	16,609[b]
Carpenters	14,204	21,422	21,984	32,890[c]
Traders	47,265	50,856	67,483	43,795
Maids	41,464	39,312	83,157	ng
Carters and coachmen	5,363	10,199	ng	ng
Harness makers	1,397	ng	ng	ng
Blacksmiths	2,398	ng	ng	3,089
Printers	1,499	ng	ng	ng
Mechanics	4,672	ng	16,633	28,581
Cigar and cigarette workers[d]	24,169	27,503	25,389	20,049
Bakers	5,444	5,162	ng	12,850
Painters	1,531	ng	ng	7,369
Tailors	3,481	ng	ng	5,773
Cobblers	6,320	6,848	6,195	25,797[e]
Railway workers	ng	951	10,429[f]	1,887
Tram workers	ng	587	ng	ng
Sugar technicians	ng	572	ng	ng
Bus drivers	ng	ng	ng	1,426
Stevedores	ng	ng	ng	3,097
Day labourers[g]	359,377	42,358	31,957	ng

ng Not given.

Notes:

[a] There is no occupational breakdown in the 1953 census.

[b] The construction industry as a whole employed 25,878.

[c] Includes wheelwrights.

[d] The occupational category used in the 1899, 1907 and 1919 censuses was 'cigar factory operatives'. This would have included cigar makers, sorters, selectors, box decorators, factory stemmers and possibly some cigarette workers, given production was not always in separate factories. The total figure for the industry was 38,692 in 1943, 36,468 in 1953.

[e] Includes shoemakers and harness makers.

[f] Refers to transport workers in general.

[g] Obviously a residual category.

Source: Compiled using figures given in the 1899, 1907, 1919 and 1943 censuses.

Table 2. *Cigar and cigarette workers, 1899–1943*[a]

	1899		1907		1919		1943	
	M	F	M	F	M	F	M	F
Havana province	15,390	1,257	15,800	3,123	11,528	3,234	7,096	516
Havana city	11,312	816	11,299	2,241	4,478	1,716	5,388[b]	
Matanzas	1,030		951	7	946	49	579	21
Pinar del Río	820	69	1,036	39	1,026	582	1,389	124
Camagüey	237	1	286	4	377	18	1,045	37
Las Villas	2,460	128	2,533	148	3,722	907	4,174	330
Oriente	2,652	22	3,495	21	2,985	115	4,601	107
Cuba	22,589	1,580	24,161	3,342	20,484	4,905	18,814	1,235[c]

Notes:

[a] The occupational category given for the 1899, 1907 and 1919 censuses was 'cigar factory operatives'. This would have included cigar makers, sorters, selectors, box decorators, factory stemmers and possibly some cigarette workers, given production was not always in separate factories. The 1943 census used the occupational category 'cigar and cigarette workers'. There is no occupational breakdown in the 1953 census.

[b] There is no breakdown for Havana city in the 1943 census. This figure is based on figures quoted in the 1945 tobacco workers' census.

[c] The figure quoted for the industry as a whole was 25,185 men and 13,507 women.

Source: Compiled using figures taken from the 1899, 1907, 1919 and 1943 censuses.

Table 3. *Unionized workers in 1944*

Industry	No. of workers	Unionized workers No.	Unionized workers %	Workers paying union dues No.	Workers paying union dues %
Sugar	497,707	122,488	25	51,775	11
Tobacco	168,467	65,695	39	31,581	18
Transport	55,342	32,467	58	23,492	42
Metallurgy	8,874	4,727	53	1,345	15
Wood	10,254	2,692	28	1,485	14
Mining	20,000	3,495	17	2,014	10
Textile	26,381	7,109	27	5,750	21
Leather	11,765	6,847	58	4,227	35
Maritime	31,421	22,638	75	15,802	50
Coffee	49,123	667	1	407	0.8
Cattle	62,261	76	0.1	72	0.2
Total	923,595	269,171	28	137,950	14

Source: Felipe Zapata, *Esquemas y notas para una historia de la organización obrera*, Havana, 1952.

Table 4. *Unionization in the tobacco industry in 1944*

Provinces	No. of work units	No. of workers	Unions affil. to CTC	Unionized workers	Workers paying dues
Cigar makers					
Pinar del Río	63	656	9	622	477
Havana	239	4,954	13	4,954	2,378
Matanzas	57	211	7	21	211
Las Villas	362	2,814	24	2,814	1,292
Camagüey	87	582	5	582	318
Oriente	115	976	11	976	511
Cuba	923	10,193	69	10,159	5,187
Cigarette workers					
Pinar del Río	3	134	0		0
Havana	9	1,920	1	950	800
Matanzas	0	0	0	0	0
Las Villas	0	540	2	517	450
Camagüey	1	56	1	56	56
Oriente	0	0	0	0	0
Cuba	16	2,650	4	1,523	1,306

Table 4. *(cont.)*

Provinces	No. of work units	No. of workers	Unions affil. to CTC	Unionized workers	Workers paying dues
Stemmers					
Pinar del Río		4,194	2	4,194	1,338
Havana		4,314	5	4,314	3,510
Matanzas		0	0	0	0
Las Villas		7,101	8	7,101	4,552
Camagüey		573	0	0	0
Oriente		271	0	0	0
Cuba		16,453	15	15,609	9,400
Leaf sorters					
Pinar del Río		19,078	2	6,405	1,113
Havana		965	2	667	201
Matanzas		0	0	0	0
Las Villas		28,030	19	26,152	13,533
Camagüey		1,765	0	0	0
Oriente		837	0	0	0
Cuba		50,675	23	33,224	14,847
Growers					
Pinar del Río	2,107	33,066	6	4,513	639
Havana	290	1,761	2	667	202
Matanzas	0	0	0	0	0
Las Villas	1,412	48,583	0	0	0
Camagüey	168	3,060	0	0	0
Oriente	170	1,448	0	0	0
Cuba	4,147	87,828	8	5,180	841

Source: Compiled from tables given in Zapata (1952).

Biographies of interviewees

During the early months of 1969, I carried out a series of interviews with old tobacco workers. This was on the basis of no sample survey and therefore cannot claim to be representative. I have chosen to include here biographies of interviewees who were workers in today's La Corona – Miguel Fernández Roig – factory. They had nearly all worked in the large factories for part, if not most, of their working lives and what they had to say was surprisingly uniform. Nearly all were born into tobacco families – the father, and in some cases the mother and some brother or sister working in the industry already. A good percentage were not born in the city but in the surrounding towns and, in a few cases, in the more outlying tobacco growing areas. This was especially common where the cigar maker was concerned. At an early age these workers had entered the industry, helping their fathers in home rolling or working in local *chinchales*. Gradually they worked their way up to the larger factories. Once there, however, they by no means always stayed. On the contrary, few were able to maintain their jobs in times of economic crises, little demand, etc., and the predominant pattern for these men and women was one of constant flux. The following are a few examples.

1. *Cigar maker:* 76 years old; began work at the age of 12 in a small shop of 7–9 workers; moved to one with 40 workers and then to a factory of 100 workers; after 9 years in that factory 'graduated' to the Fonseca factory (whose workers at times numbered some 300); after 2–3 years managed to get work at the Rey del Mundo factory, where he stayed for the next 10–12 years; lost that job at the height of the 1932 depression and went to the Gener factory in Güines; shortly after, 100 workers were laid off and he was one of them; returned to Havana to work in small shops until 1954, when able to get a job in H. Upmann.

2. *Cigar maker:* 61 years old; also began work at the age of 12 as a stemmer; when 14 learned to mend shoes and became a cobbler for five years before re-entering the tobacco industry as a sorter and cigar maker in Sancti Spíritus; over the years has worked throughout the island but mostly in Havana, in more or less all the large export factories; in 1945 was laid off from the Gener factory and was out of work 1948 to 1950; 1951–3, worked in a small shop in Luyanó, Havana, for the next few years in a second-class factory until he managed to get work in La Corona factory in 1957; when out of work would roll cigars at home with his brother.

3. *Cigar maker:* 56 years old; one of the women working for the last 40 years in the trade; father grew tobacco and mother rolled cigars in the home, her father selling the cigars she made in the local store; she and her brother learnt with her mother at home until, in 1934, entered small factory of 60–70 workers in Artemisa; over the years 1944–50 worked in the Bock factory in Marianao; in 1952 began work in Por Larrañaga; recounts that in June/July there was hardly ever enough work in the large factories and that for several days of the week there would be no work at all, or only sufficient for a few hours.

4. *Cigar maker:* 65 years old; 40 years in the industry; initially worked as a sorter on his father's tobacco farm but then moved to Güines to a small shop where he served two years' apprenticeship to cigar maker; later moved to a larger factory of some 250 workers and there stayed until the 1950s when the factory was closed down.

5. *Stemmer:* 43 years old; 27 years in the industry; began work in a small shop in Santa Clara where she stayed for five years before transferring to the General Cigar Company, a stemmery of 600-odd workers; when laid off went to work in the Company stemmery in Remedios; when out of work again, rolled cigars in the home for a short time before coming to Havana to work as a stemmer in the Gener factory.

6. *Stemmer:* 61 years old; 45 years in the industry; she and her sisters began as stemmers in Candelaria, Pinar del Río; husband a cigar maker in Romeo y Julieta and moved to work there; later found work in the Rey del Mundo factory, where she continued to work for many years; in 1949, Rey del Mundo laid off nearly all

its women workers in the stemmery and she was left redundant over the next decade.

7. *Leaf selector*: 60 years old; working in the industry since the age of 13; first worked in Manicaragua, Las Villas, where worked the sugar season at the mill, at the end of the sugar harvest sorting tobacco leaf over a period of three to four months; for 25 years worked in this way, until came to Havana in 1958 and began to work in Por Larrañaga as leaf selector.

8. *Ringer*: 44 years old; 25 years in the industry; husband a box decorator in a small shop of 20 workers and then in the Gener factory; for a period of five years or so worked in different industries (e.g., talc factory) but eventually returned to work as a ringer in Gener.

9. *Ringer*: 65 years old; 46 years in the industry; always worked in La Corona as a ringer; never out of work because women of the department shared out the little work there was in bad times.

10. *Sorter*: 62 years old; 47 years in the industry; father a cigar maker in the Henry Clay factory and there served apprenticeship to sorter; over period of 16 years or so sustained more or less regular work but then forced to work in smaller factories.

11. *Sorter*: 72 years old; began work at the age of 13; father a sorter in Gener and he and his brother had their first job there in the wetting department; worked their way up to become sorters, a job which they maintained, with the exception of periods of economic crisis and acute lack of demand for cigars.

12. *Sorter*: 72 years old; 60 years in the industry; uncle a leaf selector in Romeo y Julieta, and through him able to get an apprenticeship to cigar maker; during the years 1928–32 worked as a cigar maker in La Belinda factory but from 1932–43 forced to work in the tobacco warehouses; 1943–51, found work in the Gener factory but was out again 1951–3; after that worked more or less constantly, but often on the basis of a few days a week, especially in June/July.

13. *Box decorator*: 83 years old; began work in 1906 as apprentice to box decorator; father worked in hotel sector but knew the owner of La Belinda factory (at the time a factory of some 300 workers) and was able to secure him a place there; stayed there for some six years, then moved to Partagás and then Gener and La Corona factories; later his son began to work with him; laid off during World War I but that was the only time; son, however, as younger member of department, sometimes only worked a few hours a day or a few days of the week, often having to find work in other sectors, such as construction industry.

14. *Box decorator*: 57 years old; working in industry since 1930; when little, worked as a carpenter's mate but his father was a cigar maker and his brother a box decorator in the Por Larrañaga factory and they managed to get him a job; worked there till 1939, when laid off; found work in shoe factory until able to enter a small rolling shop and then Por Larrañaga again in 1942; from then on never again redundant, but there were many weeks when there was only sufficient work for a few hours a day.

Notes

Introduction: A changing world tobacco economy

1   The Duke story can be found in Gustavus Myers, *History of the great American fortunes*, New York, 1937.

2   Plug: the term is said to have originated in Kentucky and Missouri, when settlers first soaked the tobacco in wild honey and then 'plugged' it tightly in holes bound with hickory log or green maple.

3   This seems to have been particularly true of the British. See B.W.E. Alford, *W.D. and H.O. Wills and the development of the U.K. tobacco industry, 1786–1965*, London 1973.

4   'Tabak', *Handwörterbuch der Staatswissenschaften*, vol. 7, Berlin, 1901.

5   Flue curing is an artificial process of drying the sap from the newly harvested tobacco leaf. A milder, brighter leaf was obtained, hence the name 'Virginia Bright'.

6   Alford (1973) refers to the 1867 machine but not to its owners. Other reports refer to the success of the Susini machine at the 1867 Exhibition. It is unlikely there were two.

7   Quoted in Richard B. Tennant, *The American cigarette industry* (New Haven, 1950), p. 24.

8   See Myers, *History*, for an enlightening account of the dizzy development of the American trusts, including ATC, the early opposition they encountered, and the way they overrode opposition; Tennant, *The American cigarette industry*, for the case against American Tobacco. The US Bureau of Corporations in 1909 analysed the full story of huge profits, inflation of stock issues, etc., and this was motive enough for the Supreme Court ruling that the Trust was in violation of the 1890 Sherman Law.

9   An interesting parallel was the Camel/Lucky Strike battle in the US. For an amusing article, see 'Camels of Winston-Salem', *Fortune*, 3:1, 1931, p. 45.

10   For the growth of these companies, see *Moody's*, 1916–1936.

11   In response both to growing concern over the danger to health from smoking and to high returns on newly expanding food and cosmetics industries, all the tobacco monopolies moved fast into these two sectors. ITC acquired HP Sauce Ltd (1967) and National Canning Co. and the Ross Group (1978), changing its name to the Imperial Tobacco Group Ltd. Significantly, after more acquisitions in this field, the Wills part of the IT Group built a large new plant in Bristol fully equipped to make the changeover from tobacco to food when the time arose. The BAT group acquired Lenthéric Ltd (1965), Morny (1966), and Yardley and the Germaine Monteuil Cosmetics Group (1968). In 1969 ATC became American Brands on taking over Sunshine Biscuits and other food companies. Reynolds had early

moved into food, acquiring the Pacific Hawaiian Products Co. (1963), Penick Ford Ltd (1965), and Patio Foods Inc. (1967). Other branches include Filmco Corp. and Mclean Industries.

12 Tennant, *The American cigarette industry*.

13 See 'Rufus Lenoir Patterson's cigar machine', *Fortune*, 1:2 (June 1930), p. 56.

14 This not being a tobacco-producing country, ITC developed overseas leaf corporations. An interesting ITC study is E. Twiston Davies, *Fifty years of progress: an account of the African organization of the Imperial Tobacco Company*, Bristol, 1958.

15 CNPDTH, *Nuestros mercados de tabaco, 1902–1930*, 1931.

16 First set up by the US and UK governments as the Anglo-American Caribbean Commission, it dropped the 'Anglo-American' in 1945 when France and the Netherlands joined it. The countries included in its study were: Bahamas, Barbados, British Guiana, British Honduras, Curaçao, French Guiana, Guadaloupe, Jamaica, Leeward Islands, Martinique, Puerto Rico, Trinidad and Tobago, Virgin Islands of the US, Windward Islands, Grenada, St Lucia, St Vincent.

17 'Note on Cuban Revolution', *Fortune*, 1:2 (June 1930), p. 148.

1: Don Tabaco, 1817–88

1 For further information on the Factoría, see José Rivero Muñiz, *Tabaco: su historia en Cuba*, Havana, 1965.

2 An interesting account of this period as a whole can be found in Manuel Moreno Fraginals, *El ingenio*, Havana, 1964.

3 Samuel Hazard, *Cuba a pluma y lápiz* (1871), Havana, 1928.

4 A detailed account of the factory, plus comments in the visitors' book over these years, is included in *Projet definitif d'une fabrique de cigarettes (genre Havanais) établie a St Sebastien (frontière d'Espagne) avec les marques LA HONRADEZ (L'Honorabilité) de La Havane et foncionnant avec les MACHINES-SUSINI brevetées*, Paris, 1869.

5 *Balanza general del comercio de la Isla, 1859*, Havana, 1861.

6 *Noticias estadísticas de la Isla de Cuba en 1862*, Havana, 1864.

7 A substantial source for the late nineteenth century was the British consular trade and shipping reports, *British Parliamentary Papers, Blue Books* (BPP, BB).

8 Don Pedro López Trigo y Pezuela, *Estadística de exportación de la Isla de Cuba, 1890*, Havana 1892.

9 The Conills (Catalans) were an important business, financial and political family. Juan Conill was a founder member of the bank La Alianza, adviser to the Banco Español, member of the Ayuntamiento de La Habana and the Junta de Fomento. In his later years he wisely transferred his interests out of tobacco and into sugar.

10 Antonio Bachiller y Morales, 'Memorias sobre la exportación del tabaco', in *Memorias de la Real Sociedad Patriótica de La Habana* (Havana 1839), pp. 323–50.

11 Miguel Ferrer y Martínez, *El tabaco: su historia, su cultivo, sus vicisitudes, sus afamadas vegas en Cuba*, Madrid, 1851.

12 Rivero Muñiz, *Tabaco*, p. 280. Susini's petition was passed to José María de Las Casas, who informed that the reasons were 'so sophisticated and so contrary to good economic principles that they should not be taken into consideration.' The Superintendente de Hacienda approved Las Casas' judgement and denied Susini's petition.

13 Ramón de la Sagra, *Cuba 1860*, Havana, 1831; re-edited 1963.
14 BPP, BB, vol. 67, pp. 803–18.
15 *Revista Económica*, 1878, p. 237. By far the heaviest part of the leaf was the central stem.
16 The Bances family was an old Asturian family of bankers and industrialists. The Havana trade register revealed that Don López Bances owned El Africano cigarette factory and Partagás cigars. Francisco Granda Bances owned Palma Real cigars.
17 Texifonte Gallego y García, *Cuba por fuera*, Havana, 1890.

2: Enter monopoly capital, 1888–1902

1 Fuller information on this and subsequent developments can be gleaned from *Burdett's Official Intelligence* and the Registro Mercantil de La Habana.
2 For a discussion of interlocking land and manufacturing interests, see chapter 6.
3 No evidence has yet been found to situate these companies regarding the companies that went to form ITC, although the timing would seem to indicate that the change-over corresponded to the 1901 ATC/ITC agreement.
4 This comes through in Philip Foner, *The Spanish–Cuban–American War and the birth of U.S. imperialism*, New York, 1972, and in Karl Grismer, *Tampa*, Florida, 1950. Tampa manufacturing was later hard hit by the 1929 depression and by large northern corporations turning out machine-made cigars.
5 The full manufacturers' report, of which clause 6 is quoted here, and the central government's reply make eloquent reading and are included in Vidal Morales y Morales, *Documentos relativos a la información económica de Madrid y al Comité Central de Propaganda de La Habana (1890)*, Colección Facticia vol. 18. A good source of reference for these years is Julio Le Riverend's two-part 'Años terribles para la economía tabacalera', *Habano*, 3:1 and 3:2 (1941).
6 Clause 4 of the declaration of the Junta General de la Unión de Fabricantes de Tabacos, included in *Memoria de los trabajos más importantes realizados por la corporación desde 18 septiembre de 1890 hasta 5 de febrero de 1894 en defensa de los intereses generales de la industria que representa*, Havana, 1894.
7 Manuel Valle y Fernández, president of the manufacturers' union, to the overseas minister of Spain, also included in *Memoria* (1894).
8 *Ibid.*, p. 91.
9 Bock's report is included in Robert Porter, *Industrial Cuba. Being a study of the present commercial and industrial conditions with suggestion as to opportunities presented in the island for American capital and labour*, New York and London, 1899.
10 Other major monopolies that moved into Cuba during these years were Bethlehem Iron, Havemeyer Sugar, and United Fruit.
11 Oscar Pino Santos in *El asalto a Cuba por la oligarquía financiera yanqui*, Havana, 1973, points out that British investment continued to be greater than US investment right up to 1913–14 and that one-third of British capital in Cuba was invested during the government of José Miguel Gómez (1909–14). The real assault by the US financial oligarchy, producing a particularly prolonged rivalry between US and British capital in railways, came after 1914. Tobacco, therefore, would seem to have been exceptional.
12 Gustav Bock, *La verdad sobre la industria del tabaco habano*, Havana, 1904.
13 José Aguirre gives a full account of the Trust factories during this period in his reply to Bock, also entitled *La verdad sobre la industria del tabaco habano*, Havana, 1905.

3: Legacy to past prosperity, 1902–24

1 This and subsequent quotes are taken from the English version of Rafael García Marqués, *Account of the grave situation of the tobacco industries, the causes of their decadence, and measures which are considered necessary to save them from the ruin that menaces them*, Havana, 1900.

2 Taken from the English version of L. V. Abad, *Statement to the Committee of Ways and Means*, Washington, 1900.

3 Paul Serre, *Le tabac de Cuba et les cigares de la Havane*, Paris, 1911.

4 *Trabajo presentado al Honorable Señor Presidente de la República por la Comisión nominada que le informara al Gobierno acerca de la actual situación del cultivo y de la industria del tabaco*, Havana, 1910.

5 Rivero Muñiz, in *Tabaco*, maintains that independence changed little in terms of Spanish ownership, but it is difficult by this period to differentiate Spanish from Cuban as new generations born and resident in Cuba continued business. The important question would be the extent to which there was a drain of capital to Spain, especially in the early decades; but this has had to be left for the present.

6 This and other company information comes from the Registro Mercantil de La Habana.

4: Mechanization and recession, 1925–33

1 Leland Jenks, *Our Cuban Colony*, New York, 1928.

2 *El Mundo*, 6 December 1925.

3 *El Mundo*, 19 March 1926.

4 *El Mundo*, 9 December 1925.

5 Taken from Por Larrañaga company records in the Registro. Mercantil de La Habana.

6 The 40,000-peso contract was transferable to legitimate successors to the company but not to the American Tobacco Company and/or subsidiaries, nor to the Havana Trust.

7 Significantly, company directors Benito Santalla (founder–director of Villaamil, Santalla y Cía cigarettes), José María Díaz Villaamil (of the same), Enrique Berenguer Gispert and Rowe Hampton Nelson (of Por Larrañaga's board of directors) had no strong ties with cigar manufacturing.

8 For a fuller discussion of the struggle against the machine, see chapter 15.

9 Published in full as 'De la Unión de Fabricantes de Tabacos y Cigarros de la Isla de Cuba. Exposición al Sr. Presidente de la República', *El Mundo*, 11 October 1926.

10 Presidential Decree 266 of February 1927. An interesting aside here is that pressure on Por Larrañaga appears to have caused considerable internal rifts. Minutes of an extraordinary board meeting in 1927 quote Alonso as having said that the old board resigned 'to give freedom of action to the Antilles Cigar Corporation to provide for the same'. The new board – presumably acceptable to Antilles – had as its president Sydney Rothschild (later president of Rothschild–Samuels–Duignan leaf) and Benito Santalla as vice-president. Alonso had particularly strong ties with cigar manufacturing: he rose from apprentice in the Bock factory (1884) to become manager of La Corona (1898), then manager (1902) and managing director (1906) of Partagás. This may have been a move to pressure him into supporting the machine, and he was certainly back as Larrañaga managing director in 1928 fighting, if unsuccessfully, for the abolition of the additional band or at least for acceptance of 'machine-made' written into the normal one.

11 The text of the law creating CNPDTH in the *Gaceta Oficial*, August 1927, defines the nature and scope of CNPDTH activities.

12 Dr Antonio Valverde y Mururi, 'Producción de tabaco', lecture to the Escuela de Comercio de La Habana, 26 March 1929.

13 'Informe de la Unión de Fabricantes a la Comisión Nacional de Propaganda y Defensa del Tabaco Habano', *Boletín del Torcedor*, 1 December 1929 (middle-page supplement).

14 According to the 'Laudo impartido en el problema de Por Larrañaga', published in the *Boletín del Torcedor*, 1 August 1930, pp. 18–19, eighty trade marks in all were *not* to be machine-made.

15 *El Mundo*, 14 January 1932.

16 An indication of pressure the rest of the manufacturers exerted on Por Larrañaga can be seen in a letter from Henry Clay and Bock director Stuart Houston to Cuban Tobacco's Vice-President Gregg, on 18 January. Houston wrote: 'I have been particularly asked by the interests represented by the Havana Manufacturers' Association to explain the above fact to you, in the hope that it may be possible for you to pass a word of admonition (in case it is practicable for you to have the word spoken) to the American Machine and Foundry Company officials, if we are correct in assuming that Company controls the policies of the Larrañaga interests here, regarding the destructive effects of this action' Archivo Nacional de Cuba (ANC), CNPDTH, TCSA file 291.

17 *El Mundo*, 13 March 1932.

18 ANC, CNPDTH, TCSA, file 291.

19 *Ibid.*

20 'La Corona', *Fortune*, 7:3 (February 1933), p. 74. Cigars have two names: one is the brand name, the other is the front mark which designates shape and size. There is only one Corona brand, but all fine cigars offer a Corona size.

21 ANC. CNPDTH, TCSA, files 1 and 2.

5: New Deal for tobacco, 1934–58

1 'Cuba tiene en su tabaco un monopolio natural', *Habano*, April 1935, p. 18.

2 'Tobacco: monthly comments', *Cuba Importadora e Industrial*, February 1936, p. 44.

3 'Pasado y futuro del tabaco habano', *Cuba Importadora e Industrial*, May 1936, p. 73.

4 *El Mundo*, 6 January 1927.

5 In Las Villas province, the General Cigar Company of Cuba Ltd operated large stemming shops in Camjuaní, Cabaiguán, Remedios, La Esperanza, and Santa Clara; Rothschild–Samuels–Duignan in Placetas and Camajuaní. In Pinar del Río province, H. Duys and Co. operated in Santiago de Las Vegas, Ruppin in San Antonio de los Baños, Cuban Land in Santiago de Las Vegas, etc. See *Primer censo de los obreros de la industria tabacalera*, Havana, 1947.

6 Lee Samuels, 'Duras realidades', *Habano*, May 1935, p. 21.

7 'Otra restricción en proyecto: la tabacalera', *Cuba Importadora e Industrial*, November 1936, p. 25. Though approved by Senate, Garriga's project was rejected in the House by 90 votes to 4. The US Cigar Manufacturers' Association welcomed such opposition. The Tobacco Defense Law, they claimed, 'would impair the close interdependent relationship now enjoyed and which, for many years, has been so advantageous to both the Cuban and American cigar interests'.

8 'El embullo intervencionista: un nuevo intento de restricción tabacalera', *Cuba Importadora e Industrial*, June 1939, p. 29.

9 Leslie Pantin (then president of the Asociación de Comerciantes y Cosechadores de Tabaco), 'El clamor del sector tabacalero', *Cuba Importadora e Industrial* December 1939, p. 29.

10 Manuel Rodríguez López, 'Hay que fomentar la exportación de cigarillos', *Habano*, February 1935.

11 'Un criterio erroneo', *Tabaco*, April 1935, p. 1.

12 Ricardo A. Casado, 'En torno a nuestra industria cigarrera', *Habano*, December 1939, p. 60.

13 'No resistiría la industria cigarrera ningún aumento del actual impuesto', *Habano*, April 1941, p. 21.

14 Quoted in 'Magno desfile frente al palacio para pedir protección para el tabaco', *Habano*, April 1942, p. 6.

15 'Criterios en discrepancia sobre la suspensión de la cuota de Cuba en los Estados Unidos', *Habano*, May 1945, p. 11.

16 *Ibid.*

17 José Perdomo and Jorge Posse, *Mecanización de la industria tabacalera*, Havana, 1945.

18 López del Castillo, 'Más sobre el Fondo de Estabilización Tabacalera', *Cuba Económica*, November 1951, p. 15.

6: The peripheral mode of production

1 Oscar Pino Santos, 'Un siglo económico: la corona, el aguila y esta libertad', *Cuba*, special 1968 issue.

2 Fernando Ortiz, *Cuban counterpoint: tobacco and sugar* (New York, 1947), p. 61.

3 Cuban demographer Juan Pérez de la Riva maintained that shortage of labour was one of the most important underlying factors of nineteenth-century Cuban history.

4 While not wishing to enter the debates on slavery in Cuba at this point – my findings are scanty and the subject out of the scope of the present study – it is worth drawing attention to the need for more work on this. Ortiz was clearly mistaken when he asserted that tobacco was grown by whites 'aside from the occasional slave' and that 'although the heavy work around the factories was done by negroes, freed slaves and Chinese, the actual cigar rolling was done by Spaniards'. And his work has coloured more recent works such as Herbert S. Klein, *Slavery in the Americas: a comparative study of Virginia and Cuba*, London, 1967, and Franklin W. Knight, *Slave society in Cuba during the nineteenth century*, Madison, 1970.

5 *Noticias Estadísticas* (1864).

6 H. Friedlaender, *Historia económica de Cuba* (Havana, 1944), p. 64.

7 *Censo* was the system whereby growers yielded a percentage of utilities; *contrato de partido* was a contract stipulating a grower's conditions; *arrendamiento* was the renting of land under specific conditions.

8 Included in Antonio Bachiller y Morales, *Recortes de periódico, 1880–1881*.

9 R.P. Porter, *Industrial Cuba*, New York and London, 1899.

10 Alberto Arrendondo, *Cuba: tierra indefensa*, Havana, 1945, p. 257.

11 *Censo Oficial*, Havana, 1899, and *Estadística Agropecuria*, Havana, 1929.

12 *Problems of the new Cuba*, New York, 1935.

13   Manuel Fabián Quesada, 'La crisis del tabaco, causas y soluciones', *Carteles*, 27 October 1935.
14   Carlos M. Raggi Ageo, *Condiciones económicas y sociales de la República de Cuba*, Havana, 1944; Julián Alienes y Urosa, *Características fundamentales de la economía cubana*, Havana, 1950; CNPDTH, *Primer censo . . .* (1947); *Memoria del censo agrícola nacional de 1946*, Havana, 1947.
15   Lowry Nelson, *Rural Cuba*, Minneapolis, 1950. Interestingly, there is also evidence of increasing preference for indirect control of sorting shops in the 1940s. On interviewing old employees I learned that Kaffemburg Brothers, who owned and operated 12 sorting shops in Santa Clara, 10 in Cabaiguán and 10 in Camajuaní, plus others scattered throughout the province of Las Villas, gave employees the option of buying the sorting shops in this period. In this way the company kept first claims on the tobacco while no longer shouldering the outlay in poor market years.
16   Included in José Rivero Muñiz, 'El tabaco en la poesía', unpublished manuscript (1946) in the Institute of History library.
17   Pardo y Betancourt, *Informe ilustrado y estadístico* (Havana, 1863) records 15,000 cigarette workers for Havana, 19,600 throughout the island. 1862 Hacienda figures quote only 7,700 and 13,000 for a similar number of shops. The only feasible reason for such a large discrepancy is that slave labour was included in the former.
18   *Projet définitif . . .* (1869).
19   *Album de La Corona: Obsequio a sus favorecedores*, Havana, 1898.
20   These and other figures, unless otherwise stated, come from ANC, CNPDTH, TCSA unclassified files.
21   Detail work brought with it departmentalization of the larger factories, whose layout has survived till today. The leaf is handled on the ground floor, rolling, stemming, sorting, box decorating and ringing on the upper floors. The part where the actual rolling takes place came to be known as the gallery (*galería*), the word being brought over from the prison galleries.
22   The editorial continued: 'Speaking in general terms, the development of the tobacco industry, outside of the capital and two or three towns of the interior of the island, if it offers any characteristic it is one of misery, compelled to supply local necessities and drawn out in perpetual agony which is exacerbated by the underhand competition which the owners of the nation's shops maintain, and by the total lack of scruples which taint a great part of these proprietors'.
23   *BANFAIC* [Banco de Fomento Agrícola e Industrial de Cuba] *Industrial Directory*, quoted in *Investment in Cuba: basic information for U.S. businessmen*, Washington, 1956.
24   James O'Connor, 'Industrial organization in the old and the new Cubas', *Science and Society*, 19:2 (1966).

7: The tobacco peasantry and proletariat

1   As the variety and quality of the cigars increased, so the demand for different types and, hence, the sorting of tobacco leaf. There are, in fact, many grades, the leaf varying in quality and size, according to the different regions of Cuba and the different parts of the plant. The middle leaves are the best; they are the biggest. The bottom ones are the poorest quality. Some typical grades are: *dieciochena* (eighteenth), a lesser quality leaf from Vuelta Abajo; *dieciseisena* (sixteenth), a

better quality leaf for better cigars but too small to be used as a binder; *diecisietecena* (seventeenth), a much smaller leaf but satisfactory for filler; *octava* (eighth), a Remedios leaf of small size and light colour used in domestic blends and as export tobacco. It is the task of sorters to differentiate the grades.

2 Stemming – a manual process whereby the central stalk is deftly wound around the finger, leaving the left and right halves of the leaf intact – was first introduced for export in 1878.

3 A full list of the names of workers in all factories, shops, sorting and stemming sheds is to be found in the CNPDTH *Primer censo . . .* (1947).

4 CTC figures for the tobacco industry are quoted extensively by Felipe Zapata in the appendices to *Esquemas y notas para la historia de la organización obrera*, Havana, 1952. Useful comparisons can be made with the CNPDTH 1947 census.

5 The cigar maker fashions the filler into its proper shape and size in the palm of the hand, and rolls the tobacco into cigar form. The wrapper is then deftly cut with a special flat knife (*chaveta*) and wound round the filler, beginning at the lighting end of the cigar and finishing at the end that goes into the mouth, the head. A touch of gum is used to fasten the leaf securely at the head and a small round top is cut out from the remaining leaf and pasted on. The cigar is then held to the gauge and trimmed smoothly to proper length by a stroke of the knife. An experienced cigar maker performs the whole operation within minutes.

6 Hazard, *Cuba*, p. 75.

7 Quoted by Rivero Muñiz, *Tabaco*, p. 280.

8 Verena Martínez-Alier, *Marriage, colour and class in nineteenth-century Cuba*, Cambridge, 1974. She quotes a tailor who remarked that belonging to a trade such as his, in which there were many free coloureds, 'markedly diminishes those whites who engage in these occupations', and another who argued that 'by virtue of his poverty and mechanical trade he cannot [marry] anyone of his class' (p. 153).

9 This is dealt with more fully in chapters 9 and 10.

10 Cigars are classified according to brand, size, shape, shade, etc. Shades vary from mature dark to light through 80–100 variations of hue. Only an experienced eye can note the fine distinctions entailed. Some of the better-known shapes and sizes from the late nineteenth-century are: Británica, Británica Fina, Victoria, Victoria Fina, Victoria Especial, Victoria Chica, Corona, Imperial, Excepcional, Media Regalía Fina, Reina María, Reina Fina, Reina, Londres, Londres Chico, Princesa, Princesita, Patriota, Liliputano.

11 Quoted in Antonio Gordon y Acosta, *El tabaco de Cuba* (Havana, 1897), p. 5.

8: Labour aristocrats?

1 Two particularly long articles were written in the journal *Jurisprudencia* on this question: 'La libreta de los tabaqueros' by José Ignacio Rodríguez (1859), and 'La Libreta de los tabaqueros. Debe suprimirse ó conservarse ó extenderse a los demás obreros?' by Dr Nicolás Azcarate (1869). The latter deals more with the general moral and political issues involved in controlling 'free' labour, the former is particularly informative and fully supports my point.

2 Rivero Muñiz, *Tabaco*, vol. II, pp. 307–8.

3 *Ibid.*, p. 308.

4 Quoted in several texts, including Rivero Muñiz (1965) and Gaspar Jorge García Galló, *El tabaquero cubano*, Havana, 1936.

5 Their latter-day counterparts José Rivero Muñiz, Gaspar Jorge García Galló, and José Luciano Franco were later to become prominent tobacco historians.

6 Undated, untitled pamphlet on the government of Estrada Palma and social and political institutions, thought to have been written around 1904–5.

7 Zapata, *Esquemas y notas.* . . .

8 Abad, *Statement* . . . .

9 Manuel Rodríguez Ramos, *Siembra, fabricación e historia del tabaco . . . con el manual del tabaquero*, Havana, 1905.

10 García Galló, *El tabaquero cubano*, p. 23.

11 'Después de la jornada', *Tabaco*, August 1939.

12 'Hechos y comentarios del mes', *Cuba Económica y Financiera*, April 1951, p. 15.

13 Benjamín Estrada y Morales, *Obreros distinguidos*, Havana, 1892.

14 *Tabaco*, November 1936, p. 29.

15 Gaspar Jorge García Galló, *Biografía del tabaco habano* (Havana, 1961), p. 52.

16 *Libro de Cuba*, 1952, p. 846.

9: Militancy and the growth of the unions

1 Rivero Muñiz covers this extensively in *Las tres sediciones de vegueros en el siglo XVIII*, Havana, 1962, and *Tabaco*, vol. 1.

2 Rivero Muñiz wrote a series of informative articles on the formal history of guilds and later unions in each sector in the journal *Tabaco*, 1933–4.

3 *La lectura*, or reading, is dealt with further in chapter 10. See also Rivero Muñiz, *La lectura en las tabaquerías*, Havana, 1951.

4 It is interesting to note that according to the 1899 census cigar makers accounted for 40% of literates in Havana.

5 García Galló, *Biografía*. . . .

10: Early reformism and anarcho-syndicalism

1 The school had been set up in 1838 and within a couple of years there were 178 apprentices training to be cigar makers. To become a master cigar maker, an apprenticeship of 2–4 years was necessary.

2 The importance of *la lectura* in the tobacco sector is a point made in most studies. The germ of the idea seems to have come from a Spanish traveller to Cuba, Jacinto de Soler y Quiroga, who saw it as a way of alleviating the work of slaves on sugar, coffee and other plantations.

3 An informative work on this is José A. Portuondo's book *La Aurora*, Havana, 1961.

4 This and subsequent quotes are taken from an unpublished and uncatalogued collection of documents and notes compiled by Rivero Muñiz in the Institute of History library.

5 Cultural circles also remained important. In 1881, the Círculo de Artesanos de San Antonio de los Baños was set up after an incident recorded by Diego González in his *Historia de San Antonio de los Baños* as follows: 'An incident that came of a decent, well-behaved citizen of the people, a cigar maker by trade, having attended a dance held by aristocratic circles of the township, moved worker elements to band together to establish a society whose need was felt in the middle and working class.' The aims of the circle were largely educational and

recreational and included adult education classes, public talks, a library and school for the children of workers.

6 This is clear from the workers' biographies in Estrada y Morales (1892).

7 For further details of the strike see Antonio González y Acosta, *Reflexiones económico-político-sociales y memoria de la huelga de los tabaqueros de La Habana*, Havana, 1887. Earlier strike movements had been quickly quelled.

8 This and subsequent quotes have been taken from Aleida Plascencia's excellent collection of documents, *El Productor*, Havana, 1967.

9 Martínez might well have been identifying more with manufacturers by this time. This labour leader of 1888 was in 1891 representing the chamber of commerce, industry and navigation on a commission to the central Spanish government.

10 Gallego y García, *Cuba por fuera*, p. 9.

11 González y Acosta, *Reflexiones*. . . .

12 Estrada y Morales *Obreros distinguidos*.

13 José Martí maintained that the colonial authorities on occasion supported the anarcho-syndicalists as a divisory tactic.

11: Revolutionary nationalism of the 1900s

1 The American Cigar Manufacturers' Association sent a commission to Cuba in the early 1890s to make offers to workers to tempt them to emigrate to Tampa and Key West. It is recorded that so many left from San Antonio de los Baños that the town was virtually left without an industry. The reason the manufacturers gave was shortage of labour but it has been pointed out that 800 strike-breakers were recruited in 1893 to weaken the cigar makers' support for the Cuban revolutionary party.

2 Zapata (1952), appendix xxv, 'La cuestión del 75%'.

3 Rivero Muñiz, 'La primera huelga general obrera en Cuba repúblicana', *Islas*, 3:3 (May–August 1961).

4 In September 1899, General William Ludlow proclaimed 'To the People of Havana' that: 'The worker in Havana is being induced to take a fatal step which, if realized, will hold back the exercise of freedom and the enjoyment of individual rights over an indefinite period of time. He is being pushed toward a general strike, that is a total stoppage of customary work, of essential daily tasks on which the existence of the people depends . . . The authorities know that only a small part of the workers sympathize with the movement and that the great majority is not ready to give its consent. But the consequences of this should be made clear. Order will be maintained and any violence or disturbance whatsoever will be put down and, if necessary, radical measures will be taken to maintain peace and the security of the people'. (Retranslated from the Spanish).

5 This is quoted in many different sources, including Foner, *The Spanish–Cuban–American War*. Foner also states that the league had a membership of 10,000 in the early days but that this dwindled to 300.

6 Sociedad de Escogedores, 'A los Compañeros de la industria del Tabaco y obreros en general', 15 June 1902, in Zapata (1952), appendix xxviii, 'La cuestión de los aprendices'.

7 *Ibid.*, appendix xxvi, 'Huelga general de 1902'.

8 ANC, SCR, Senado: Secretaría de Actas, Segunda Legislatura, 1902. Expediente iniciado a virtud de un proyecto de Ley proponiendo el amparo a la clase obrero en las fábricas y talleres, no. 47.

9 El Crédito, a small *chinchal* run by Calixto and Faustino Rodríguez Maurí, grew rapidly over the months of the lock-out to the point, it is said, of establishing El Crédito cigars as favourites among consumers.

10 Carlos Baliño, 'Independencia económica', *La Discusión*, Havana, 5 July 1902.

11 Carlos Baliño, *Verdades socialistas* (Havana, 1905), p. 20.

12 Letter from Baliño to Miranda dated 9 February 1909, quoted in Rivero Muñiz, *Carlos Baliño* (Havana, 1962), p. 30.

13 Letter from Baliño to Miranda dated 25 February 1909, in *Ibid.*, p. 32.

12: Cigar makers on the defensive

1 Serre, *Le tabac de Cuba*, p. 36. Serre makes the point that Bock was very paternalistic as far as the workers were concerned and had all sorts of welfare schemes going. He argues that this was not to the liking of the Trust and one of the main reasons for what was virtually an 'enforced' retirement when he became ill.

2 *Trabajo presentado . . .*, Havana, 1910.

3 *Ibid.*

4 Quoted by Zapata, *Esquemas y notas.*

5 Quoted in Carlos del Toro, *El movimiento obrero cubano en el año 1914*, Havana, 1969.

6 León Primelles, *Crónica cubana 1919–1922*, Havana, 1958. See 1919 under 'Proletariado'.

7 Quoted in Olga Cabrera, *El movimiento obrero cubano en el año 1920*, (Havana, 1969), p. 65. Havana cigar makers were in conflict with their fellow workers in Tampa over this. In April, the Havana and Pinar del Río cigar makers' federation laid down that cigar makers returning to Cuba had to present official union cards. Tampa cigar makers, however, had formed their own Tampa cigar makers' society, not wanting to belong to the Cigar Makers' International 'because we cannot go along with them knowing, as we do, that many of our brothers are in jail and others deported because of its leaders, and they know as well as we do their position on the European war, aligning themselves with the government and the bourgeoisie'. See Tranquilo Martínez, 'A los torcedores', *La Opinión*, 17 April 1920.

8 Cabrera, *El movimiento obrero*, p. 70.

9 1966 interview with Octavio Mesa, Las Villas Central University.

13: The sleeping lion awakes

1 Martín Duarte Hurtado, *La máquina torcedora de tabaco y las luchas en torno a su implantación en Cuba* (Havana, 1973), p. 41.

2 'Laudo impartido en el problema de Por Larrañaga', *Boletín del Torcedor*, August 1930, pp. 18–19.

3 Zapata, *Esquemas y notas.*

4 Eduardo Plochet, 'Las máquinas torcedoras de tabacos', *Boletín del Torcedor*, November 1929, p. 31.

5 'Informe de la Comisión de Reorganización al Comité Central de la FNT de Cuba', *Boletín del Torcedor*, February 1930, p. 24.

6 According to the Trust study, for the year 1929 a total of 3,539,535 cigarettes were manufactured by unionized labour, 1,987,868 by non-union labour. In Havana, only nine out of a total of sixteen factories employed unionized labour, In 1918, it was claimed, total production was worked by unionized labour.

7 This blackleg labour was later unionized in Juan Arévalo's Unión Federativa Obrera Nacional, in opposition to the FNT.
8 Coupons read: 'People. – The Trusts are the workers' guillotine. Aguilitas, Bock, Susini, Bellamar, Bellamarcitos, Bellamar No. 5, Dos Ríos and Liborio cigarettes belong to a US Trust. Do not smoke them even if given them. You will be aiding the destruction of 800 Cuban homes.
'Unión de Obreros de la Industria de Cigarrería. Unión de Dependientes del Ramo del Tabaco. Unión de Cigarreros y Similares.
'Do not drop this on a public thoroughfare.'
9 ANC, CNPDTH, TCSA, files 291 and 292.
10 *Ibid.*
11 'Note on Cuban Revolution', *Fortune*, 1:2, p. 148.
12 'La Corona', *Fortune*, 7:3
13 *El Mundo*, 1 September 1931.
14 ANC, CNPDTH, TCSA files 291 and 292.
15 'La Corona', *Fortune,* 7:3

14: The big tobacco unions of 1936–48

1 'Informe de la Comisión de Reorganizaciónal Comité Central de la FNT de Cuba', *Boletín del Torcedor*, February 1930, p. 24.
2 'Memoria al Congreso (Sancti Spíritus), *Boletín del Torcedor*, March 1930.
3 José Beltrán, 'No retrocedemos, progresamos', *Boletín del Torcedor,* June 1930, p. 9.
4 'Circular de la Federación Nacional de Torcedores de Cuba a la opinión pública y a los torcedores en particular', *Boletín del Torcedor*, April 1930, p. 6.
5 'A nuestros lectores', *Boletín del Torcedor*, May 1929, p. 11.
6 Guillermo Gener, 'Banzay', *Boletín del Torcedor*, May 1929, p. 33.
7 Teodoro Cabrero, 'El triunfo de un compañero', *Boletín del Torcedor*, June 1929, p. 13. The short stories and plays were often understandably melodramatic but the moral was constant: the suffering of the working class and the role education and culture can play in struggle.
8 'Manifiesto a la opinión pública y a los tabaqueros en particular', published in *Tabaco*, November 1933.
9 'Tribuna obrera', *Tabaco*, December 1933, p. 9.
10 1966 interview with José Alejandro Reyes, Las Villas Central University.
11 Interview (1966) with Pedro Arboláez, Comisión de Activistas de Historia del Partido Comunista de Cuba (PCC).
12 ANC, Fondo Especial (FE).
13 *Ibid.*
14 *Memoria del Congreso Nacional de Tabaqueros*, Havana, 1938.
15 Interview (1966) with Reinaldo Fundora, Comisión de Activistas de Historia del PCC.

15: The machine and the anti-union war

1 Manifesto of the anti-machine committee to the authorities, the people and cigar makers of Havana, reproduced by Duarte, *La máquina torcedora*, p. 245.
2 'Traición y máquinas' in Duarte, p. 212.

3 Parallel developments in the peasant sector were growers' associations – in the case of tobacco the Asociación Nacional de Cosecheros de Tabaco – and a new Confederación Nacional Campesina.

4 The 1950 Truslow Report on Cuba observed the large gap between leadership and rank and file, commenting that unions had little worker participation and were lacking any strong democratic base.

5 ANC, CNPDTH, TCSA, unclassified files.

6 *Ibid.*

7 *Ibid.*

8 *Ibid.*

9 *Hoy*, 13 February 1948.

10 *Hoy*, 24 April 1948.

11 *Ibid.*

12 ANC, CNPDTH, TCSA, unclassified files.

13 'Máquinas, monopolios y desempleo en masa', *Fundamentos*, 95 (1950), p. 566.

14 Interview (1969) with Manuel Duke Linero carried out by the author.

15 Quoted in Duarte (1923), pp. 239–41.

16 Interview (1966) with Vicente Avelado carried out by the Communist Party history commission.

17 ANC, CPDTH, TCSA, unclassified files.

18 *Libro de Cuba* (1952), p. 58.

19 Ministry of labour records included correspondence testifying to this. One such letter from CTC general secretary Eusebio Mujal, dated 16 January 1957, denounced six communists of the Marianao cigar makers' union and two in the José L. Piedra cigar factory. An earlier letter of 9 November 1956 was from the tobacco section of the vehemently anti-communist Asociación Cubana Pro-democrática, denouncing the FTN national and Santa Clara executives for non-aggression pacts with the communists and deploring the number of communists in union posts, along with the open distribution of 'communist propaganda' in factories and the recent provincial FTN plenary in Santa Clara that had come out against the machine.

20 *Revolución* (official publication of the underground 26th of July Movement), September 1958.

Epilogue: A new twist

1 These and subsequent figures are taken from Adelfo Martín Barrios, *La ANAP: 20 años de trabajo*, Havana, 1982.

2 An informative article is Brian Pollitt, 'The transition to socialist agriculture in Cuba: some salient features', *Institute of Development Studies Bulletin,* 13:4, 1982.

3 See *Memorias del V Congreso de la ANAP*, Havana, 1978.

4 Figures supplied by ANAP.

5 Archivo del Ministerio del Trabajo, General Cigar Company files.

6 *Ibid.*

7 The economic planning and management system, along with the role of the trade union movement, etc., was set out in the Resolutions to the 1975 Party Congress.

8 These and other figures are taken from the various years' *Anuario Estadístico de Cuba*.

9 Interview with the director of Tabacalera S.A., entitled 'In Spain when one says "cigar", one means Havana Cigar', *Cubatabaco International*, 6 (1982), 62.

10 Quoted in 'A magnificent harvest in quality and quantity', *Cubatabaco International*, 1 (1980), 29.

11 Karl Avery Werner, *Tobaccoland,* New York, 1922, quoted on p. 1.

Bibliography

1. Archival sources

Archivo Nacional de Cuba, Havana
Fondo de la Comisión Nacional de Propaganda y Defensa del Tabaco Habano (CNPDTH).
Uncatalogued, although certain files bore old classification numbers. This section
largely comprises the archive of the American Tobacco Company subsidiary,
Tabacalera Cubana, S.A. (1932–58) and provided much information on this and other
tobacco firms and on strikes and industrial action.

Fondo Especial (FE). Uncatalogued but an inventory by year is in process. This
section includes valuable manifestos of the labour movement.

Fondo de Donativos y Remisiones. Catalogued by author but not subject and, therefore,
difficult to work with. This section, however, contains important documents on
varied subjects.

Fondo de Audiencia

Fondo de Tribunales de Urgencia. Court cases indexed chronologically and not by subject
matter.

Fondo de Senado y Cámara de Representantes. Uncatalogued. Some debates on tobacco
matters were found.

Registro Mercantil de La Habana
Libro de Sociedades. Indexed volumes according to company names. The bulk of
company information comes from this trade register.

Archivo del Banco Nacional de Cuba, Havana
Sección de seguros. Catalogued by firm. Contains reports on tobacco firms but largely
duplicates information in the trade register.

Archivo de Seguro Social, Havana
Catalogued by sector and by firm and comprehensive data contained on employment,
wages and hours of work.

Archivo del Ministerio del Trabajo, Havana
This vast archive is largely composed of individual files on Cuban workers. One
section is classified according to company and covers collective labour contracts.

Archivo de la Fábrica La Corona, Havana
Contains time-sheets for La Corona, 1950–60.

Archivo de Santa Clara
Copies of rules and regulations of old guilds of the province and useful pamphlets were found.

Comisión de Activistas de Historia del Partido Comunista de Cuba, Havana
Special collection of oral material on the history of the labour movement, 1920–58 (transcribed).

Universidad Central de las Villas, Santa Clara
History Department. Special collection of oral material on the history of the labour movement, 1920–58 (transcribed).

2. Printed collections of documents, censuses and statistical publications

Anuario Estadístico de Cuba, Havana, 1946–82
Anuario del Tabaco Habano, Havana, 1944 and 1945
Bachiller y Morales, Antonio, *Recortes de periódicos, 1880–1881,* Colección Cubana, Biblioteca Nacional José Martí, Havana
Balanza general de comercio de la Isla de Cuba, 1859, Havana, 1861
British Parliamentary Papers, Blue Books, Cuban Consular Commercial Reports, London–Havana Trade and Shipping, 1850–1890, British Museum, London
Burdett's Official Intelligence, London, 1888–1933
Censos Oficiales de Cuba: Report on the Census of Cuba, 1899, Washington, 1900; *Censo de la República de Cuba, 1907,* Washington, 1908; *Censo de la República de Cuba* (1919, 43 and 53), Havana
Comisión Nacional de Propaganda y Defensa del Tabaco Habano, *Nuestros mercados de tabaco,* Havana, 1931
  Primer censo de obreros de la industria tabacalera, Havana, 1947
  Producción agrícola tabacalera de Cuba, 1929–56, Havana, 1957
  Comercio exterior tabacalero, 1952–58, Havana, 1959
  Resumen analítico de las exportaciones de tabaco, 1950–1959, Havana, 1960
  Informes del mercado tabacalero, 1951–59, Havana, 1960
  Estimado general de la cosecha de tabaco, 1951–59, Havana, 1960
Cuadro estadístico de la siempre fiel Isla de Cuba, correspondiente al año de 1846, Havana, 1847
Documentos de Carlos Baliño, Biblioteca Nacional José Martí, Havana, 1964
Documentos del IV Congreso Nacional Obrero de Unidad Sindical, Havana, 1934
Erenchum, Félix, *Anales de la Isla de Cuba: diccionario administrativo, económico, estadístico y legislativo,* 5 vols, Havana, 1861–5
Estadística agropecuaria, Havana, 1929
Ferrara y Marino, Orestes, *Anuario estadístico,* Havana, 1914
García de Arboleya, José, *Manual de la Isla de Cuba: compendio de su historia, geografía, estadística y administración,* Havana, 1852
Handwörterbuch der Staatswissenschaften, Berlin, 1901
Informations Internationales, Paris, 1960–70
Memoria de los trabajos presentados al Congreso Nacional Obrero de La Habana, Havana, 1915

Memoria del Congreso Nacional de Tabaqueros, Havana, 1938
Memoria del censo agrícola de 1946, Havana, 1947
Memorias de la Real Sociedad Patriótica de la Habana, Biblioteca Nacional José Martí, Havana
Memorias de la Sociedad Económica de Amigos del País, Biblioteca Nacional José Martí, Havana
Moody's Industrial Manual, New York, 1901–58
Morales y Morales, Vidal, *Documentos relativos a la información económica de Madrid y al Comité Central de Propaganda de la Habana, (1890)*, Colección Facticia, vol. 18, Colección Cubana, Biblioteca Nacional José Martí, Havana
Noticias estadísticas de la Isla de Cuba en 1862, Havana, 1864
Pardo y Betancourt, Valentín. *Informe ilustrado y estadístico*, Havana, 1863
Pezuela y Lobo, Jacobo de la, *Diccionario geográfico, estadístico, histórico de la Isla de Cuba*, 4 vols, Madrid, 1863–6
Pichardo, Hortensia, *Documentos para la historia de Cuba*, 4 vols, Havana, 1973–81
Plascencia, Aleida, *El Productor*, Biblioteca Nacional José Martí, Havana, 1967
Primelles, León, *Crónica cubana 1919–1922*, 2 vols, Havana, 1955 and 1958
Primer Anuario Comercial de Cuba, Havana, 1953
Saco, José Antonio, *Colección de papeles científicos, históricos, políticos y de otros ramos sobre la historia de Cuba ya publicados, ya inéditos*, Paris, 1858–9
United Nations Food and Agriculture Organization, *Tobacco*, Commodity Series Bulletin 20, Rome, 1952
United Nations *Statistical Yearbook*, 1948–60

3. Cuban national newspapers

El Mundo
El País
Diario de la Marina
Hoy (Official paper of the Cuban Communist Party)

4. Periodicals

Boletín del Torcedor (Journal of the Havana cigar makers and later the national cigar makers' federation)
Carteles
Cuban Foodstuff Record (1926–27). Title changed to *Cuba Importadora e Industrial* (1928–44). Title changed to *Cuba Económica y Financiera* (1944–56)
Cubatabaco International
El Cigarrero (Journal of the cigarette workers' union)
El Tabacalero (Journal of the cigar makers' union)
Fortune (New York)
Fundamentos (Official journal of the Cuban Communist Party)
Graceta de la Habana (Official legal publication of the Spanish colonial government and provisional military government of 1898–1902). Title changed to *Gaceta Oficial de la República de Cuba* after July 1902
Habano (Journal of the manufacturers' association)
Revista Económica
Tabaco (Originally the official organ of the Alianza Tabacalera)
Trabajo (Journal of the ministry of labour)

5. Contemporary pamphlets and descriptive accounts

A los trabajadores de Cuba. Informe al Senado de la República que presentan sobre la cuestión social en Cuba, Havana, 1919

Abad, L.V., *Statement submitted to the Committee of Ways and Means of the House of Representatives*, Washington, 1900

Aguirre, José C. *La verdad sobre la industria del tabaco habano*, Havana, 1905

Album de la Corona: Obsequio a sus favorecedores, Havana, 1898

Álvarez, Celestino, 'La industria del Tabaco', *Diario de la Marina*, Edición Extraordinaria, August 1918

Asociación de Almacenistas y Cosecheros de tabaco de Cuba, *Nuestro problema tabacalero*, Havana, 1941

Baliño, Carlos, *Verdades socialistas*, Havana, 1905

Bock, Gustav, *La verdad sobre la industria del tabaco habano*, Havana, 1904

Cárdenas, Fernando, *Memoria: sobre la gran importancia que tienen en la riqueza nacional cubana, la industria y negocio del tabaco en rama*, Havana, 1934

Carvajal, Leopoldo, *Respuesta que da cierto oficio de la dirección general de rentas estancadas sobre algunos particulares de la contrata de tabacos para la península*, Havana, 1885

Casado, Ricardo A., *Nuestro tabaco*, Havana, 1939

Cuestionario relativo a la producción, elaboración y exportación del tabaco en Cuba, Havana, 1909

Dana, Richard H. Jr., *To Cuba and back: a vacation voyage*, Boston, 1859

Estrada y Morales, Benjamín, *Obreros distinguidos* [tabaqueros], Havana, 1892

Ferrer y Martínez, Miguel, *El tabaco: su historia, su cultivo, sus vicisitudes, sus afamadas vegas en Cuba*, Madrid, 1851

Gallego y García, Texifonte, *Cuba por fuera*, Havana, 1890

García Marqués, Rafael, *An account of the tobacco industries, the causes of their decadence and measures which are considered necessary to save them from the ruin that menaces them*, Havana, 1900

González y Acosta, Antonio, *Reflexiones económico-político-sociales y memoria de la huelga de los tabaqueros de la Habana*, Havana, 1887

Gordon y Acosta, Antonio, *El tabaco en Cuba*, Havana, 1897

Hazard, Samuel, *Cuba a pluma y lapiz* (1871), Havana, 1928

Kimball, Richard Burleigh, *Cuba and the Cubans: comprising a history of the island of Cuba and its present social, political and domestic conditions; also its relations to England and the United States*, New York, 1850

Madden, Richard Robert, *The island of Cuba*, London, 1849

Más y Otzet, Francisco, *El tabaco y la industria tabacalera en Cuba*, Havana, 1886

Project définitif d'une fabrique de cigarettes (genre Havanais) établie à St. Sebastièn (frontière d'Espagne) avec la marque LA HONRADEZ (L'Honorabilité) de la Havane at foncionnnant avec les MACHINES SUSINI brevetées, Paris, 1869

Rodríguez Acosta, Rafael, *Album de la fábrica de cigarros, la Belleza*, Havana, 1892

Rodríguez Ramos, Manuel, *Siembra, fabricación e historia de tabaco . . . con el manual del tabaquero*, Havana, 1905

Sagra, Ramón de la, *Historia económica-política y estadística de la isla de Cuba*, Havana 1831; 2nd edn 1963

   Cuba en 1860 ó sea cuadro de sus adelantos en la población, la agricultura, el comercio y las rentas públicas, Paris, 1863

Tellería, Evelio, *Los congresos obreros de Cuba*, Havana, 1973

Trabajo presentado al Honorable Señor Presidente de la República por la Comisión nominada
  para que le informara al Gobierno acerca de la actual situación del cultivo y de la industria
  del tabaco, Havana, 1910
Unión de Fabricantes de Tabaco de la Habana, *Memoria de los trabajos más importantes*
  realizados por la corporación desde 16 septiembre 1890 hasta 5 de febrero 1894 en defensa de
  los intereses generales de la industria que representa, Havana, 1894
Villaverde, Civilo, *Excursión a Vueltabajo,* Havana, 1861

6. Books and articles

Aguilar, Luis E, *Cuba 1953; prologue to revolution,* New York, 1972
Alba, Victor, *Historia del movimiento obrero en América Latina,* Mexico, 1964
Alexander, R.J. *Communism in Latin America,* New Brunswick, 1957
  Organized labour in Latin America, New York, 1965
Alford, W.B.E., *W.D. and H.O. Wills and the development of the U.S. tobacco industry,*
  1786–1965, London, 1973
Alienes y Urosa, Julián, *Características fundamentales de la economía cubana,* Havana, 1950
  Economía de post-guerra y desempleo, Havana, 1949
American Tobacco Company, *The American Tobacco story,* New York, 1960
Arcos, Juan, *El sindicalismo en América Latina,* Bogotá, 1964
Arnault, J., *Cuba et le marxisme,* Paris, 1962
Arredondo, Alberto, *Cuba: tierra indefensa,* Havana, 1945
Azcarate Rosell, Rafael, *Nicolás Azcarate el reformista,* Havana, 1939
Barbarrosa, Enrique, *El proceso de la República: análisis de la situación política y económica*
  de Cuba bajo el gobierno provisional de Ramón Estrada Palma y José Miguel Gómez, con
  datos e informaciones estadísticas, Havana, 1911
Blackburn, Robin, 'Prologue to the Cuban Revolution', *New Left Review* 21 (1963)
Bonnell Philips, Ulrich, *American Negro slavery,* New York, 1952
Cabrera, Olga, *El movimiento obrero cubano en el año 1920,* Havana, 1969
Caribbean Commission, *The tobacco trade of the Caribbean,* Washington, 1949
Carr, Raymond, *Spain 1808–1939,* Oxford, 1966
Cepero Bonilla, Raúl, *Azúcar y abolición,* Havana, 1948
Chapman, Charles Edward, *A history of the Cuban Republic,* New York, 1927
Chia Garzón, Jesús A., *El monopolio del jabón y el perfume en Cuba,* Havana, 1977
Comisión Nacional de Economía, *El programa económico de Cuba,* Havana, 1955
Cuba: economic and commercial conditions, HMSO, London 1954
Davies, I.D. and Miranda, S. de, 'The working class in Latin America; some
  theoretical problems', in John Saville and Ralph Milliband (eds), *Socialist*
  Register, London, 1967
Deschamps Chapeaux, Pedro, *El negro en la economía habanera del siglo XIX,* Havana,
  1971
Deschamps Chapeaux, Pedro, and Pérez de la Riva, Juan, *Contribución a la gente sin*
  historia, Havana, 1974
Duarte Hurtado, Martín, *La máquina torcedora de tabaco y las luchas en torno a su*
  implantación en Cuba, Havana, 1973
Dumoulin, John, 'Monocultivo y proletarización: dos ejemplos de Las Villas',
  Ciencias Sociales, 1 (1965)
  Azúcar y lucha de clases 1917, Havana, 1980
Ely, Roland, *Comerciantes cubanos del siglo XIX,* Bogotá, 1961

Fitzgibbon, Russell, *Cuba and the United States, 1900–1955*, Menasha, 1935

Foner, Philip Sheldon, *A history of Cuba and its relations with the United States*, 2 vols, New York, 1973

    The Spanish–Cuban–American War and the birth of American imperialism, 2 vols, New York and London, 1972

Franco, José Luciano, *Ensayos históricos*, Havana, 1974

Friedlaender, Heinrich, *Historia económica de Cuba*, Havana, 1944

Furtado, Celso, *Obstacles to development of Latin America*, Berkeley, 1964

Galeano, Eduardo, *Open Veins of Latin America*, New York, 1974

García Galló, Gaspar Jorge, *El tabaquero cubano: psicología de las profesiones*, Havana, 1936

    Biografía del tabaco habano, Havana, 1961

Grismer, Karl, *Tampa*, Florida, 1950

Grobart, Fabio, 'El movimiento obrero cubano de 1925 a 1933', *Cuba Socialista*, 60 (1966)

Guerra y Sánchez, Ramiro, *En el camino de la independencia; estudio sobre la rivalidad de los Estados Unidos y la Gran Bretaña en sus relaciones con la independencia de Cuba*, Havana, 1930

    Guerra de los diez años, 1868–1878, Havana, 1960

    Azúcar y población en las Antillas, Havana, 1961

    Manual de historia de Cuba, Havana, 1964

Guerra y Sánchez, Ramiro, et al., *Historia de la nación cubana*, 10 vols, Havana, 1952

Gunder Frank, André, *Capitalism and underdevelopment in Latin America*, New York and London, 1969

    Lumpenbourgeoisie, lumpendevelopment, New York, 1972

Gutierrez, Gustavo, *Presente y futuro de la economía cubana*, Havana, 1952

Halper, S.A., and Sterling, J.H., *Latin America: dynamics of social change*, London, 1972

Hennessy, C.A.M., 'The roots of Cuban nationalism', *International Affairs*, July 1963

Hidalgo, Ariel, *Orígenes del movimiento obrero y del pensamiento socialista en Cuba*, Havana, 1976

Hobsbawm, Eric, *Primitive rebels*, London, 1959

    Labouring men, London, 1964

    Bandits, London, 1968

    Captain Swing, London, 1969

    'The labour movement and military coups', *Marxism Today*, October 1974

Huberman, Leo, and Sweezy, Paul M., *Cuba: anatomy of a revolution*, New York, 1961

Ibarra, Jorge, *Historia de Cuba*, Havana, 1965

    Ideología Mambisa, Havana, 1967

    José Martí, dirigente político e ideológico revolucionario, Havana, 1980

Imperial Tobacco Company (of G.B. and Ireland) Ltd, *The Imperial Tobacco Company 1901–1951*, Bristol, 1952

International Bank for Reconstruction and Development (IBRD), *Report on Cuba*, Washington, 1950. *Investment in Cuba. Basic Information for U.S. businessmen*, Washington, 1965

Jenks, Leland, *Our Cuban colony*, New York, 1928

Klein, Herbert S., *Slavery in the Americas. A comparative study of Cuba and Virginia*, London, 1967

Knight, Franklin W., *Slave society in Cuba during the nineteenth century*, Madison, 1970

Lenin, V.I., *The development of capitalism in Russia*, Moscow, 1977

Imperialism, the highest stage of capitalism, Moscow, 1975
Le Riverend Brusone, Julio, 'Años terribles para la economía tabacalera', (pts 1 and 2), *Habano*, 3:1 and 3:2 (1941)
Historia económica de Cuba, Havana, 1965
La República, dependencia y revolución, Havana, 1966
Libro de Cuba, Havana, 1952 and 1953
Libro de la vida nacional, Havana, 1931
López Segrera, Francisco, *Cuba: capitalismo dependiente y subdesarrollo* (1510–1959), Havana, 1972
Lugo de la Cruz, Evelio, 'La industria del tabaco torcido y sus perspectives', *Cuba Socialista*, 21 (1963)
MacGaffey, Wyatt, and Barnett, Clifford Robert, *Twentieth Century Cuba, the background of the Castro Revolution*, New York, 1965
Magdoff, Harry, *The age of imperialism*, New York, 1969
Marrero y Artiles, Levi, *Geografía de Cuba*, Havana, 1955
Martí, Carlos, *Catalanes en América (Cuba)*, Havana, 1921
Martí, José, *Obras completas*, Havana, 1979
Martín Barrios, Adelfo, *La ANAP: 20 años de trabajo*, Havana, 1982
Martínez Alier, Juan and Verena, *Cuba: economía y sociedad*, Paris, 1972
Martínez-Alier, Verena, *Marriage, class and colour in nineteenth-century Cuba*, Cambridge, 1974
Memorias del V Congreso de la ANAP, Havana, 1978
Moreno Fraginals, Manuel, *El ingenio: el complejo económico-social del azúcar*, 2nd edn, 3 vols, Havana, 1978
Myers, Gustavus, *History of the great American fortunes*, New York, 1937
Nelson, Lowry, *Rural Cuba*, Minneapolis, 1950
Nun, José, *Latin America. The hegemonic crisis and the military coup*, Berkeley, 1969
O'Connor, James, 'The foundations of Cuban socialism', *Studies on the Left*, 4:4 (1964)
'*The Political economy of pre-revolutionary Cuba*', unpublished thesis, Columbia University, 1964
'Industrial organisation in the old and the new Cubas', *Science and Society*, 19:2 (1966)
'The labour force, employment and unemployment in Cuba', *Social and Economic Studies*, June 1966
'The organised working class in the Cuban Revolution', *Studies on the Left*, 6:2 (1966)
The origins of socialism in Cuba, Cornell University Press, 1970
Ordoquí, Joaquin, *Elementos para la historia del movimiento obrero en Cuba*, Santa Clara, 1961
Ortiz, Fernando, *Cuban counterpoint: tobacco and sugar*, New York, 1947
Perdomo, José E., *Brief history of tobacco*, CNPDTH, Havana
Perdomo, J.E., and Posse, Jorge, *Mecanización de la industria tabacalera*, Havana, 1945
Pérez de la Riva, Juan, *El barracón y otros ensayos*, Havana, 1975
Petras, James, and Zeitlin, Maurice, *Latin America: reform or revolution*, Greenwich, Conn., 1968
Pino Santos, Oscar, *Historia de Cuba: aspectos fundamentales*, Havana, 1964
'La Corona, el águila y esta libertad', *Cuba*, no. especial, 1968
El asalto a Cuba por la oligarqía financiera yanqui, Havana, 1973
Poblete Troncoso, Moíses, *The rise of the Latin-American labour movement*, New York, 1960

Pollitt, Brian, 'Estudio acerca del nivel de la vida rural en la Cuba prerevolucionaria', *Teoría y Práctica*, Nov.–Dec. 1967
'The transition to socialist agriculture in Cuba: some salient features', *Institute of Development Studies Bulletin*, 13:4 (1982)
Portell Vilá, Herminio, *Historia de Cuba en sus relaciones con los Estados Unidos y España*, 4 vols, Havana, 1941
Porter, Robert P., *Industrial Cuba. Being a study of present commercial and industrial conditions with suggestions as to opportunities in the island for American capital enterprise and labor*, New York and London, 1899
Portuondo, Fernando, *Estudios de la historia de Cuba*, Havana, 1973
Portuondo, José A., *La Aurora*, Havana, 1961
Poyo, Gerald E., 'Cuban emigré communities in the United States and the Independence of their homeland, 1852–1895', University of Florida PhD dissertation, 1983
'José Martí, architect of social unity: class tensions in the Cuban emigré communities of the United States, 1887–1895', Occasional Paper No.5, Caribbean Migration Program, Center for Latin American Studies, University of Florida, 1984
Problems of the New Cuba, New York, 1935
Quintero-Rivera, A.G. 'Socialist and cigarmaker: Artisans' proletarianization in the making of the Puerto Rican working class', *Latin American Perspectives*, 10:2 and 3 (1983)
Raggi y Ageo, Carlos M., *Condiciones económicas y sociales de la República de Cuba*, Havana, 1944
Ravelo, Sergio N., 'Algunos comentarios sobre la industria tabacalera cubana', *Comercio Exterior*, July–September, 1965
Rivero Muñiz, José, 'El tabaco en la poesía', Havana, 1946 (unpublished)
'Pequeña antología del tabaco', Havana, 1946 (unpublished)
La lectura en las tabaquerías, Havana, 1951
Los cubanos en Tampa, Havana, 1958
'La primera huelga general obrera en Cuba republicana', *Islas*, 3:3 (May–August 1961)
El movimiento obrero durante la primera intervención: apuntes para la historia del proletariado en Cuba, Santa Clara, 1961
El movimiento laboral cubano durante el período 1906–1911: apuntes para la historia del proletariado en Cuba, Santa Clara, 1962
El primer partido socialista: apuntes para la historia del proletariado en Cuba, Santa Clara, 1962
Las tres sediciones de vegueros en el siglo XVII, Havana, 1962
Tabaco: su historia en Cuba, 2 vols, Havana, 1965
Roca, Blas, *Por la consolidación de la república democrática y los avances obtenidos*, Havana, 1939
Por la defensa nacional y el progreso de Cuba, Havana, 1941
Tabaco y economía de post-guerra, Havana, 1945
Los fundamentos del socialismo en Cuba, Havana, 1961
Roig de Leuchsenring, Emilio, *La Habana, apuntes históricos*, 3 vols, Havana, 1964
Los Estados Unidos contra Cuba Republicana, 2 vols, Havana, 1964
Scheer, Robert, and Zeitling, Maurice, *Cuba: an American tragedy*, London, 1964
Seers, Dudley, *Cuba, the economic and social revolution*, Chapel Hill, 1964

Serre, Paul, *Le tabac de Cuba et les cigares de la Havane*, Paris, 1911
Serviat, Pedro, *40 aniversario de la fundación del Partido Comunista*, Havana, 1965
Shurcliffe, Alice W., *Labour in Cuba*, Washington, 1957
Smith, Robert E., *The U.S. and Cuba: business and diplomacy, 1917–1960*, New York, 1960
   Background to revolution: the development of modern Cuba, New York, 1966
Stokes, W.S., 'The Cuban Parliamentary system in action, 1940–7', *Journal of Politics*, May 1949
Tabares del Real, José A., *La revolución del 30*, Havana, 1971
Tennant, Richard B., *The American cigarette industry: a study in economic and public policy*, Yale University Press, New Haven, 1950
Thomas, Hugh, *Cuba, or the Pursuit of Freedom*, London, 1971
Thompson, Claudia, *The tobacco industry of the Philippines and its relations to the United States*, Washington, 1946
Thompson, E.P., *The making of the English working class*, London, 1963
Toro, Carlos del, *El movimiento obrero cubano en el año 1914*, Havana, 1969
Touraine, Alain, 'Mobilité sociale, rapports de classe et nationalisme en Amérique Latine; *Sociologie du Travail*, 1965
   'Industrialisation et conscience ouvrière a São Paulo,' *Sociologie du Travail*, 41 (1961)
Trelles, Carlos Manuel, *El progreso (1902–1905) y el retroceso (1906–1922) de la República de Cuba*, Havana, 1923
Truslow Report on Cuba, Havana, 1950
Twiston Davies, E., *Fifty years of progress. An account of the African organization of the Imperial Tobacco Company*, Bristol, 1958
Varona, Enrique, *De la colonia a la república*, Havana, 1919
Vega Cobellas, Ulpiano, *Los doctores Ramón Grau San Martín y Carlos Saladrigas Zayas*, Havana, 1944
Veliz, Claudio (ed.), *The politics of conformity in Latin America*, London, 1967
   Latin America and the Caribbean: a handbook, London, 1968
   Obstacles to change in Latin America, Oxford, 1970
Vivó, Hugh, *El empleo y la población activa de Cuba*, Havana, 1950
Wade, Richard, *Slavery in the cities: the South, 1820–1860*, Oxford, 1967
Wallich, Henry Christopher, *Monetary problems of an export economy: the Cuban experience, 1914–1947*, Cambridge, Mass., 1950
Werner, Karl Avery, *Tobaccoland*, New York, 1922
Williams, Eric, *From Columbus to Castro. A history of the Caribbean, 1492–1969*, London, 1971
Wood, Dennis B., 'The long devolution. Class relations and political conflict in Cuba, 1868–1968', *Science and Society*, 34
Wright, Philip Green, *The Cuban situation and our treaty relations*, Washington, 1931
Zanetti, Oscar, and García, Alejandro, *United Fruit Company: un caso de dominio imperialista en Cuba*, Havana, 1976
Zapata, Felipe, *Esquemas y notas para una historia de la organización obrero en Cuba*, Havana, 1952
Zeitlin, Maurice, 'Labour in Cuba', *The Nation*, 20 Oct. 1962
   'Political generations in the Cuban working class', *American Journal of Sociology*, 1966
   'Economic insecurity and political attitudes of Cuban workers', *American Sociological Review*, Feb. 1966
   Revolutionary politics and the Cuban working class, Princeton, 1967

Index

Partagás, Jaime, 17
Partido Auténtico, 137, 147, 148, 149, 150, 151, 152
Partido Obrero de la Isla de Cuba, 115
Partido Revolucionario Cubano, 109
Partido Socialista Cubano, 111
patriotic clubs, 109
Patterson, Rufus Lenoir, 6, 7
Peña, Lazaro, 89–90, 138, 142, 143, 144, 159, 168
Philippines, 3, 8, 9
Por Larrañaga: factory founded, 17; introduction of machinery in, 36–9, 124–5, 126, 133, 135, 147; Eustaquio Alonso manager of, 74
protectionism, 3, 8, 9, 19–20, 23, 24, 26, 28–9, 44–51, 97
Puerto Rico, 5, 8, 44–5

race, 68–70, 72; *see also* blacks, slave labour
reading, 88–9, 98–9
redundancy: US, 7; Cuba, 39, 88, 147, 148
reformism, 89–91, 99–100, 106, 107, 121, 129
Rhodesia, Imperial Tobacco Co. in, 9
Rivero Muñiz, José, 18–19, 53, 73, 74
Roig San Martín, Enrique, 89–90, 99, 104, 107, 108–9
Romeo y Julieta, 33, 166

Sagra, Ramón de La, 19
sharecropping, 52–7, 65
Sherman Anti-Trust Law, 5
Sindicato de Obreros de Maquinistas Elaboradores de Tabacos y sus Anexos de La Habana, 156
Sindicato de Torcedores de La Habana, 128, 148, 149, 153
Sindicato Nacional de Obreros de la Industria Tabacalera, 141
skill, concept of, 70–3, 79
slave labour, 53, 57, 65, 68, 69, 74, 105
slavery, abolition of, 74, 100, 101
socialism, 11, 89–90, 91, 92, 94, 96, 100–1, 107, 115–16; *see also* communism
Sociedad de Anilladoras y Envolvedoras, 139
Sociedad de Escogedores de La Habana, 111, 139
Sociedad de Fileteadores, 139
Sociedad Económica de Amigos del País, 18, 32, 97
sorters: of leaf, 66–7, 78–9, 144; of cigars, 77, 101; unionization of, 86, 94, 140–1;

apprenticeship of, 102–6, 111–12; *see also* Sociedad de Escogedores de La Habana
sorting: US, 7; Cuba, 11, 57
Spain: production in, 2, 3, 6, 8; tobacco monopoly in Cuba, 15; antagonisms with Cuba, 19, 24–5, 29, 44; strike over currency of, 75; labour ideology, in, 100; post-revolutionary trade with, 166–7
state farms, 160, 161, 162
stemmers, 66, 67; as woman's job, 71; conditions of, 77–8; unionization of, 86, 90, 94; unemployment of, 117, 141, 144, 145; 1948 strike of, 153; *see also* Gremio de Despalilladoras
stemming: US, 7; Cuba, 11, 57
strikes, 26, 87, 90, 91, 94, 100, 117, 118, 120, 141, 144; 1866 Cabañas strike, 99; late 1880s Cuban strikes, 101–7; late 1880s Key West strikes, 108; 1902 strike, 110, 112–15; 1907 American Currency strike, 32; 1925 Por Larrañaga strike, 125; 1931–3 strikes, 39, 129, 130–6, 139, 140; 1935 General Strike, 137–8, 145
Sumatra, 8, 9
Susini: cigarette machine, 3–4; company, 21, 57
Susini, Luis, 18–19
Susini y Rioseco, José, 16
sweatshop production, *see* outwork

Tabacalera Cubana SA (TCSA), 39–43, 61, 136, 150, 153; *see also* American Tobacco Co., Bock, Cuban Land and Leaf Tobacco Co., Havana Tobacco Co., Henry Clay, La Corona
Tabaco, 140
Tampa: Cuban tobacco development in, 23–5; returning Cuban cigar makers from, 70, 87; exodus to, 71, 105, 115, 135; labour activities in, 108–9, 133; support for Cuban workers from, 113; transfer of production from, 133
tariffs, *see* protectionism
taxes, *see* protectionism
trade: world, 2–3, 5, 7–11; *see also under* France, Germany, Holland, United Kingdom, United States
trade treaties, 24, 31, 35, 44, 46, 48
transfer of production: from Cuba to US, 10, 23–5, 39–42; from Tampa to New York, 133; from Havana to cheap labour areas, 75; Cuban legislation against, 143
Trenton, New Jersey: American Tobacco Co. move from Cuba to, 39–42, 133, 135–6

CAMBRIDGE LATIN AMERICAN STUDIES

Cambridge Latin American Studies